Big Book of
CRAFTS

NORTH LIGHT BOOKS

CINCINNATI, OHIO

www.artistsnetwork.com

Table of
CONTENTS

Greeting Card Magic
with Rubber Stamps...................... 5

Quick & Easy
Decorative Painting 130

Easy Mosaics for Your Home and Garden

....................253

Wreaths for Every Season

................377

Introduction

Here's a book you have to love. It's a book of everything craft. You've got paper crafts, wreath making, decorative painting and mosaics. Make a card using rubber stamping to send to a friend. Paint a candle holder to complement your home décor. Brighten up your home inside or out with mosaic garden stepping stones or wall hangings. Make a wreath for every door and every season.

We've collected tons of projects in four crafty areas to provide you with infinite ideas and ways to satisfy your need to be creative. That's why it's called *Big Book of Crafts*! In addition to the projects, you'll find basic materials and techniques information at the beginning of each section to help get you started, plus specific materials, hints and tips for each project so anyone can do it. Check out the Table of Contents at the beginning of each section for a list of projects and the resource page at the back of each section for help locating materials.

There are over 500 pages and 70 projects waiting for you.

You'd better get started!

greeting card magic
with RUBBER STAMPS

MaryJo McGraw

NORTH LIGHT BOOKS
CINCINNATI, OHIO
www.nlbooks.com

table *of* contents

1
POCKETS AND MINI ENVELOPES
12

Basic Envelopes With Templates
14

Mini Message Card
17

2
DIORAMA CARDS
22

Doggy Diorama
24

3
CUTTING CORNERS
30

Simple Cut-Up
33

Tumbling Triangles
36

4
EXQUISITE PAPER MOSAIC
42

Mosaic Technique
44

Deluxe Mosaic
48

Glitzy Mosaic
50

5
GLAZING WITH GLUE
54

Pear Card
56

Dreamy Face
61

Elegant Women
65

6
COLLAGE VENEERS
70

Holiday Card
72

7
PASTELS AND CRAYONS
78

Basic Pastel Background
80

Simple Watercolor Wash
83

Artful View Card
84

Fun Face Card
86

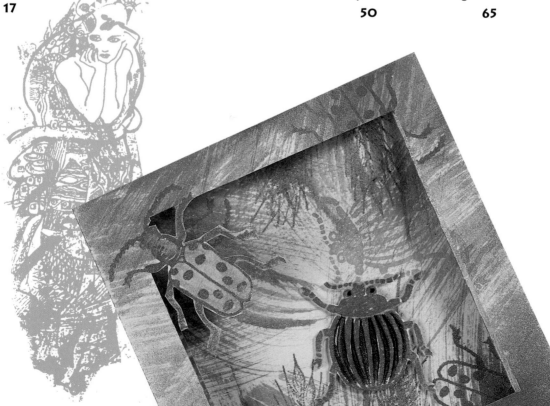

introduction **8**

tools and materials **10**

resources **128**

8

SHRINK
PLASTIC
92

Abstract Elegance
94

Catalina Tiles
99

Beaded Tiles
105

9

NATURAL
ADORNMENTS
110

Silver Cups
112

Worldly Leaf
117

Stone Tablets
122

Sea Shells
125

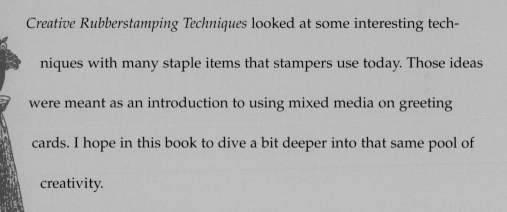

Creative Rubberstamping Techniques looked at some interesting techniques with many staple items that stampers use today. Those ideas were meant as an introduction to using mixed media on greeting cards. I hope in this book to dive a bit deeper into that same pool of creativity.

introduction

Many of the ideas in this book can be taken even further than the greeting card. Again I will use some items that are familiar: paper, metallic pens and embossing powders. The unusual—acetate, glazing glue, shrink plastic, laminating sheets and templates—will become familiar quickly. These items are all easy to use and create fabulous effects on cards. Be adventurous! Use these techniques on other surfaces too. Limiting yourself to using only paper for your creations will obstruct your creativity. Expand beyond the greeting card onto other surfaces, such as cardboard frames, wooden boxes and even your windows and walls.

Above all else, PLAY! *All of these techniques are simple and easily mastered with a bit of practice. Get out all your craft and stamping stuff and* ENJOY!

Tools and Materials

Rubber stamps
There are generally three parts to a rubber stamp: the mount, the cushion and the die. Quality mounts are made from hardwood. The cushion is made of foam from ⅛" to ¼" thick. The die, the most important part of the stamp because it transfers the design, should be closely trimmed.

Paper
Most of the projects in this book require high-grade papers and cardstock. Don't skimp on the paper—it will show. One of the papers you need to find is a translucent vellum. Be sure you can see through it, as there are many types of vellum that are opaque.

Inks
There are three basic ink types: dye, pigment and solvent. Dye-based pads are the type you see lying around the house or office. Dye-based ink is water-soluble. Pigment inks are now widely available through stamp and gift stores and are a good choice when using uncoated papers. They are also used for embossing and for archival applications, such as scrapbooking. Solvent-based inks are used mainly for stamping on unusual surfaces like wood, plastic and ceramic. I use them for a nice, crisp, black outline that won't smear like dye inks do.

Dye re-inkers
Dye re-inkers are the small bottles of ink you normally use to refill your dye-based ink pads. In this book they will be used to color Diamond Glaze: By adding a few drops of re-inker to Diamond Glaze, you can make a paint that dries transparent. Be careful when using inks straight from the bottle; they are very concentrated and will easily stain clothing. Be sure to use the smallest amount possible; you can always add more.

Embossing powders
Embossing powders are required for many of the cards in this book. To use embossing powder, stamp an image with pigment or embossing ink. Sprinkle the powder over the wet ink and shake off the excess. Use a heat gun to melt the powder and create a raised design. Be sure to have a variety of colors; embossing looks great in almost any color. Embossing powder comes in solid-color and multicolor forms.

Double-sided tapes
Double-sided tapes come in a variety of forms. The double-sided tapes used in this book include mosaic tape, a paper-lined tape that is thin, embossable, heat resistant and good for layering. Cellophane double-sided tape is also great for layering, especially with transparent papers. Double-sided foam tape is perfect when you need to add height to a layered piece.

Accessories
Accessories such as threads, beads, paper cord, tassels and gift tags can be found at most stamp stores. I also find these items in specialty stores for beads and needlecrafts. Office supply stores are great for unusual items too.

Acetate
The acetate used in this book can be found in stamp stores. You want to be sure to get embossable acetate (also known as "window plastic") in case you want to heat the piece. The same is true of the heavy cold laminate used here; it should be embossable. The thicker the laminate is, the better for the projects in this book because of the beating the pieces will take.

Beads
The glass beads I use in the projects in this book are tiny and have no holes. They also have a metallic finish.

Bone folder

The bone folder is a great tool for scoring paper and smoothing down creases. Bookbinders use it for turning corners and scoring. Some are made from bone, while others are made from resin or wood. They come in several lengths and are very helpful in several crafts.

Brayers

Brayers come in so many varieties it is hard to choose which to buy. For my money, the best all-around brayer is a detachable 4" soft rubber brayer. It will handle most jobs and it is easier to clean. You will also find sponge, acrylic, hard rubber and wood brayers. Each yields a different result.

Craft knives

A craft knife is an invaluable tool when creating greeting cards or other stamp projects. The blade should be pointed and very sharp. Change your blades often to ensure clean cuts.

Heat gun

Look for a heat gun that is specially made for stamping: They are usually geared at a safe temperature for paper projects. Keep your heat gun away from your cutting mat, as it can distort the surface. (It's hard to cut on a warped mat.)

Pastels and water-soluble crayons

Pastels and water-soluble crayons are available in stamp and art supply stores. I prefer crayons that are soy based because they have a creamy texture and are loaded with pigment.

Powdered pigments

Powdered pigments are raw pigments used for a variety of purposes, including making your own paints. You can also use these pigments as a surface coating on paper or collage projects. Powdered pigments do need what is known as a "binder" to keep them adhered to your proj-ect. In this book we will be using Diamond Glaze as a binder. Other options include white glue, paint mediums, gum arabic or spray fixative. Mixing any of these with the powdered pigments will create a colored medium you can apply to surfaces as you wish.

Shrink plastic

Several projects in this book call for shrink plastic, so I want to give you some tips for using it. Most shrink plastics shrink by 40 to 50 percent. You can shrink the plastic using a heat gun on a heat-safe surface (not your cutting mat), but be aware that the heat will not be even over the piece and consequently the plastic may become distorted.

You can also shrink the plastic in your oven. To ensure distortion-free results, place the plastic in a hot spot. It is easy to test your oven for hot and cold spots. Create several 1-inch squares of shrink plastic. Place these squares on a parchment-covered cookie sheet, spreading the pieces evenly on the sheet. Be sure to put a piece in each corner. Place the cookie sheet in a hot oven, and watch through the oven door to see which pieces begin to shrink first. This will tell you where your oven hot spots are. That is where to place the pieces you are shrinking.

Tassels and cords

Tassels make a great addition to a beautiful card. The ones used in this book are available at most stamp stores. Paper cord is also available. As you will see in this book, paper cord is an extremely versatile decorative item. Both tassels and cords are usually sold in assortments of colors.

Templates

Plastic and brass templates are a great investment. They last forever, are inexpensive, and there are many types available. Look for envelope, box and card templates at stamp stores.

CHAPTER 1

pockets and mini envelopes

*E*veryone loves a little surprise. The cards in this chapter feature built-in pockets and envelopes for mysterious correspondence. The basics are simple folds and the use of envelope templates, which are perfect for those tiny messages. These are great cards for extravagant embellishments: silk, velvet, gold or specialty threads and small charms or tags. You might also enclose a pair of earrings or a gift certificate in the envelope.

Basic Envelopes With Templates

What you'll need:

- vellum
- envelope template (see page 16)
- bone folder
- white glue
- envelope glue (see recipe on page 16)

For this envelope I have used a type of vellum that is tinted but transparent. There are many colors available. Some even have embedded glitter or confetti. You should be able to find this at your local stamp, craft or paper store.

Materials, clockwise from upper left: stamped and unstamped papers and vellum, gift tags, envelope templates, bone folder, craft knife, cutting mat.

1 *Trace the envelope template.* Begin by tracing the template lightly onto the vellum with a pencil.

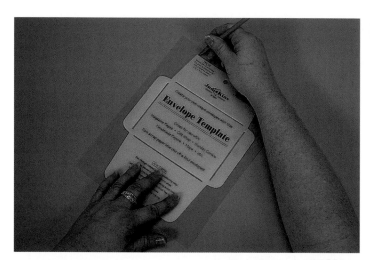

2 *Score the vellum.* Using a bone folder or a stylus, score the vellum using the slots in the template.

3 *Cut out the envelope.* Cut out the envelope along the pencil lines. Remove any pencil marks with a soft eraser.

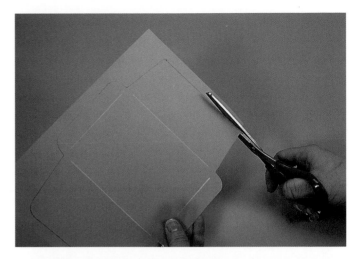

4 *Fold the envelope.* Fold along the score marks and burnish the creases with the side of the bone folder.

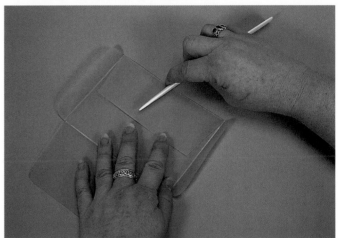

5 *Glue the seams.* Using a paintbrush and a small amount of clear-drying glue, cover the lower half of the envelope seams. Fold and seal the seams. Do not use this glue for the envelope flap.

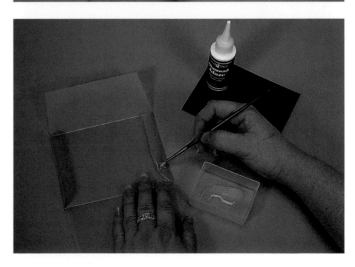

TIP

✧ Recycle old magazines, calendar pages and gift wrap into new envelopes. For a more personal envelope, copy your family photos on a color copier!

6 *Apply envelope glue.* Using the recipe on this page, make a batch of "lickable" envelope glue. Apply the glue to the top flap of the envelope.

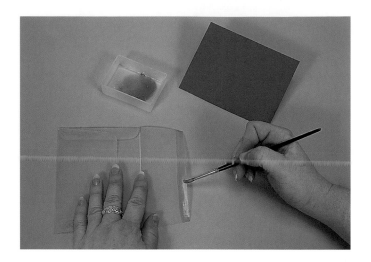

Cut line

Fold line

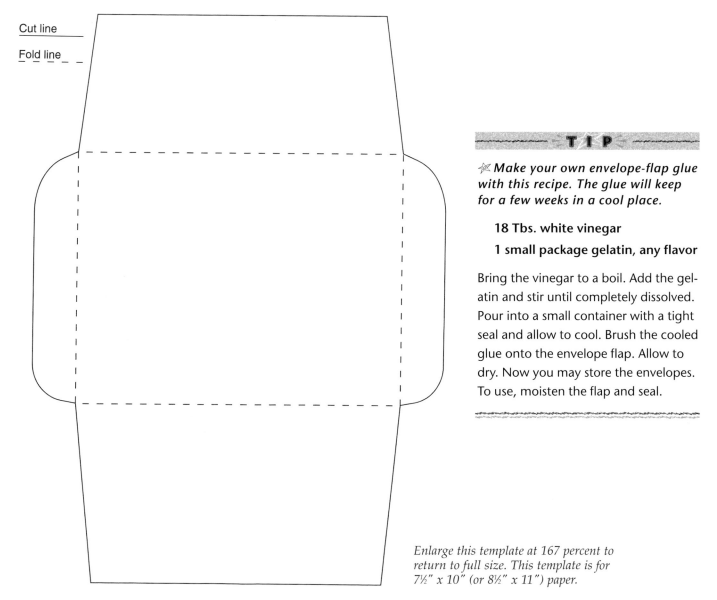

Enlarge this template at 167 percent to return to full size. This template is for 7½" x 10" (or 8½" x 11") paper.

Mini Message Card

What you'll need:

- small round stamp from JudiKins
- rectangular stamp from Stampers Anonymous
- word stamp from Zettiology
- brown paper—text weight
- tall notecard
- round gift tag
- white glue
- mini square envelope template
- pencil
- bone folder
- scissors
- metallic embossing powder
- heat gun
- gold thread
- double-sided tape
- metallic pigment ink
- black and green dye inks

1 *Make a mini envelope.* Stamp plain brown lightweight paper with black dye ink. Trace the mini square envelope template following the basic envelope instructions on pages 14–16. Score and cut out the envelope. Set it aside.

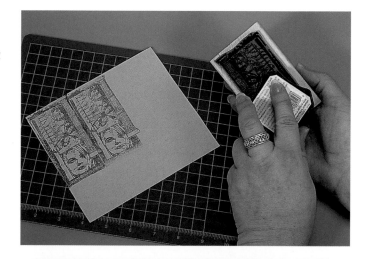

2 *Make a liner.* To make a liner for the envelope, use a pencil to trace the square interior through the template slots. Continue tracing around the top flap. Cut along the pencil lines.

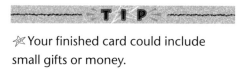

⭐ Your finished card could include small gifts or money.

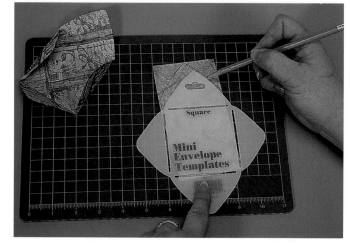

3 *Attach the liner.* Trim ¼" off the liner on all sides and glue the liner to the inside of the envelope. Glue the seams of the envelope and set it aside.

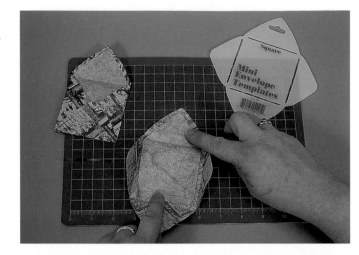

4 *Dye the tag.* Color the tag with dye ink. Wipe off any excess ink on the metal rim of the tag. Allow to dry.

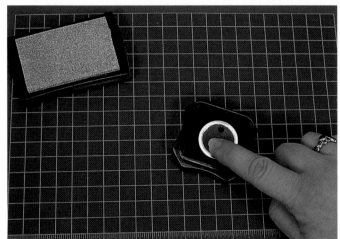

5 *Stamp the tag.* Stamp a design on the tag with pigment ink. Again wipe away any excess on the rim with a paper towel.

TIP

✯ Many types and sizes of tags are available at your local office supply store.

6 *Add embossing powder.* Sprinkle embossing powder over the wet pigment ink and shake off the excess.

7 *Emboss the tag.* Use a heat gun to heat the embossing powder until it melts.

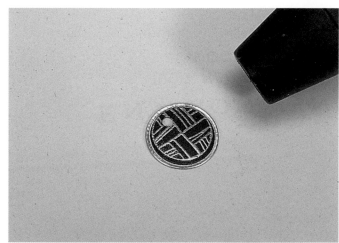

8 *Make the mini card and finish the mini envelope.* Using the template, trace just the inside square and cut it out. Trim this piece as necessary to fit inside the envelope perfectly. Write or stamp your message on the card and slip it in the envelope. Wrap gold thread around the envelope several times and tie on the tag. Trim away excess thread with scissors.

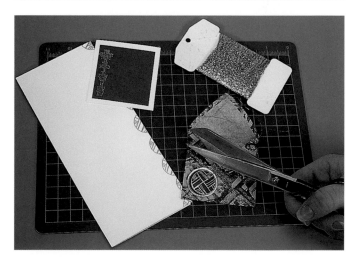

TIP

⭐ Raffia, yarn and narrow ribbons also work well for trims on greeting cards. Be sure to keep the size of the trim in proportion to the card.

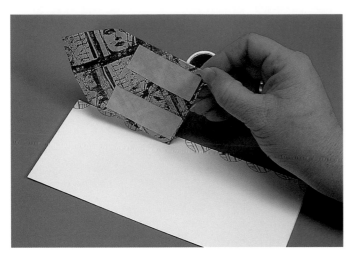

9 *Attach the envelope to the card.* If you wish, stamp the tall notecard along the edge with a coordinating design. Apply the piece to the front of the card with any double-sided tape.

The finished card and enclosure.

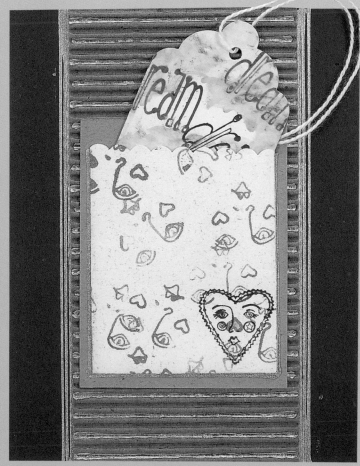

CHAPTER 2

Queen of Last Minute

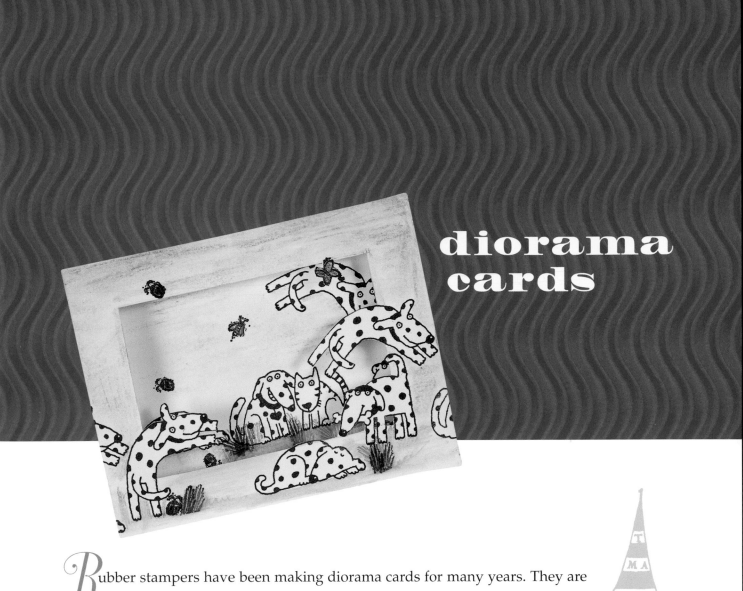

diorama cards

*R*ubber stampers have been making diorama cards for many years. They are wonderful cards to receive and unique enough to treasure as a keepsake of holidays, birthdays and vacations. Although the card looks complicated, the use of a template makes the whole process fast and easy.

Doggy Diorama

What you'll need:

- dog stamps by Rubber Zone
- butterfly stamps by Claudia Rose
- 11" x 17" cardstock in your choice of color
- diorama template
- watercolor crayons or pens
- black dye ink
- bone folder
- double-sided masking tape
- craft knife

Create a theme by selecting stamps of similar styles or subjects. Here I have chosen a set of active dogs. Landscape and collage stamps work well for dioramas.

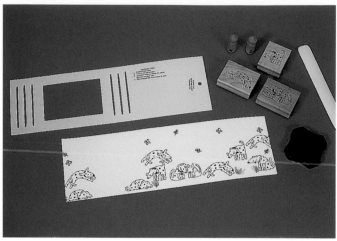

Materials, clockwise from upper left: diorama template, stamps, bone folder, ink pad, cardstock (already cut and stamped).

1 *Cut cardstock, stamp image and score.* Cut a piece of cardstock-weight paper to the size of the template. Stamp the characters in black dye ink. After the ink has dried, lay the template back over the paper and use a bone folder to score through the slots.

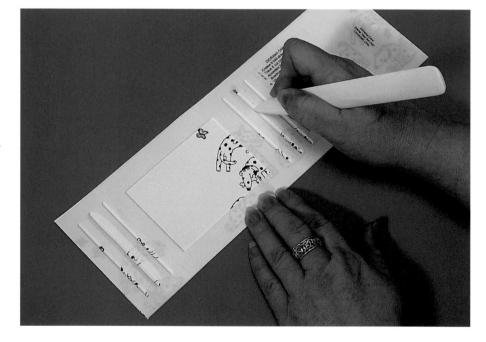

T I P

✯ If you have a hard time holding the template and paper together, use removable tape to secure the two pieces, score them, then remove the tape.

---

2 *Mark the window area.* With a pencil, mark out the window area of the template.

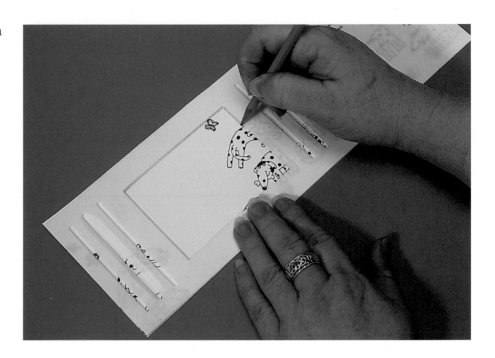

3 *Add extra elements.* Now that you know where the window will be, you can add extra elements jutting out of the window. I have placed the stamp to make it look as if the dog is jumping halfway out of the window.

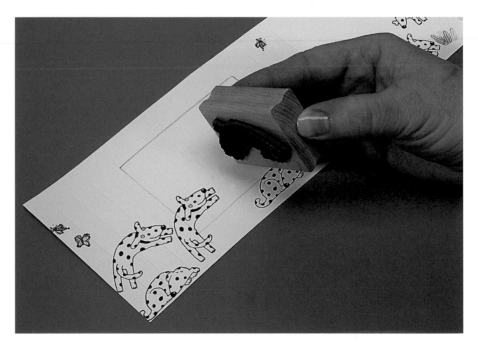

4 *Cut out the window.* Now cut out the window section with a craft knife, being careful to cut around the designs stamped inside the window.

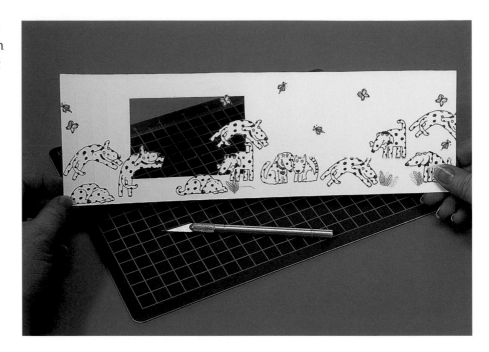

5 *Fold.* Fold the score marks accordion style. Crease each fold with the bone folder. Do not overwork the creases by folding back and forth. The card will stand better with crisp creases.

The folds should look like this from above.

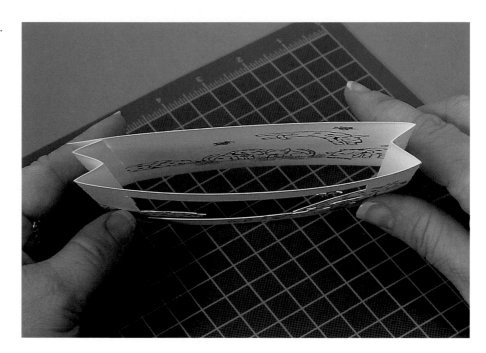

6 *Color the design.* Lay the entire card out flat again and add color to your design with colored pencil, markers, crayons or watercolors.

7 *Finish the card.* Apply double-sided tape to the side seam. Fold the entire card flat to seal it. Trim any uneven edges with a sharp knife—slowly. Change your knife blade before making your final trims.

The finished card.

To add dimension to your diorama, use double-sided foam tape to adhere cutouts to the back of the diorama behind the window.

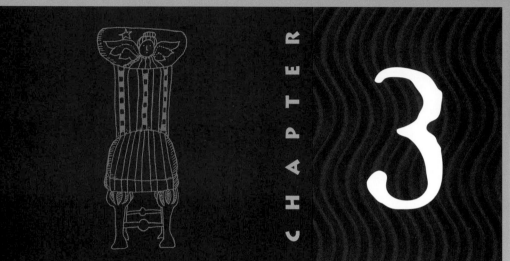

CHAPTER

3

(STAMPS CLOCKWISE FROM LEFT) **Rubber Moon, Acey Duecy, Stamp Camp.**

cutting corners

$\mathcal{U}$se your tools! That ruler you have can create interesting designs out of paper you have

stamped! These cards can be quick to make, too, because you can cut enough pieces

for several cards in no time. You'll also have plenty of leftovers for emergencies.

Simple Cut-Up

What you'll need:

- rectangular stamp by JudiKins
- cardstock
- pigment ink
- embossing powder
- heat gun
- craft knife
- double-sided tape
- tassel

Though this is an easy technique, most folks who receive this card will be very impressed with your cutting skills.

1 *Stamp your image.* Begin by stamping an image in pigment ink on cardstock.

2 *Emboss the image.* Sprinkle embossing powder over the still-wet ink and shake off the excess. Use a heat gun to melt the embossing powder.

3 *Cut in half.* To start making a pattern, use a sharp craft knife to cut the image in half lengthwise.

4 *Cut in quarters.* Cut those pieces in half again.

5 *Seal the embossing.* Reheat the edges of each piece to reseal the embossing. This will keep the embossing from flaking off along the edges.

6 *Build your card.* Affix double-sided masking tape to the back of each stamped piece. Then layer the pieces onto contrasting cardstock leaving ¼" between the pieces.

7 *Finish and embellish the card*. Finish the greeting by adhering the cardstock to a dark-colored notecard and tying on a matching tassel.

> ### TIP
>
> ✴ To create a more intricate pattern, cut the pieces into smaller sections and use several colors of paper or embossing powders.

Tumbling Triangles

What you'll need:

- small stamps by Paula Best
- cardstock
- paper in several colors/patterns
- dye ink
- double-sided masking tape
- 8½" x 11" Cosmic vellum
- hole punch
- tassel

This card is fun, quick and easy to create. Cube stamps work well in this project, since their designs fit well into a square.

1 *Cut squares.* Begin with three different colors of paper. Cut at least three 1½" squares out of each color. Here I have used cinnamon, forest and white.

TIP

⭐ The width of most rulers (1½ inches) is perfect for this project. Align the edge of your ruler with one edge of the paper, and then slice it on the other side. Repeat for the top and bottom.

2 *Stamp the papers.* Use one color of ink to impress all the squares with different stamp patterns. Allow the ink to dry.

3 *Cut triangles.* Cut the squares diagonally to make triangles.

4 *Stick triangles to card.* Apply small pieces of double-sided masking tape to the backs of the triangles. Position the triangles, alternating the colors, on a tall card.

5 *Make the overlay.* For this card I made a vellum overlay. It goes over the card and tucks under the triangles. Fold a piece of 8½" x 11" Cosmic vellum in half lengthwise and trim to fit the tall card. Unfold the vellum and lay your ruler along the fold so the ruler is on the right of the fold. Cut away the vellum to the right of the ruler, leaving about 1½". Fold the vellum overlay onto the card.

6 *Attach the tassel.* You can attach the overlay with a tassel by punching two holes on the crease of the card and the overlay.

The finished card. If you are making a card for a wedding, try this card using shades of white and cream.

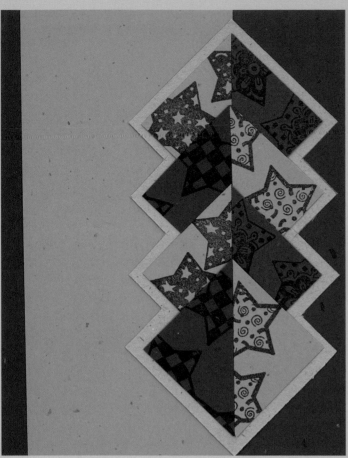

Here are a few examples of alternating different colors of paper. When using this technique, be sure to choose a color of embossing powder that is compatible with both papers. Don't choose a color that is too light.

For these two cards, the stamped and embossed images were stacked, then cut. If
you stack the images before cutting them,
you'll end up with images that match perfectly across the cut.

CORPUS

CHAPTER 4

exquisite paper mosaic

This is by far the most rewarding concept I have ever found because literally *everyone* can

do it. Paper mosaic is quick, easy and beautiful. It can look modern, elegant, country or

just pretty. Best of all you can do this project with a variety of paper scraps, including

stamping leftovers or mistakes, magazines, gift wrap and wallpaper—even old photos.

The unfortunate thing is you'll never want to throw any paper away ever again.

Mosaic Technique

What you'll need:

- colorful stamped and unstamped scraps of paper
- double-sided masking tape
- paper cording
- craft knife
- cardstock

This is hands-down the easiest way to create elegant greeting cards: The lovely patterns you'll create will amaze you. Pull together many types of stamped papers. Include in your selection large stamped backgrounds, metallic or shiny papers, embossed pieces, leftover glazed strips (see chapter five) and anything you were tempted to throw away! Once you have assembled the papers, cut them into strips with your craft knife and ruler. Even strips cut on the diagonal will work. Be sure that all the strips have straight edges on all sides. Sort the strips into color combinations for each mosaic.

All of these cards were made with scraps of paper, double-sided tape and paper cording.

1 *Cut mosaic strips.* Use a craft knife to cut strips of colorful, stamped or unstamped paper. Make sure the sides are straight and parallel.

T I P

✳ I like to use at least two patterned or stamped papers for each mosaic—it makes for a much more interesting pattern.

44

2 *Add strips to tape.* Start with a 4"-long section of double-sided masking tape. Lay the tape sticky side up on your cutting mat. Put one strip of paper at an angle across the center of the tape. Carefully lay another strip next to it, followed by another. Do not trim the strips just yet.

3 *Add cord and perpendicular strips.* Lay a paper cord on either side of the strips and press firmly. Once you have several strips across the center, begin laying strips perpendicular to your original strips.

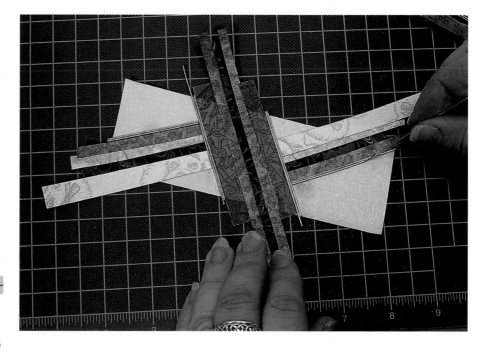

T I P

✯ I prefer to use double-sided masking tape for this project because it is very forgiving. At times, you'll want to move the strips after you've put them on the tape. With this tape, you will be able to do so.

4 *Fill the tape.* Repeat the process until the tape is covered.

5 *Trim the mosaic.* When the tape is covered, turn the piece over with the backing face up. Trim ⅛" off of each side of the tape.

6 *Finish the card.* Peel the liner off the tape and layer it onto cardstock. Trim the cardstock to about ½" around the mosaic. Apply double-sided tape to the back and layer it all onto a tall notecard.

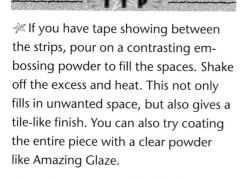

T I P

✣ If you have tape showing between the strips, pour on a contrasting embossing powder to fill the spaces. Shake off the excess and heat. This not only fills in unwanted space, but also gives a tile-like finish. You can also try coating the entire piece with a clear powder like Amazing Glaze.

Deluxe Mosaic

What you'll need:

- a completed mosaic
- craft knife
- double-sided masking tape
- paper cord
- notecard

Now let's create a more intricate piece. By cutting the mosaic into smaller strips, you can create more interesting looks and even patterns.

1 *Make a mosaic.* Begin by completing a mosaic as in the previous project (steps 1 through 5). Before removing the backing of the double-sided tape, cut this piece into four ⅜" strips.

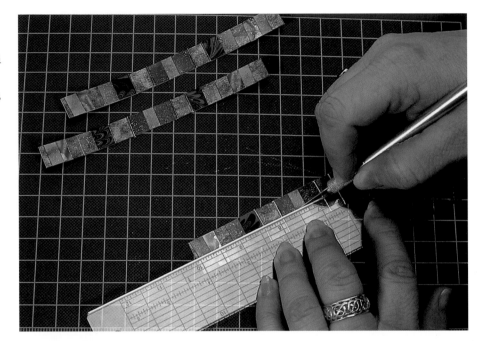

2 *Place strips on tape.* Cut another section of tape long enough to place your newly cut strips on. Remove the liner of each mosaic piece before placing it onto the the sticky side of the second piece of tape.

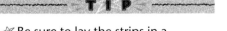
T I P

✧ Be sure to lay the strips in a different pattern from which they are originally cut. By turning every other strip you'll achieve a much more eye-catching pattern.

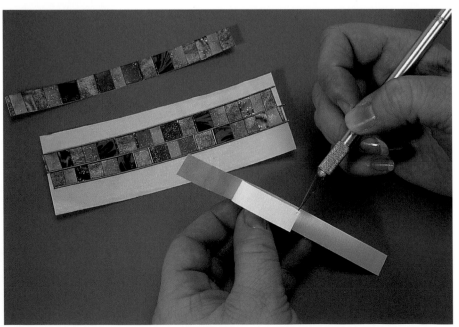

48

3 *Add cording and finish card.* Place a paper cord between each strip. Continue until all four pieces are in position, and then trim away the remaining exposed tape. Peel off the liner and place directly on a notecard.

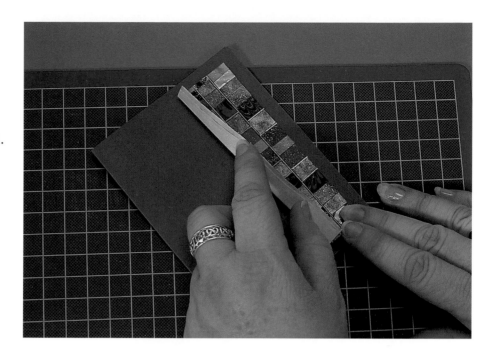

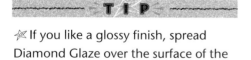
TIP

✦ If you like a glossy finish, spread Diamond Glaze over the surface of the mosaic.

The finished card.

Glitzy Mosaic

What you'll need:

- scraps of paper

or

- scraps from the projects in chapter five
- double-sided masking tape
- glass beads
- square notecard

Try the underglazing technique in chapter five and then use the leftover scraps on your latest mosaic. This mosaic uses blue and pink underglazed scraps, but you can use paper scraps with this technique as well.

1 *Arrange mosaic pieces on tape.* Begin with small, square chunks of colored plastic or small leftover paper strips. Here I am using two 4" sections of tape that will create a square-finish mosaic. Place the largest pieces toward the center of the double-sided tape and surround each piece with tiny scraps of strips. Leave ⅛" of exposed tape showing between each piece.

2 *Add glass beads.* In a box lid, lay the tape exposed side up and then pour tiny glass beads over the entire surface. Gently roll the beads over the tape with your fingertips. Lift the tape and tap off any excess beads.

T I P

✳ Pour the beads over the surface of the tape instead of turning the tape over and rolling it in the beads. You'll see where the beads should go so you can press them in with your fingers.

3 *Attach mosaic to card.* Remove the liner from the back of the tape and place each piece on the notecard as shown.

T I P

⭐ Make several of these beaded mosaics and put them all together on a piece of matboard. Frame for an interesting piece of abstract art.

The finished card.

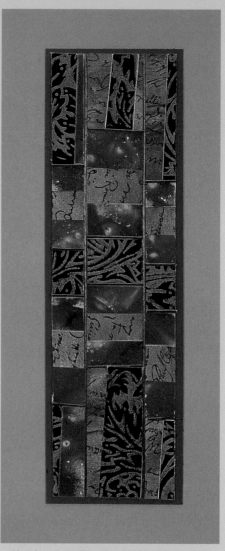

This mosaic was cut in half diagonally, creating two triangles. A spare mosaic strip was used to separate them.

Check out quilting books for some great patterns you can create using this technique.

Tall cards are perfect for mosaic sections, and are very elegant. These cards are perfect for men or women.

As you can see, paper cords add dramatic effect to mosaics. Simply wrapping a cord around a mosaic before layering the mosaic on a card adds lots of texture.

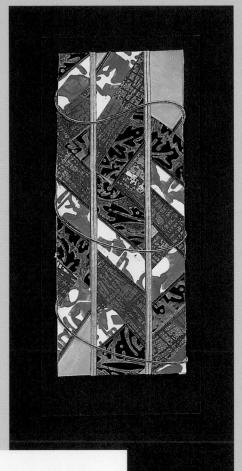

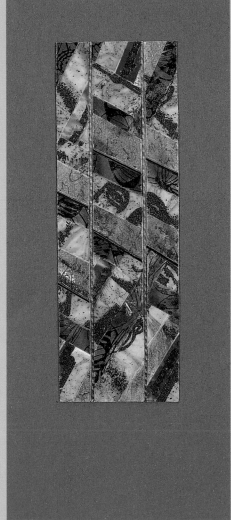

Try small, uniform squares as a central element in a mosaic.

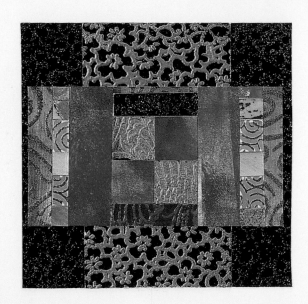

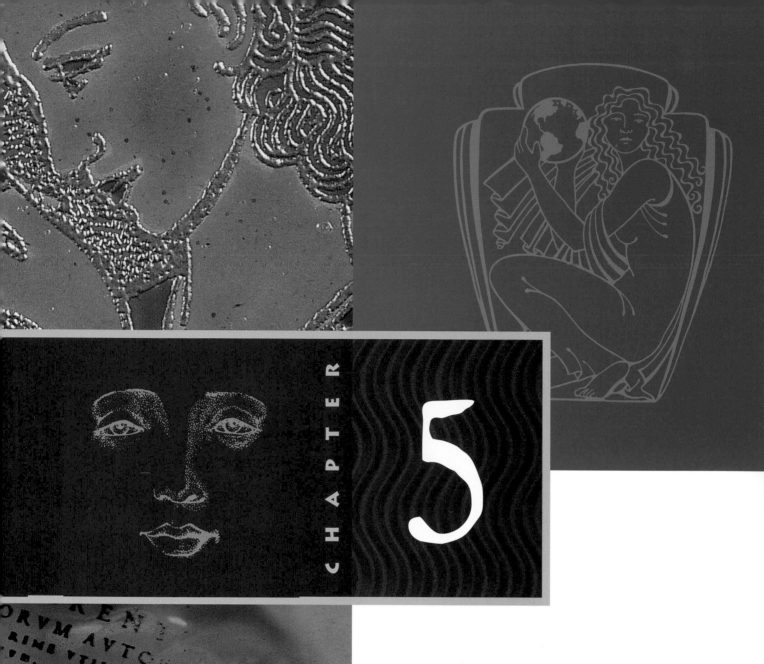

C H A P T E R

5

(STAMPS CLOCKWISE FROM LEFT) JudiKins, JudiKins, JudiKins.

glazing with glue

This is a great idea for those who love a little glitz. Make up several pieces at a time so you'll have extra cards on demand. Underglazing is a technique in which Diamond Glaze and dye re-inkers are used to create a colorful background on the reverse side of transparent acetate. You can also cut these into smaller pieces and add them to your latest mosaic. Overglazing uses a mixture of Diamond Glaze and dye re-inkers to make a transparent, glossy paint.

Pear Card

What you'll need:

- pear stamp from Stampers Anonymous
- word stamp from Zettiology
- clear acetate with tissue liner
- Diamond Glaze
- dye stamp pad re-inkers in several colors
- black permanent (solvent) ink
- craft knife
- ruler (preferably clear)
- double-sided masking tape
- notecard

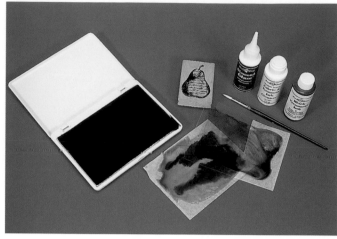

Materials, clockwise from upper left: permanent (solvent) ink pad, stamp, Diamond Glaze, stamp cleaner for permanent ink, permanent ink, a small paintbrush, acetate.

This project uses acetate that is embossable and that usually comes with a tissue liner. Remove the liner and set it aside. In the photo at right the tissue has not been removed so that you can see the plastic.

1 *Add glaze to the acetate.* Squirt on a half-dollar-size amount of Diamond Glaze.

T I P

✍ If you can't find Diamond Glaze, you can substitute the following:

> **gloss medium**
>
> **clear-drying glues**

Test several colors first—these items may not dry as clear.

Your local stamp or art supply store should carry acetate. You can also find it at:

> **copy shops**
>
> **office supply stores**
>
> **teacher supply stores**

2 *Add ink to the glaze.* Open your re-inkers and carefully add a drop or two of ink to the glaze. Let the ink blend into the glaze. Add a couple of drops of another color, allowing the inks to blend. Caution: Adding too much ink can cause the Diamond Glaze to stay soft. A basic mixing ratio is three parts Diamond Glaze to one part ink.

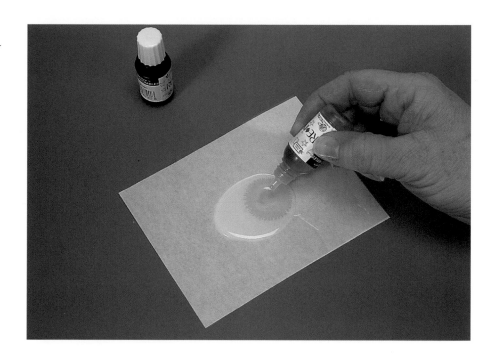

3 *Mix the colors.* If you feel the colors have not meshed well, use a paintbrush to swirl the inks together while the glaze is still very liquid. Do not overmix or the color will become muddy. Spread the mixture over the surface of the plastic.

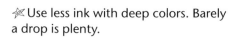

TIP

✯ Use less ink with deep colors. Barely a drop is plenty.

4 *Dry and stamp.* Allow the mixture to dry completely. This should take about 15–20 minutes. (It can take longer in a humid climate.) Once the glue is dry, turn the plastic over and stamp your images with permanent (solvent) ink (dye ink will bead up on the acetate). For this particular technique I like to use dreamy or collage-style images.

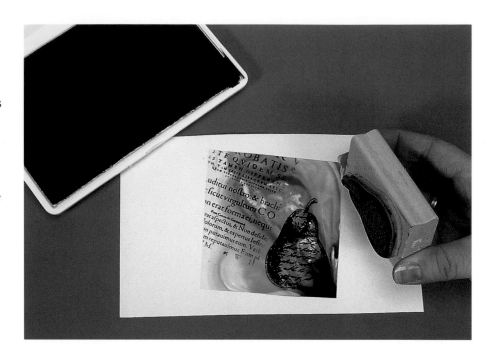

5 *Trim the acetate.* Cut a ½" frame out of a 4" x 4" piece of cardstock using a craft knife and your see-through ruler.

6 *Apply tape.* Center the plastic onto the back of the frame. Apply double-sided tape to the frame, slightly covering the edges of the plastic. Remove the liner from the tape.

7 *Finish the card.* Layer the framed acetate on a square notecard.

The finished card.

Dreamy Face

What you'll need:

- face stamp from Rubber Zone
- permanent ink
- acetate
- Diamond Glaze
- glitter
- dye re-inkers
- scissors
- tissue paper
- brayer (or other smooth cylindrical object)
- notecard

This underglazing technique puts the acetate's paper liner to work.

1 *Stamp, glaze and apply glitter.* On this card, the image of the face was stamped in permanent ink first. Once the design is dry, turn the plastic over and pour on the Diamond Glaze. Then add your ink. Spread the mixture over the surface of the plastic. Do not go all the way out to the edge of the plastic—leave at least a ½" margin around the edge. While the mixture is still very wet, sprinkle on a medium grind of glitter.

TIP

✯ You can use printed tissues for added interest. Also try crinkling the tissue for a textured look.

2 *Apply tissue.* Lay the piece of liner tissue over the entire mixture.

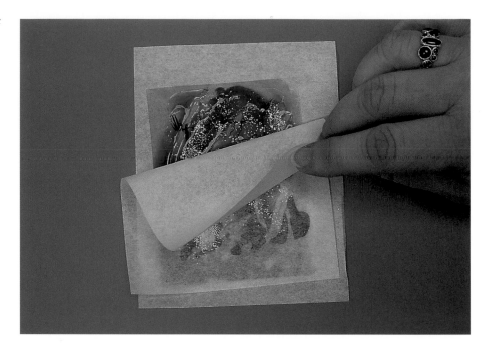

3 *Roll with brayer.* With a rubber brayer, slowly and gently roll over the tissue, sealing the plastic and tissue together. Doing this allows you to work with the piece sooner than allowing it to dry on its own because the tissue absorbs much of the liquid.

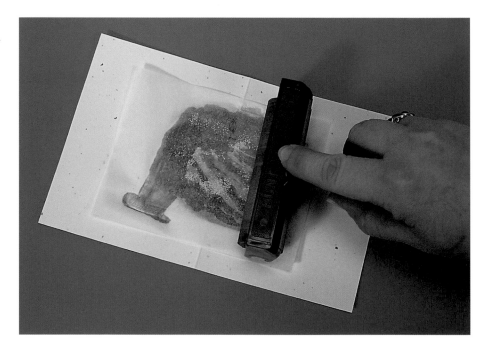

TIP

✦ For a smooth look, use the brayer. If you like more texture, simply lay the tissue on the glaze and pat the surface of the tissue down.

4 *Trim the acetate.* In 5 to 10 minutes the piece should be ready to cut. Test the piece for dryness by touching the tissue. Cut the piece down to approximately 3¼" x 4". Trim away the excess.

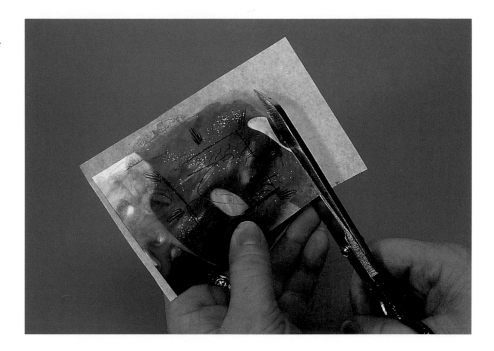

5 *Apply acetate to card.* Apply a few drops of Diamond Glaze to the tissue side of the piece and spread the glaze well. Adhere the piece to the front of a notecard.

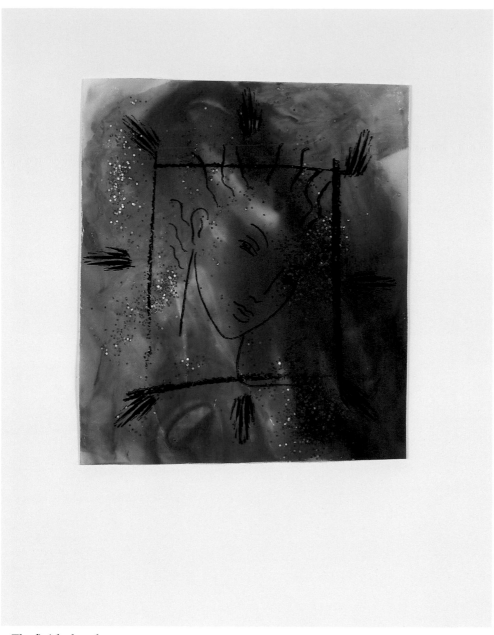

The finished card.

Elegant Women

What you'll need:

- stamp by JudiKins
- dye re-inkers
- brown kraft cardstock
- gold embossing powder
- craft knife
- Diamond Glaze
- small paintbrush
- paper cords
- tall notecard
- white colored pencil

Another idea to try with Diamond Glaze is to mix it with dye re-inkers and then use it as a translucent paint. I call this technique "overglazing."

1 *Emboss your image.* Emboss an image in gold on brown kraft cardstock. This image is long, so I cut it into three separate images.

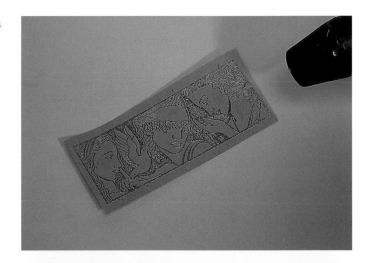

2 *Mix glaze and paint image.* Mix one drop of each color dye with five drops of Diamond Glaze in a paint tray or small plastic dish. Paint the images, being careful to keep the glazing mixture off of the gold embossing. The dove in the second section should be white, so I used a white pencil on it.

3 *Create the cord border.* While the pieces are drying, create the border strip by cutting a piece of double-sided masking tape ½" wide and at least 8½" long. Cover the tape with paper cord, starting at the center and working out.

4 *Finish the card.* Attach the stamped images to the left side of the front of a tall card. Remove the liner from the tape and lay the border as shown.

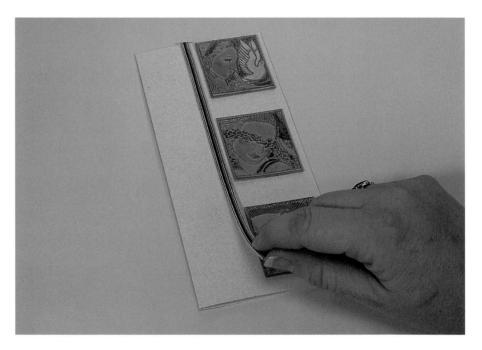

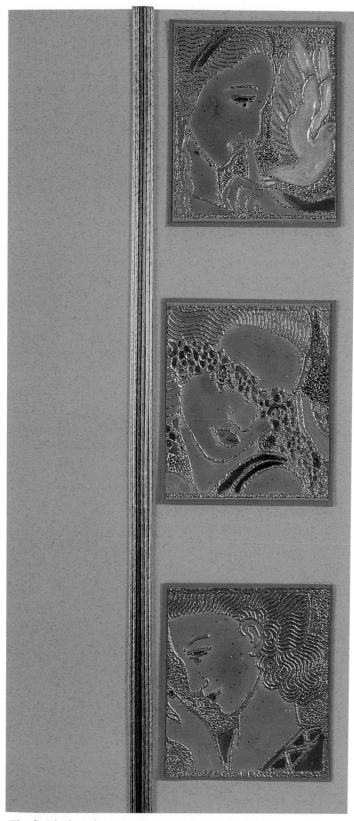

The finished card.

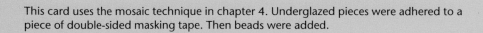

This card uses the mosaic technique in chapter 4. Underglazed pieces were adhered to a piece of double-sided masking tape. Then beads were added.

I stamped and overglazed the image of the woman, then cut it out and placed it over an underglazed panel.

I usually stamp my image on the front of the acetate, but you can also stamp on the back. Remember that your image will be reversed if you stamp on the back of the acetate.

CHAPTER

6

(STAMPS CLOCKWISE FROM LEFT) Zettiology, Acey Duecy, Zettiology.

collage veneers

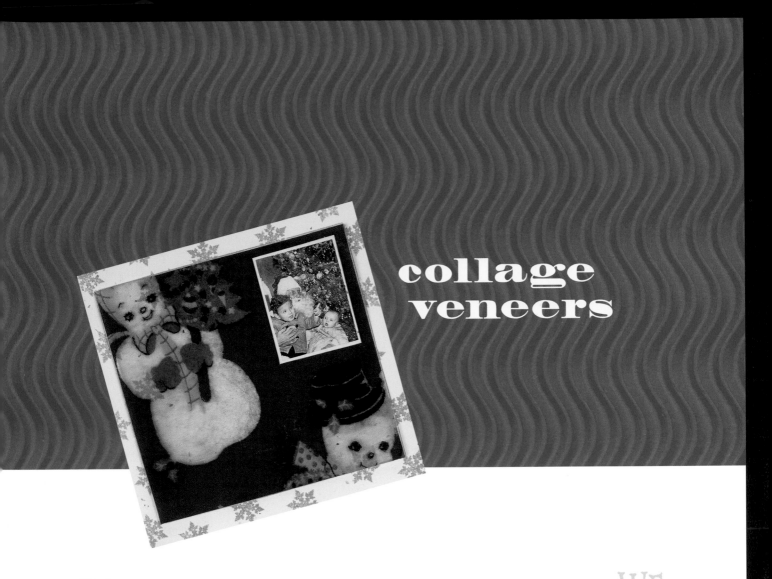

This is an interesting technique you might recognize. Many people who create their own overhead-projector transparencies use this method. The technique can also be used to create greeting cards or in building a collage. It is relatively simple, which makes it very fun and a great project for kids as well as adults.

WE ARE SHAPED AND FASHIONED BY WHAT WE LOVE

Holiday Card

What you'll need:

- snowflake stamp by JudiKins
- color photocopy in a design of your choice
- heavy clear self-adhesive laminate or acetate
- bone folder
- craft knife or scissors
- bowl of water big enough to hold laminate

- square notecard
- metallic gel ink pen
- double-sided clear tape
- double-sided foam tape
- copy of a small vintage photograph

This process transfers an image from paper to the adhesive side of heavy clear acetate or laminate. You will get the best results using photocopies (color or black and white) because the paper is thin and does not take long to remove from the adhesive. Magazines and many other printed materials will work, but can take longer. Ink jet printers do not work! Here I have started with a color copy of an old piece of holiday fabric. The copy was cut to 4" x 4".

Once you've tried this project, try collaging several images together directly on the sticky side of the laminate. Apply metallic pens, powdered pigments or gold leaf foils to the sticky side of the acetate for a dramatic effect.

1 *Adhere copy to laminate.* Apply the copy to the sticky side of a piece of heavy clear laminate.

2 *Burnish.* Carefully burnish the back side of the copy with a bone folder or brayer.

3 *Trim.* Trim any excess laminate.

4 *Immerse in water.* Immerse the entire piece in plain water for 3 minutes.

5 *Rub off the paper.* Place the piece on paper towels face (shiny side) down. Begin rubbing the paper off the laminate with the tips of your fingers. It is very important not to use a sharp object to do the rubbing because it could scrape the veneer. Be sure to remove as much paper as possible. If you see a feltlike residue when the piece is dry, dip the piece in water again and continue rubbing.

TIP

✺ Keep your fingers wet when rubbing off the paper. This helps speed the removal process.

The finished veneer should be translucent when all the paper is rubbed off. Notice that the portion that was white is now clear.

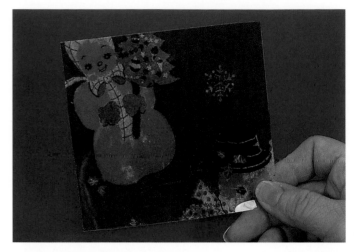

6 *Stamp.* Stamp a border around a square card.

7 *Create a metallic border.* I used a metallic gel ink pen to trace a border on the notecard around the trimmed laminate.

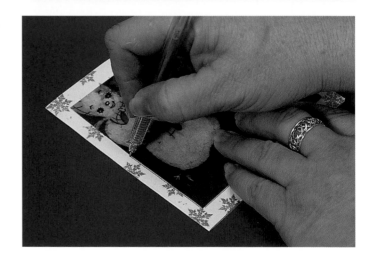

8 *Finish.* Finish the card by using clear double-sided tape to adhere the small photocopy of a vintage photograph to the veneer. To create a 3-D effect, I used double-sided foam tape squares to adhere the veneer to the card. You can also use clear double-sided tape.

The finished card.

The card at the left incorporates a picture of my grandmother and aunt. The background of the card above is made up of old advertising. I added the Hotel Victoria image and the cancelled stamp image.

The background of the card above is a collage of images from a magazine. I added the Eiffel Tower stamp (which is from Carmen's Veranda).

You can add a variety of materials to the adhesive side of the laminate in order to create some stunning special effects. Try powdered pigments, metallic paint pens and gold leaf. Add a few drops of Diamond Glaze for a very modern metal look.

The card above was made with a black and white photocopy of an image of an angel given to me by Zelda of Cleveland. I have photocopied it so many times that the picture has become grainy. I really like that effect.

CHAPTER

7

pastels
and
crayons

Remember the feeling of new crayons in your hand? Experience the joy of simple color-

ing and messy fingers with water-soluble crayons and pastel chalks.

Basic Pastel Background

What you'll need:

- passion flower stamp by Stamp Camp
- pastel sticks
- craft knife
- uncoated (not glossy) postcard
- sponge
- pigment ink pad
- embossing powder
- heat gun
- double-sided tape

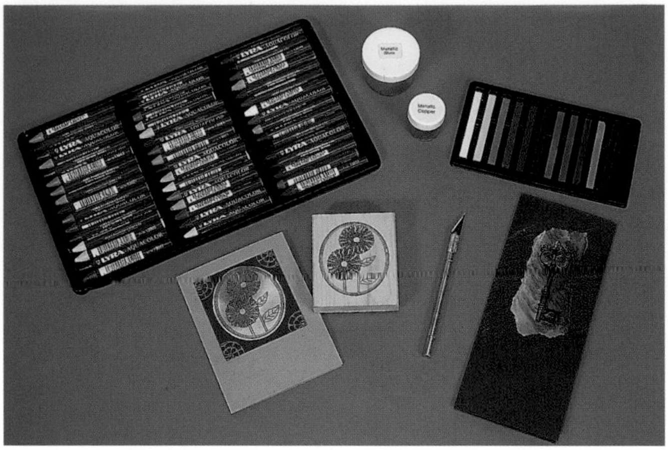

Materials, clockwise from top left: water-soluble crayons, metallic embossing powders, pastel sticks, craft knife, stamp.

Some of the most fun I have with stamping is with water-soluble crayons and regular chalk pastels. They are easy to use on many surfaces and are quick to clean up since they don't stain your fingers!

1 *Scrape the pastel stick.* Scrape the pastel stick with a craft knife, allowing the dust to fall onto an uncoated postcard.

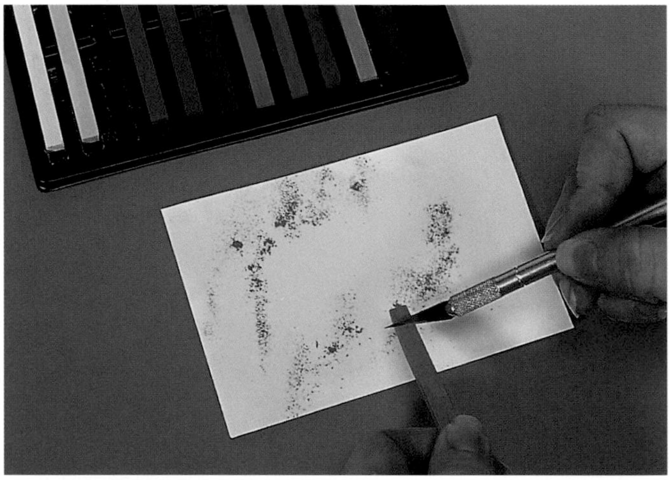

2 *Smear the pastel dust.* Smear the dust into the paper with your fingers or a sponge. Add several more colors in the same manner, blending as you go. Carefully blow away the excess chalk.

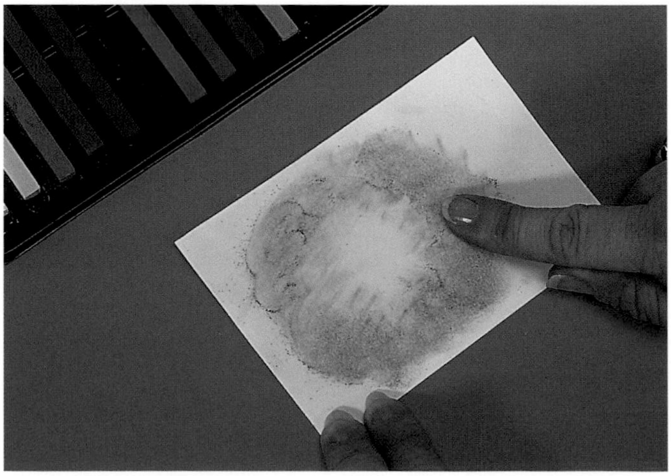

TIP

Begin with the lightest color in the center and then blend with medium and darker colors.

3 *Stamp the image.* Stamp a favorite image onto the paper with pigment ink.

4 *Apply embossing powder.* Pour on a dark embossing powder such as Galaxy. Shake off the excess.

5 *Melt the powder.* Use a heat gun to melt the powder.

6 *Finish the card.* Trim the excess paper from the edge of the image and then use double-sided tape to adhere the finished part to a tall notecard.

Simple Watercolor Wash

What you'll need:

- water-soluble crayons
- uncoated postcard
- water
- small paintbrush

Water-soluble crayons are simple and fun to use. Create watercolor washes for backgrounds or to color in stamped designs. They work on most kinds of paper and can be permanently fixed with a matte spray fixative or even hairspray.

This is a great way to do quick backgrounds for stamping landscapes.

1 *Apply color.* In the center of a postcard scribble a section of color, and then a section of a contrasting color.

2 *Add water.* Spritz generously with water. Allow to dry.

3 *Blend.* Try blending the colors together while wet for a smoother look. Use these postcards to create background layers for notecards, or stamp large designs over the colors once they have completely dried.

Artful View Card

What you'll need:

- face stamp by JudiKins
- water-soluble crayons
- black dye ink pad
- water
- small paintbrush
- paper
- square notecard

1 *Stamp the face.* Begin by ink-ing a large face stamp with black dye ink. Stamp the face.

TIP

✯ To get a perfect print with large stamps, use a brayer to apply pressure evenly.

2 *Apply color.* Apply the crayons in a variety of colors around—but not over—the face design. Carefully apply color to the eyes and lips.

3 *Blend the colors.* With a small amount of water on a paintbrush, gently blend the outside colors in toward the center, but not over the face. Rinse the brush and squeeze out most of the water. Blend the color on the eyes and lips. Follow the shading of the stamp design for shadows. Once the piece is dry, apply small dabs of white crayon to the whites of the eyes and as a highlight in the irises. This makes the face light up and stand out against the background.

4 *Tear the paper.* Tear away the edges of the paper and apply it to a deeper shade of paper with double-sided tape. Tear the edges of this second piece of paper slowly. Tearing the paper toward you will leave a rough appearance on the front of the piece; alternating tearing toward you and away from you can give an interesting texture to the collage. Add tape to the back of the deeper paper and layer the whole piece onto a square notecard. Finish it off with a tassel.

TIP

✫ For a glossy appearance, try spreading Diamond Glaze over the piece and then adding a small amount of glitter.

Fun Face Card

What you'll need:

- stamps by Paula Best
- pigment ink pad
- embossing powder heat gun
- water-soluble crayons
- water
- small paintbrush
- double-sided masking tape

1 *Stamp the background.* Stamp a background with a fun word stamp. Here I have used two light shades of dye inks. Don't use more than three colors; limiting the colors will keep the pattern harmonious.

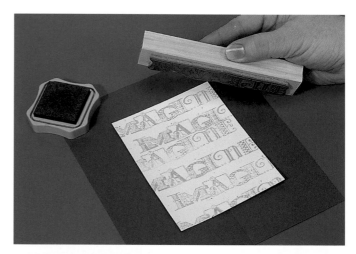

2 *Stamp the face.* Stamp the large face stamp using a pigment ink.

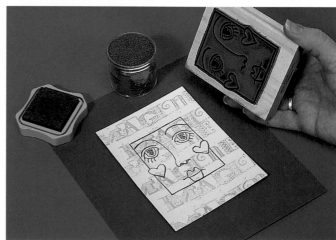

3 *Add embossing powder.* Cover the image in embossing powder and then shake off the excess.

4 *Heat powder.* Heat the powder thoroughly and allow the piece to cool.

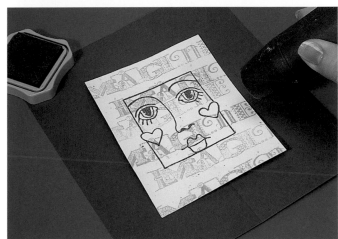

5 *Color.* Color in the open sections of the stamps with colors similar to those used in the background.

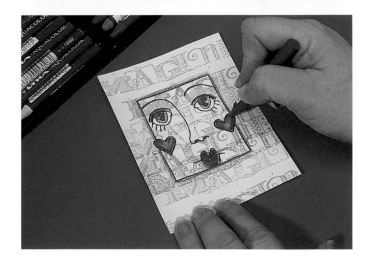

6 *Blend.* With a slightly damp paintbrush, blend the crayon colors.

7 *Add more color.* Add a rim of green around the outside edge of the face stamp and then blend that out with a bit more water.

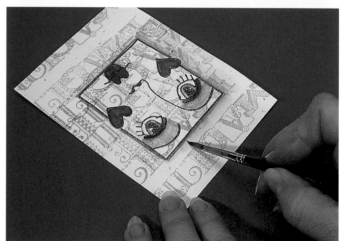

8 *Finish.* When the piece has dried, trim off any excess and apply to a notecard with double-sided tape.

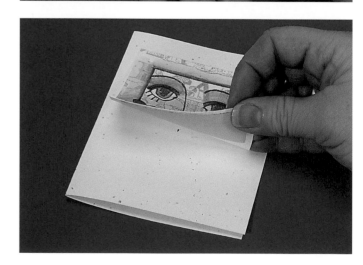

The finished card. I like to add the texture of a soft background to an open image like this face. It gives the card more interest, especially when you hve a simple white card as your base.

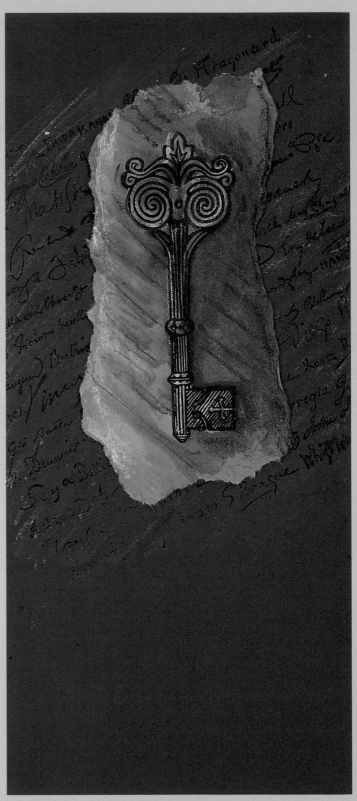

Use colored pencil to add even more detail.

I stamped this image and colored it with crayons, being careful to blend loosely. Don't overdo it.

After stamping the words and the face, I added color by smudging pastels.

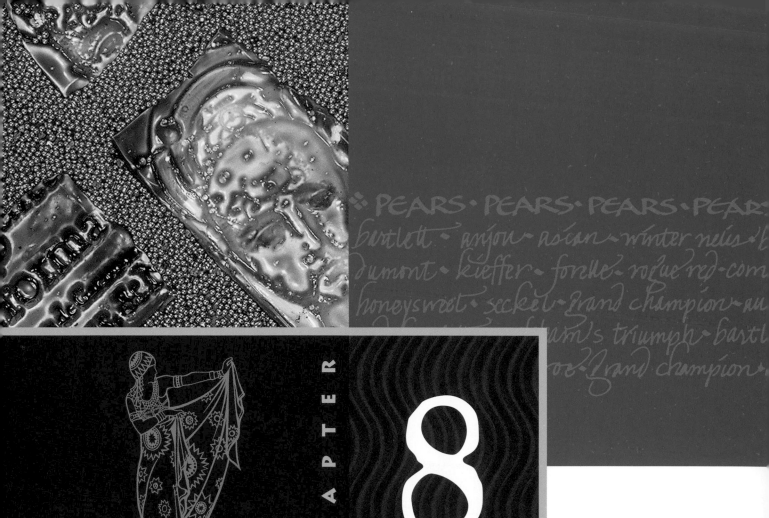

CHAPTER

8

PEARS · PEARS · PEARS · PEAR
bartlett · anjou · ascan · winter nelis ·
dumont · kieffer · forelle · rogue red · com
honeysweet · seckel · grand champion · au
... ... triumph · bart
... grand champion ·

(STAMPS CLOCKWISE FROM LEFT)
JudiKins, A Stamp in the Hand, A Stamp in the Hand

shrink plastic

Shrink plastic came out as a kids' craft item in the late 1960s. It was fun for kids—and easy to use because the images came preprinted on the plastic. With rubber stamps you can create your own images or scenes to shrink. Practice makes perfect with shrink plastic, so be sure you have enough on hand to play with. Always stamp a few extra images to use as charms. This stuff is fun!

Abstract Elegance

What you'll need:

- swirl stamps by Paula Best
- white or translucent shrink plastic
- heat gun (or oven)
- translucent gold embossing powder
- craft knife or scissors
- glass beads
- two colors of metallic pigment ink
- white and dark-purple cardstock
- black corrugated paper
- paper cord
- double-sided masking tape

There are many kinds of shrink plastics out there: white, super clear, translucent (or frosted) and black. There are even some colored varieties. I prefer the super clear for many of my projects because it has a glasslike finish once it is heated.

Permanent ink is the best on plastic since it does not run or bead up. If you want to add color, you can use colored pencils. On translucent or white plastic you may want to sand the surface lightly with an emery board before coloring. This adds some tooth to the surface, and the plastic will accept the colored pencils more easily. Be sure to sand in both directions so the plastic will shrink evenly. Super clear can be stamped on one side and colored on the reverse with water-based metallic markers.

Shrink plastic shrinks down to 40 to 50 percent of the original size. The oven is absolutely the best method for heating and shrinking the plastic. Follow the directions on the package for oven temperature and time. You can also use a heat gun, but this method is sometimes tricky. Be sure to practice!

This project is good for a beginner because it doesn't matter if the plastic is bumpy or doesn't lie flat.

1 *Tear the plastic.* Tear a piece of white or translucent shrink plastic into an unusual shape approximately 2" x 2".

TIP

✐ You can use a hold punch to cut ⅛" holes before shrinking to create jewelry pieces or charms for cards.

2 *Shrink it.* Shrink the piece with a heat gun. Don't worry if the piece is bumpy or doesn't flatten out completely.

T I P

✦ Here I am using the heat gun, which can be tricky. Uneven heating could distort the shape of the piece. Always use a heat gun on a heat-resistant surface (such as a ceramic tile), and use something long to hold the plastic down; a craft knife, chopstick or bone folder will do well.

---

3 *Add embossing powder.* Cover the warm plastic with embossing powder and shake off the excess. Here I have used Translucent Gold.

4 *Heat the powder.* Use the heat gun to melt the embossing powder.

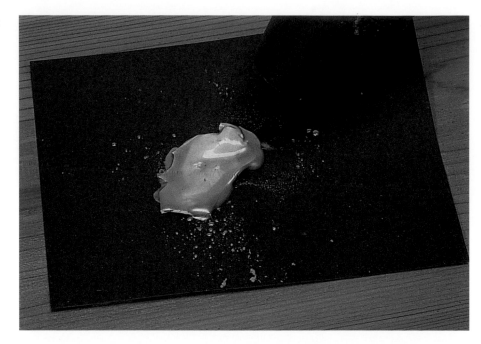

5 *Add glass beads.* While the powder is in a liquid state, sprinkle on a few colored glass beads.

T I P

✵ Try adding glitter instead of beads to the hot embossing powder for a brilliant sheen.

6 *Reheat.* Reheat the whole piece lightly to seal everything together.

7 *Stamp your card.* Set the piece aside to cool. For the card, stamp two colors of metallic pigment ink on a white and dark-purple piece of cardstock.

8 *Cut the card.* Cut the dark-purple cardstock down to 4½" x 3½". Cut a piece of 3½" x 2½" black corrugated paper. Punch two ¹⁄₁₆" holes in the corrugated paper approximately 1" apart, as shown. Thread the paper cord through the holes and tie on the abstract piece of plastic.

9 *Layer.* Layer all the parts together with double-sided masking tape.

Catalina Tiles

What you'll need:

- border stamp by Paper Parachute
- white shrink plastic
- craft knife or scissors
- heat gun
- several colors of dye re-inkers
- Diamond Glaze
- small paintbrush
- powdered pigment
- double-sided masking tape
- copper embossing powder

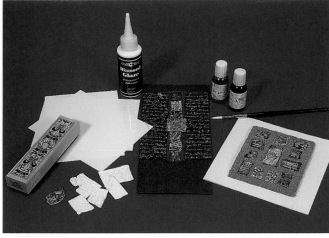

Materials, clockwise from upper left: stamp, shrink plastic, Diamond Glaze, dye re-inkers, paintbrush.

Here is an easy and fun alternative to stamping an image on the plastic. These tiles can be used for jewelry or as embellishments on cards or boxes. This is also a great technique for decorating small box lids.

1 *Cut and shrink tiles.* Cut small squares of white shrink plastic of various sizes. Irregular shapes work well too and have the appearance of broken tile. Shrink the pieces with a heat gun until they become flat.

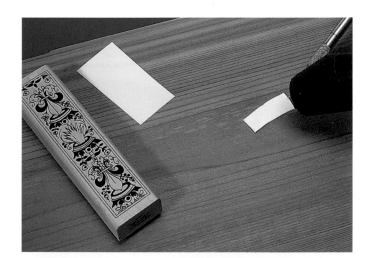

2 *Stamp.* Quickly impress a stamp image into the hot plastic. Make up several of these pieces before moving on to the next step.

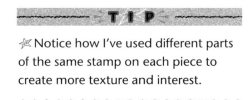

TIP

✸ Notice how I've used different parts of the same stamp on each piece to create more texture and interest.

3 *Make colors.* Make glazes of three or four different colors by adding a drop of dye re-inker to a nickel-size dollop of Diamond Glaze.

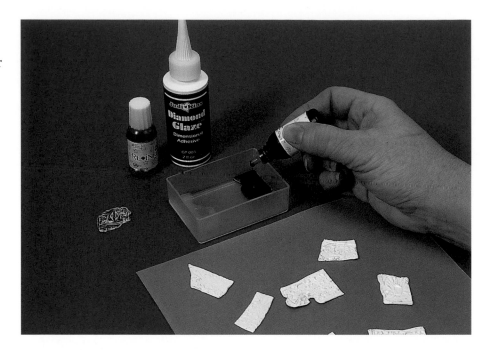

4 *Paint the tiles.* Paint the tiles starting with the lightest color, adding dots or highlighting edges using the darker colors in different parts of each tile.

5 *Add powdered pigment.* If you like a metallic finish, add a little powdered pigment with your paintbrush while the tiles are still wet.

TIP

✦ Powdered pigments come in a wide range of colors and are available at stamp and craft stores. These pigments must be mixed with a liquid like Diamond Glaze or acrylic medium to adhere to surfaces. If applied in their powdered state, a spray fixative should be used to adhere them to the surface and prevent smearing.

6 *Apply embossing powder to tape.* While the tiles are drying, cut a 6" piece of double-sided masking tape. Lay the tape exposed side up and pour copper embossing powder over the entire surface.

7 *Heat.* Heat the powder and while it is hot, pour on another layer of copper powder. Repeat this step. Heat the piece completely and then set it aside to cool. The tiles must be completely dry and cool before the next step.

8 *Reheat.* Reheat the powder on the tape until it is very fluid. Carefully add the tiles onto the tape on top of the liquid embossing powder.

9 *Adhere tiles.* Press each tile down firmly. Adhere tiles on top of the base tiles with Diamond Glaze. Let dry.

10 *Finish card.* Remove the backing from the tape and apply the tape directly to a tall card.

T I P

✯ To secure the tiles, be sure to allow some of the embossing powder to melt over the edges of the tile.

The finished card.

Beaded Tiles

What you'll need:

- stamp by Zettiology
- fifteen or more shrink plastic tiles
- heavy chipboard
- tray or box lid
- Diamond Glaze
- glass beads
- double-sided masking tape
- square notecard

This technique creates a very heavy card, but it is so intriguing you won't mind the extra postage. You can also try this technique on a cardboard picture frame. Before you begin, make up at least fifteen shrink plastic tiles and color them with the Diamond Glaze/re-inker mixtures described previously.

1 *Prepare the chipboard.* You'll need at least fifteen dry tiles. Place a 3½" x 3" piece of heavy chipboard in a small tray or box lid. Spread a thick layer of Diamond Glaze over the chipboard.

2 *Arrange the tiles.* Arrange the tiles in a pleasing pattern on top of the glaze. Leave space between each tile.

3 *Pour on the beads.* Pour glass beads over the glaze. Do not move the tray for at least 20 minutes.

TIP

✯ If all your tiles are the same color, try sprinkling on a second color of beads while the glaze is still wet for more interest.

4 *Finish the card.* After the time has elapsed, shake off the excess beads. Apply the double-sided tape to the chipboard, then layer the piece onto a square note card. For this project I have layered two of these beaded pieces together.

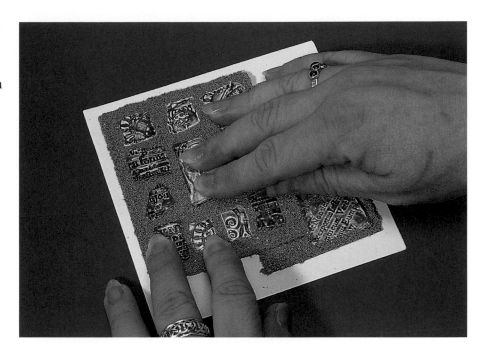

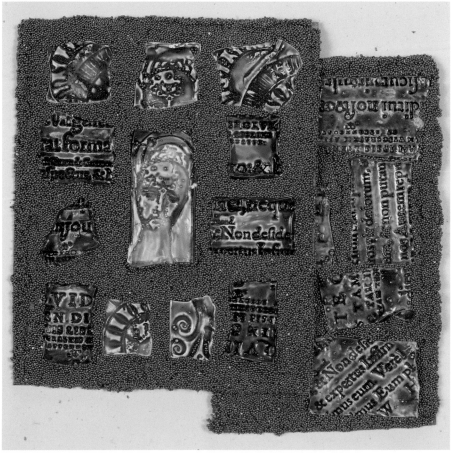

The finished card. If the chipboard starts to curl after you have applied the Diamond Glaze, don't worry. As you press in the tiles, the chipboard will relax.

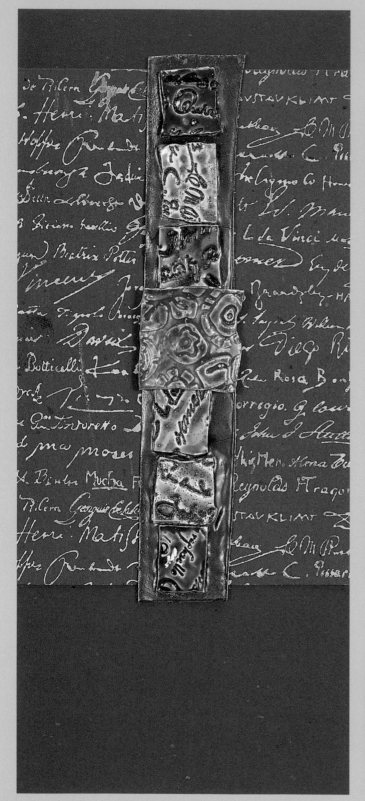

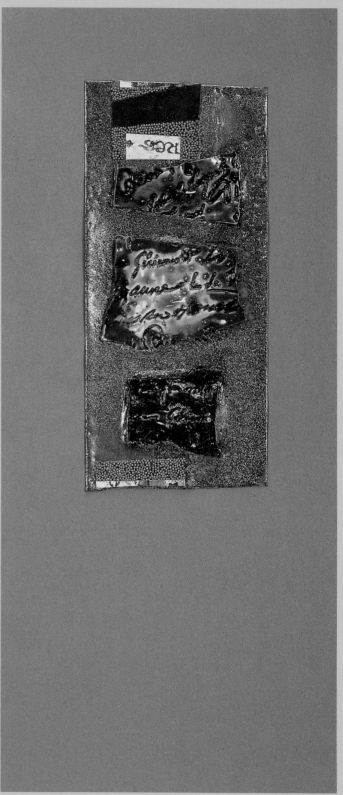

This design incorporates stamped paper.

These square pieces and the long rectangular piece were cut from wood veneer that you can find at most home centers.

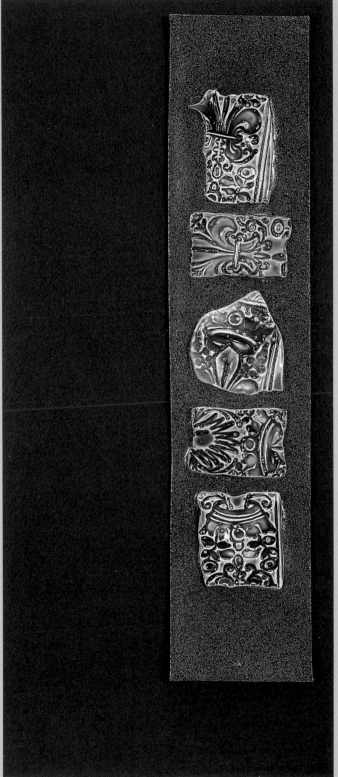

CHAPTER 9

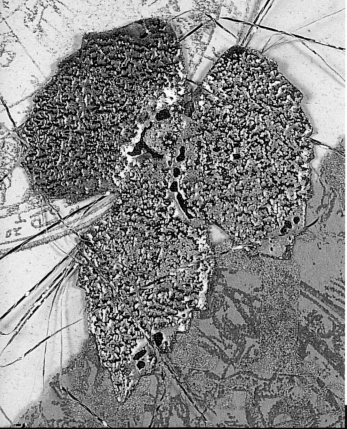

(STAMPS CLOCKWISE FROM LEFT) Acey Duecy, Toy Box, Stampers Anonymous.

natural adornments

Stones, leaves, shells, pods and bark—all of these natural elements can be used on your greeting cards. You can even stamp or emboss most of these surfaces. Slate works very well as a card embellishment because it is relatively thin and lightweight. It also embosses well for those same reasons. Leaves, seeds, bark and pods should be relatively flat. These elements cannot be too bulky or too heavy to attach to paper or board: It would make the card too difficult to mail in an envelope. Of course, you can solve the problem by sending the piece in another container, such as a box or a tube. Silk leaves can also be used in place of dried leaves for a more permanent display.

Silver Cups

What you'll need:

- embossing ink
- small dried flowers
- paper towels
- silver embossing powder
- heat gun
- cancelled postage stamps
- double-sided tape
- scissors
- hole punch
- thin gold thread
- square notecard

Dried flowers are available everywhere—you probably have a few around the house. This is a great technique to use when they start looking a bit worn out. Pour your embossing ink into a small container for ease of use. (You can also roll sturdy flowers in pigment ink to add color.)

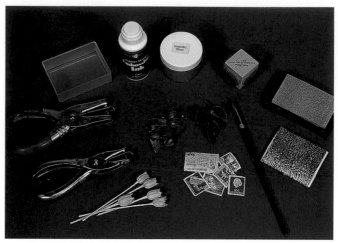

Materials, clockwise from upper left: small tray, embossing ink, embossing powders, stamp, metallic ink pad, gold thread, small paintbrush, cancelled postage stamps, dried or silk flowers and leaves, hole punches.

1 *Dip flowers in embossing ink.* Pour embossing ink into a small tray. Dip each flower into the embossing ink to coat.

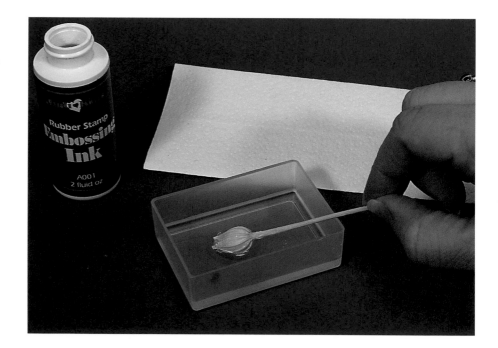

2 *Blot flower.* Blot each flower lightly to remove excess ink.

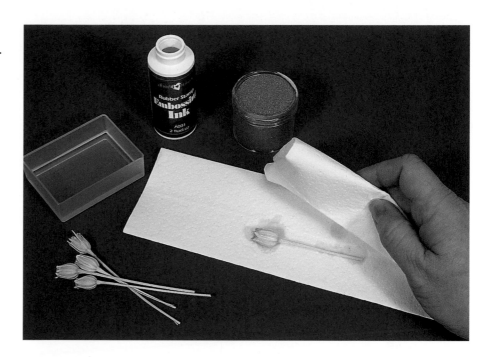

3 *Dip flowers in embossing powder.* Coat the flowers in silver embossing powder.

4 *Heat.* Heat the powder. If the flowers have long stems, and you are doing several at once, stick them into a stiff foam block. Don't get the heat gun too close to the foam because it will melt.

5 *Create the card.* Set the flowers aside. Affix cancelled postage stamps to one side of double-sided masking tape. Trim the edges away with scissors.

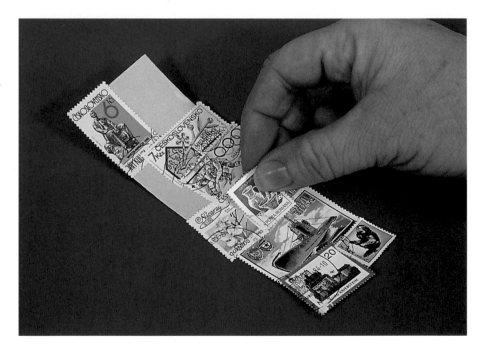

6 *Punch holes.* Punch two small holes about ¼" apart in the center of the tape.

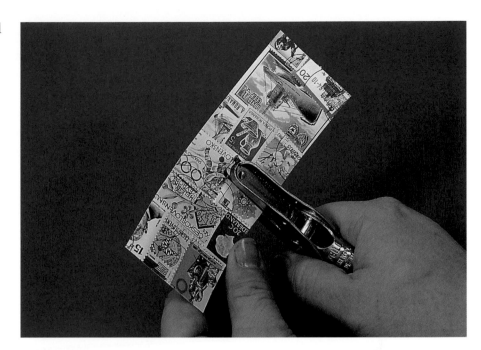

7 *Tie on flowers.* Use decorative gold thread to tie on the silver-cup flowers.

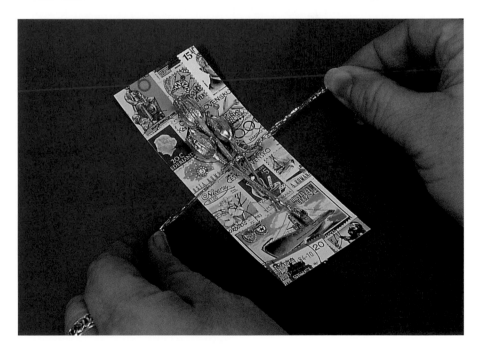

8 *Finish card.* Remove the backing from the tape and adhere the tape directly to a square notecard.

The finished card.

Worldly Leaf

What you'll need:

- zodiac stamp by Toy Box
- large word stamp by Stampers Anonymous
- silk or dry leaf
- embossing ink
- silver embossing powder
- translucent gold embossing powder
- paper towels
- heat gun
- cardstock in sage green and gray-green
- white postcard
- deep-green dye ink
- gold pigment ink
- double-sided masking tape
- natural fibers

The greatest success in embossing leaves is usually achieved with a sturdy dry leaf or a silk leaf. Of course, the older the leaf, the greater the chance it will fall apart. I like to use real leaves for temporary items such as centerpieces or other decorations. For greeting cards it is easier to use silk leaves.

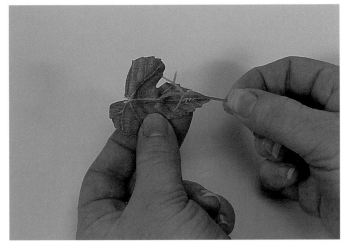

If you plan to use silk leaves, be sure to remove the plastic stems before embossing.

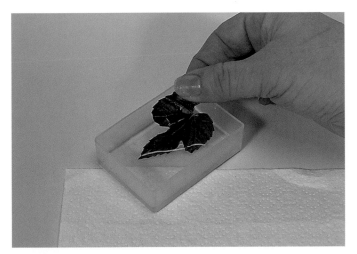

1 *Dip leaves in embossing ink.* For this project we will be embossing with two different powders, Silver and Translucent Gold. Dip the leaf into embossing ink and then blot off any excess.

2 *Add embossing powder.* Pour silver powder on half of the leaf. Shake off the excess and return the remainder to the jar.

3 *Repeat.* Repeat the process with Translucent Gold on the other half of the leaf.

4 *Heat.* Heat the powder and then set the leaf aside to cool.

5 *Assemble the card.* To create the card you'll need a sage green square card, a white post-card and a piece of gray-green cardstock. Tear the gray-green cardstock diagonally as shown. Stamp this piece several times with the zodiac stamp in deep-green dye ink.

6 *Stamp.* Stamp the large word stamp over the same piece with gold pigment ink. On the white postcard, stamp the zodiac stamp once in the corner.

7 *Build the card.* Affix the cards to the sage square card with double-sided tape as shown. Apply the same tape to the back of the leaf.

8 *Place leaf.* Lay the leaf down lightly for placement.

9 *Add fibers underneath.* Lift half of the leaf up and tuck a few fibers under it. Reposition the leaf and apply pressure to the entire leaf.

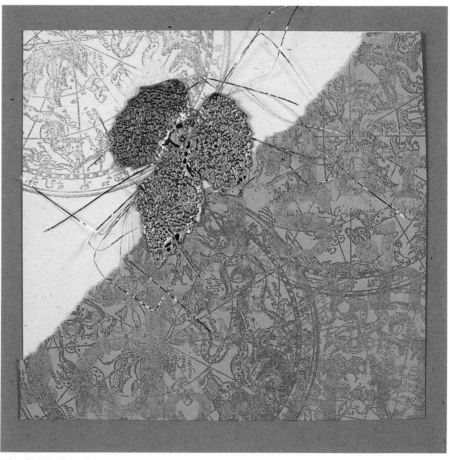

The finished card.

Stone Tablets

What you'll need:

- handwriting stamp by JudiKins
- leaf stamp by Rubber Monger
- small, flat piece of slate
- metallic pigment ink
- gold embossing powder
- heat gun
- black corrugated paper
- Diamond Glaze
- double-sided tape
- cardstock
- notecard

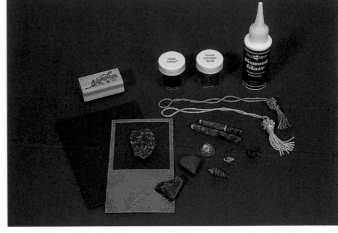

Materials, clockwise from upper left: stamp, embossing powder, Diamond Glaze, tassels, shells, dried flowers and small rocks.

Small pebbles and slate can be very effective on cards. Slate works very well because it is flat.

1 *Stamp the slate.* Here I am using a small piece of slate. Ink the stamp with a metallic pigment ink and lay the stone on the stamp.

2 *Add embossing powder.* Pour on the gold powder.

3 *Heat.* Heat the stone carefully. It takes longer to emboss rocks because of the density, so be sure to emboss on a heat-resistant surface.

TIP

✯ Your cutting mat is not heat resistant, so don't use your heat gun too close to it.

---

4 *Glue stone to paper.* Attach the stone to a piece of black corrugated paper with a dab of Diamond Glaze. Allow the piece to dry thoroughly.

5 *Finish the card.* Use double-sided tape to apply the stone and black paper to a layer of stamped cardstock. Finish by layering onto a notecard and wrapping gold thread through and around the card fold.

Sea Shells

What you'll need:

- stamp by JudiKins
- small sea shells
- pigment ink or embossing ink
- bronze embossing powder
- heat gun

You can emboss sea shells just like slate. Attach shells to tassels or use them as central ornaments. To attach to thread, drill a small hole in the shell before inking and embossing.

1 *Ink shells.* Try to roll long shells across the stamp.

2 *Emboss.* Roll the shells in bronze embossing powder and heat.

For this card, holes were drilled in the long shells before they were stamped (you can purchase some types of shells pre-drilled), then cords were run through the holes once the shells had cooled from the heat gun. A square scrap of stamped paper provided the foundation for a spiral shell that I had immersed in embossing ink and embossing powder and then heated.

The edges of the eucalyptus bark were coated with the same metallic pen used on the edges of the paper.

This face was stamped on a broken piece of wood veneer. You could also use tree bark or stained balsa wood.

The shells on both of these cards were secured with layers of melted embossing powder, then coated with Amazing Glaze for a clear finish. The card on the right has colored powders incorporated into the Amazing Glaze. Glitter and beads can also be added.

Resources

stamp companies

The companies listed in this directory sell high-quality rubber stamps. All the companies listed have different policies regarding copyrights, catalogs, stamps and supplies. Many companies now have Web sites you can visit.

ACEY DUECY
P.O. Box 194
Ancram, NY 12502

ALICE IN RUBBERLAND
P.O. Box 9262
Seattle, WA 98109

AMERICAN ART STAMP
3892 Del Amo Blvd. Suite 701
Torrance, CA 90503
(310) 371-6593
Fax 310-371- 5545

ART GONE WILD
3110 Payne Ave.
Cleveland, OH 44114
(800) 945-3950
artgwild@aol.com

CARMEN'S VERANDA/POSTSCRIPT
P.O. Box 1539
Placentia, CA 92871
(888) 227-6367
http://www.carmensveranda.com

CLAUDIA ROSE
15 Baumgarten Road
Saugerties, NY 12477
(914) 679-9235

COFFEE BREAK DESIGNS
P.O. Box 34281
Indianapolis, IN 46234
coffeebreakdesign@ameritech.net

**THE CREATIVE BLOCK/
STAMPERS ANONYMOUS**
20613 Center Ridge Road
Rocky River, OH 44116
(440) 333-7941

CURTIS UYEDA/CURTIS' COLLECTION
3326 St. Michael Drive
Palo Alto, CA 94306

DENAMI DESIGN
P.O. Box 5617
Kent, WA 98064
(253) 639-2546

DRAGGIN' INK
P.O. Box 24135
Santa Barbara, CA 93121
(805) 966-5297

FEBRUARY PAPER
P.O. Box 4297
Olympia, WA 98501
(360) 705-1519

GUMBALL GRAPHICS
1417 Creighton Ave.
Dayton, OH 45420
(513) 258-2663

HOT POTATOES
2805 Columbine Place
Nashville, TN 37204
(615) 269-8002
http://www.hotpotatoes.com

JUDIKINS
17803 S. Harvard Blvd
Gardena, CA 90248
(310) 515-1115
http://www.judikins.com

LOVE YOU TO BITS/TIN CAN MAIL
P.O. Box 5748
Redwood City, CA 94063
(800) 546-LYTB

MAGENTA
351 Blain, Mont-Saint-Hilaire
Quebec, Canada J3H3B4
(514) 446-5253

MEER IMAGE
P.O. Box 12
Arcata, CA 95518
http://www.meerimage.com

MOE WUBBA
P.O. Box 1445, Dept. B
San Luis Obispo, CA 93406
(805) 547-1MOE

PAM BAKKE PASTE PAPERS
303 Highland Dr.
Bellingham, WA 98225
(360) 738-4830

PAPER PARACHUTE
P.O. Box 91385
Portland, OR 97291-0385

RUBBER BABY BUGGY BUMPERS
1331 W. Mountain Ave.
Fort Collins, CO 80521
(970) 224-3499
http://www.rubberbaby.com

RUBBER MONGER
P.O. Box 1777
Snowflake, AZ 85937
Fax: (888) 9MONGER

RUBBERMOON
P.O. Box 3258
Hayden Lake, ID 83835
(208) 772-9772

RUBBER ZONE
P.O. Box 10254
Marina del Rey, CA 90295
http://www.rubberzone.com

RUBY RED RUBBER
P.O. Box 2076
Yorba Linda, CA 92885
(714) 970-7584

SKYCRAFT DESIGNS
26395 S. Morgan Rd.
Estacada, OR 97023
(503) 630-7173

STAMPACADABRA
5091 N Fresno St. Suite 133
Fresno, CA 93710
(209) 227-7247

STAMP CAMP
P.O. Box 222091
Dallas, TX 75222
(214) 330-6831

STAMPSCAPES
7451 Warner Ave. #E124
Huntington Beach, CA 92647

STAMPS HAPPEN, INC
369 S. Acacia Ave.
Fullerton, CA 92631
(714) 879-9894

A STAMP IN THE HAND
20630 S. Leapwood Ave. Suite B
Carson, CA 90746
(310) 329-8555
http://www.astampinthehand.com

**STAMP YOUR ART OUT/
ENVELOPES PLEASE**
9685 Kenwood Rd.
Cincinnati, OH 45242
(513) 793-4558

THE STUDIO
PO Box 5681
Bellevue, WA 98006

TOYBOX RUBBER STAMPS
P.O. Box 1487
Healdsburg, CA 95448
(707) 431-1400

TWENTY-TWO
6167 North Broadway, No. 322
Chicago, IL 60660

VIVA LAS VEGASTAMPS
1008 East Sahara Ave.
Las Vegas, NV 89104
(702) 836-9118

WORTH REPEATING
227 N. East St.
New Auburn, WI 54757
(715) 237-2011

ZETTIOLOGY/THE STUDIO
P.O. Box 5681
Bellevue, WA 98006

publications

For more information (including stamp-related Web sites) on stamping or stores in your area, try these stamping publications:

THE RUBBERSTAMPER
225 Gordons Corner Road
P.O. Box 420
Manalapan, NJ 07726-0420
(800) 969-7176

RUBBERSTAMPMADNESS
408 SW Monroe #210
Corvallis, OR 97330
(541) 752-0075

**RUBBERSTAMP SOURCEBOOK &
TRAVELERS GUIDE TO RUBBERSTAMPING**
Cornucopia Press
4739 University Way NE
Suite 1610-A
Seattle, WA 98105
(206) 528-8120

STAMPER'S SAMPLER & SOMERSET STUDIO
22992 Millcreek, Suite B
Laguna Hills, CA
(714) 380-7318

VAMP STAMP NEWS
P.O. BOX 386
Hanover, MD 21076-0386

favorite products

My favorite rubber-stamping products are listed below.

COLORBOX
pigment inks

DRAGGIN' INK
embossing powders

ENCORE
pigment inks

ENVELOPES PLEASE
diorama template

FEBRUARY PAPERS
decorative threads and yarns

JUDIKINS
card stock
detachable brayer
embossing powders
Amazing Glaze
Diamond Glaze
permanent ink
paper cord
tassels
glass beads
Wax Wafers
envelope templates

shrink plastic
acetate
laminating sheets
mosaic tape

LYRA
watercolor crayons
pastel chalks

MARVY
dye inks

PAM BAKKE PASTE PAPERS
specialty papers

PEARL EX
powdered pigments

SCOTCH
double-sided cellophane tape
double-sided foam mounting tape

SKYCRAFT DESIGNS
specialty papers

SPEEDBALL
C-thru ruler
detachable brayer

stamps used in this book

Here is a list of all the stamps used in this book.

PAGE 8, planeterium by Toy Box, wave woman by Stampers Anonymous, script by A Stamp in the Hand. **PAGE 9,** clown girl by Zettiology. **PAGE 12,** butterfly woman by Stampers Anonymous, chair by Rubber Moon, script background by Zettiology, tiny wax seal by JudiKins. **PAGE 17,** butterfly woman by Stampers Anonymous. **PAGE 18,** deco cube by JudiKins. **PAGE 20,** sentiment by Zettiology. **PAGE 21,** Japanese mum and bird of paradise by Stamp Camp, tiny swirl by Twenty Two, paula best cubes by JudiKins. **PAGE 22,** large print background by Stampers Anonymous, statue by Toy Box, fish background by American Art Stamp, "Queen of Last Minute" by Paper Parachute, keys and crown by JudiKins. **PAGE 23,** bugs by Meer Image, clown girl by Zettiology. **PAGE 24,** dogs by Rubber Zone. **PAGE 29,** large print background by Stampers Anonymous, statue by Toy Box, bugs by Meer Image. **PAGE 30,** stars by paula best, chair by Rubber Moon, kissing couple by Curtis Uyeda. **PAGE 31,** oranges by Stamp Camp, deco panel by JudiKins. **PAGE 32,** deco panel by JudiKins. **PAGE 36-40,** stamps by paula best. **PAGE 41,** sun by A Stamp in the Hand, kissing couple by Curtis Uyeda. **PAGE 42,** floral background by American Art Stamp, "corpus" by Stampers

Anonymous. **PAGE 50,** wave woman by Stampers Anonymous. **PAGE 52-53,** baroque, origami, relish, deco swirls backgrounds by JudiKins. **PAGE 54,** three sisters, Lisa face, deco woman by JudiKins; pear by Stampers Anonymous; words by Zettiology. **PAGE 55,** dreamy lady by Rubber Zone, deco lady by JudiKins. **PAGE 58-60,** pear by Stampers Anonymous, words by Zettiology. **PAGE 62-64,** dreamy lady by Rubber Zone. **PAGE 65-67,** three sisters by JudiKins. **PAGE 68,** wishing and hoping deco ladies by JudiKins, dragonfly by Hot Potatoes, tiny swirl by Meer Image. **PAGE 69,** deco lady, Lisa face, square swirl by JudiKins; moon face by Rubber Moon. **PAGE 70-71,** Madrid, Eiffel tower by Carmen's Veranda; book by Acey Duecy; moon dial, "we are shaped" by Zettiology. **PAGE 74,** snowflake by JudiKins. **PAGE 76,** row of chairs by A Stamp in the Hand; cancellation, world tour background by Carmen's Veranda. **PAGE 77,** Eiffel tower by Carmen's Veranda. **PAGE 78,** flowers by Paper Parachute; butterflies background, Lisa face, artists' signatures by JudiKins; clock face by Stampers Anonymous. **PAGE 79,** heart face, "imagine" by paula best; three sisters by JudiKins. **PAGE 80,** flowers by Paper Parachute. **PAGE 81-82,** passion flower by Stamp Camp. Page **84-85,** Lisa face, artists' signatures by JudiKins. Page **86-89,** heart face, "imagine" by paula best. **PAGE 90,** willow, key butterflies by JudiKins. **PAGE 91,** artists' signatures, Mona face, deco cube by JudiKins; flowers by Paper Parachute; planeterium by Toy Box. **PAGE 92,** celestial woman by JudiKins, border by Paper Parachute, head by Zettiology, pears by A Stamp in the Hand. **PAGE 93,** pillar by A Stamp in the Hand. **PAGE 93-98,** paula best swirl cube by JudiKins. **PAGE 99-104,** border by Paper Parachute. **PAGE 105-107,** head, words by Zettiology. **PAGE 108-109,** artists' signatures, deco flowers by JudiKins; border by Paper Parachute. **PAGE 110,** world map by Toy Box, postoid by Acey Duecy. **PAGE 111,** leaf by Rubber Monger. **PAGE 119-121,** world map by Toy Box, large words by Stampers Anonymous. **PAGE 122-125,** leaf by Rubber Monger, artists' signatures by JudiKins. **PAGE 126,** paula best star cube by JudiKins, squared face by Rubber Moon. **PAGE 127,** swirl cube by JudiKins.

QUICK & EASY
decorative
painting

Peggy Jessee

NORTH LIGHT BOOKS
CINCINNATI, OHIO
www.nlbooks.com

Table of Contents

Introduction 134

Where do you get those ideas? . .135

What You'll Need

Chapter 1 136
General Supplies
Brushes
Surfaces

Colors

Chapter 2 140

What You'll Need to Know

Chapter 3 143
Crackling
Sponging
Filbert Brush
    Comma stroke
    Leaf stroke
Flat Brush
    S-stroke
    Comma stroke
Sandy's Sure-Stroke Brush
    Comma stroke
    Daisy stroke
Liner Brush
    Comma stroke
    Squiggles or Vines
Miracle Wedge Brush

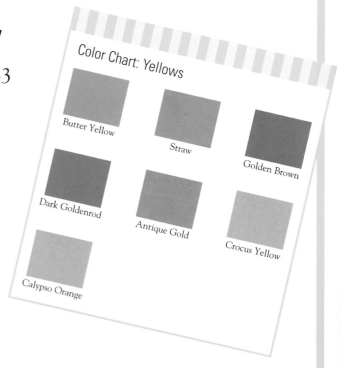

Color Chart: Yellows

Butter Yellow

Straw

Golden Brown

Dark Goldenrod

Antique Gold

Crocus Yellow

Calypso Orange

Leaves and Twigs

Project 1 150

Filler Flowers

Project 2 166

Focal Flowers

Project 3 182

Fruits and Berries

Project 4 216

Pull It All Together

Project 5 236

Design Your Own

. 250

Resources 252

Introduction

Welcome to *Quick & Easy Decorative Painting*. You'll find that by practicing your brushstrokes you'll be able to decorate everything from coasters to furniture pieces with designs that are truly your own.

There are many ways to paint flowers, fruit and foliage that can take a long time, but as I tell my students—I am the Queen of "Instant Gratification." I like to see progress in a short time.

When I start a project, I don't have a clue what it will look like when I am finished. I start by selecting the flower or fruit that will be my focal point and I build from there. I select the area where I want the focal point, and paint around that fruit or flower. I love painting freehand because tracing is time consuming. However, don't feel you have to do the same. Use the patterns included in this book, but with practice you'll soon be painting without patterns, too.

My rules for painting are simple:

1. Play with color combinations to find the colors you *love*.

2. Practice and enjoy your time painting. I believe,

"If you paint what you love, and with the colors you love, you'll love what you paint."

-Peggy Jessee

Where do you get those ideas?

There are a lot of places to look for design ideas and color schemes. Look at greeting cards, especially when you travel. Check out the local gift shops for cards and wrapping paper from small companies. They have beautiful art work. I often find a flower in a design or just a color combination I like, so I buy the card to add to my "idea book."

Look at the bargain books in bookstores. I have found several gardening books with fantastic pictures of flowers and fruit that give me ideas for easy designs. For example, while doing this book, I found a picture of "Johnny-jump-ups" and realized the flowers could be painted with a few basic strokes and a little line work.

Don't forget to look at seed packets and seed catalogs for ideas, especially for color and flower details. When I find pictures in catalogs or magazines I cut them out for my "idea book." And remember to take your camera wherever you go. Your photographs will make a nice addition to your "idea book," too.

What is an "Idea Book"?

I use a sketch book I purchased at a local craft supplier. It has a heavy cover so it won't get bent. Some books have plain paper and some have a few lines for notes. I tape or glue my magazine pictures or photos on the pages, and make a few notes about colors or designs to use at a later time. I often go to department stores and look at the bath towels on display. I find this an easy way to visualize color combinations. Seeing different solid colors together

helps me plan color schemes and gives me a lot of ideas. Fabric stores are another great place to look for color combinations.

I also love to go through the silk flowers at craft stores. I often buy a single stem of flowers and keep all my finds in a huge container in my studio for inspiration. Once, when I was purchasing a sprig of flowers at my local craft store a clerk told me, "God never made that flower in that color." My reply was ". . . but, God made all the colors."

Practice, play and most of all, have fun. You'll be surprised at the wonderful color combinations you discover and how creative you can be.

WHAT YOU'LL NEED

General Supplies

Brush Basin: A good brush basin has two or three compartments for water and grooves for brushes to rest on without touching the sides or bottom of the container. Brush basins usually have a set of ridges to rub the bristles over to help remove paint. To avoid damaging your brushes, never jam them on the ridges, but rub gently.

Sandpaper: Most of the wood pieces in craft stores today are very good and need only light sanding with a no. 220 grit sandpaper. I usually use the sanding pads purchased in craft, hardware and paint stores. They are more expensive than regular sandpaper, but last a long time and usually have a different grit on each side, some are very rough and some are very fine. Check out the variety and you'll find what works best for you.

Tack Rag: Tack rags are usually cheesecloth that has been soaked in a liquid (usually varnish) then dried to a tacky feel. Tack rags are used to remove sanding dust from your wood surface. Store your tack rag in an airtight container to keep it sticky. A Ziploc bag or a glass jar with a lid works fine.

Palette: There are many types of palettes. You'll find paper palettes at your local art supply store. Make sure they are suitable for acrylic paint. Styrofoam plates, glazed ceramic tile or metal pans can also be used.

Paper Towels: I like to use soft paper towels to clean my brushes, so as not to cause damage to the bristles. It is important that the paper towel not leave lint. It will get into your paint.

Wood Sealer: I recommend a water- based wood sealer, so you

can mix your sealer with your basecoat color. There are many good sealers on the market: Delta's wood sealer, Jo Sonja's All Purpose sealer or J.W. Etc. wood sealers are all great.

Varnish: If you start reading the labels on varnish cans, it will drive you crazy. There are so many from which to choose—oil-based, water-based, acrylic or polymer. Stick with a water-based product. My favorites are Delta and J.W. Etc. Right-Step Varnish. Most varnishes come in a variety of finishes including satin, gloss and flat. Choose the type of sheen you like best. Most water-based varnishes can be used inside, because they have low odor and dry quickly. Make sure you read the instructions carefully.

Crackle Medium: I think it best to use the crackle medium made to go with the brand of paint you use. Crackle mediums can be difficult to use, but if you read and follow the directions, you'll get good results. Be sure not to brush over the medium once you apply it, simply let it dry. Also, the topcoat will crack in the direction the crackle medium is brushed. To find the look you like, brush the crackle medium on a scrap of wood—thick in some areas, and thin in others. Vary the direction in which you apply the crackle—up and down, side to side and in different directions. This will help you decide on the look of the background.

Glazing Medium: This medium is used either for staining wood with the acrylic color of your choice or

to mix with one of the browns like Burnt Umber to antique your painting after you're done.

Stencils: I like to use stencils for welcome signs and for backgrounds such as checks and stripes. There are thousands of stencils available for these purposes. They are easy to use and clean up with soap and water.

Gesso: Use gesso when you are wanting to seal a surface such as the back of linoleum.

Sponges: You should have a variety of sponges on hand including sea sponges, make-up sponges and regular sponges. This will help you with spills, applying paint to presses or stamps and faux finishes.

Brushes

Brushes are your most important tool when it comes to decorative painting. It is important to purchase the proper brushes for the type of work you do. You should purchase the best brushes you can afford, and take proper care of them to keep them in good shape.

The following are my brush choices. I believe that the best brush for any project is the one that works best for you. After you work with brushes, you'll discover your favorite brands, shapes and sizes. You'll want synthetic bristles for painting with acrylics.

Liner Brushes: Liners come in a variety of lengths and sizes. You'll want several sizes. I prefer the

medium-length liners such as the Loew-Cornell JS liners or Robert Simmons Expressions E51. They are easier to handle than script liners and hold more paint than the short liners.

Flat Brushes: Flats are a standard in every painter's brush caddie. I don't use a lot of flat brushes in my style of painting, but you'll want several different sizes. My choice is the Loew-Cornell series 7300 shaders. I use these for foliage and basecoating.

Filbert Brushes: I use filberts most of the time rather than flat brushes, because they make great strokes with rounded ends for flowers and foliage. My choice of filbert brushes is Loew-Cornell series 7500.

Rake Brushes: I use the flat and filbert rake brushes by Loew-Cornell series 7120 and 7520. These are used for creating texture in leaves or flower petals. They can also be used for painting blades of grass.

Round Brushes: Round brushes are used for daisy petals and foliage.

All-Purpose Brush: This is a round, natural bristle brush that is available from several companies. Ceramic shops call it a ceramic dusting brush; Loew-Cornell calls it an All-Purpose Brush. It comes in several different sizes. I use one that is approximately 1-inch (2.5cm) in diameter. This is an inexpensive brush, so you may want more than one size. I use this brush to pounce in background foliage color, or to add texture to my backgrounds. It is important to use this brush dry. When you want to change colors, wipe as much of the paint as possible out of the the brush onto a paper towel.

Stencil Daubers: Stencil daubers can be used to create lettering like the Welcome Sign on page 209, or the fabulous berries on pages 217-221. Stencil daubers are usually round and come in several sizes. The size you'll need depends on the size of the berries or the size of the stencil. Stencil daubers can be found in your local craft supply store.

Miracle Wedge: The wedge is a three-sided brush with a long point. At first I was unsure what to do with it. I found it a lot of fun to use be-cause it makes quick and easy petals and leaves.

Ultra-Round by Loew-Cornell: This round brush has a long point and holds a lot of paint. After experimenting with it, I found it makes great foliage and flower petals.

Worn Brushes: Make sure you save your old worn-out brushes, they are great for putting in background foliage. Sometimes they'll make a pretty flower or baby's breath.

Sandy's Sure Stroke: This is my favorite brush. It comes in two sizes: the original Sandy's Sure Stroke by Royal Brush or Eagle Brush's Sandy's Easy Stroke, and the Sandy's Sure Stroke Mini by

Royal Brush or Eagle Brush's Sandy's Easy Stroke Mini. I saw Sandy Aubuchon use this brush to paint a carnation at the Heart of Ohio Tole Convention. I knew it would make wonderful flowers, quickly and easily. I use this brush for everything that calls for a round brush. It holds its shape well and takes the abuse of decorative painting. I recommend having both sizes handy.

Leaf Press: A press is like a rubber stamp. It can be used to quickly add leaves or even flowers. You can embellish them after you've pressed it on the surface or you can add different colors to the press itself.

Surfaces

My goal with this book is not to focus on the surfaces, but more on the techniques you'll need to do quick and easy decorative painting. Often I used to feel I couldn't paint a pattern from a book I liked, unless I had the exact surface on which the original was painted. The truth is you can paint any design on anything with a few modifications. I have painted on a canvas-covered journal I picked up in a local mall. It comes in many colors and makes a great surface for a quick painting. Every year the craft stores have a new variety of wood, glass and ceramic items. Check out the hardware stores for buckets, watering cans, mail boxes and other metal items to decorate. In my local hardware superstore I found a wonderful line of do-it-yourself furniture such as coffee tables and end tables. I also found the plain wooden ball feet that are used on a lot of sofas. They make great candleholders. You can find other items such as lamps, window shades and more at your local hardware store. A lot of stores sell glass jars of all sizes that have varnished wood lids on them. Just sand the lids a little and you're ready to basecoat and paint. Keep your eyes open and you'll be amazed at all the inexpensive, easy-to-paint-on surfaces you find.

CHAPTER 2

COLORS

A World of Colors

Colors make the world go round. Without them life would be very dull and boring. The following colors are the ones I use most often in my painting. I enjoy using Delta Ceramcoat acrylic paint because it is creamy, and flows well when I'm doing stroke flowers. Of course, being acrylic it cleans up quickly too. If you have a favorite brand of paint, feel free to use it. The color charts on these pages will help you match colors. Also, feel free to use other colors. Make notes of the colors that harmonize especially well, or that go with your home decor. Enjoy experimenting with colors; most of the time you'll get some surprising and beautiful results.

Color Chart: Yellows

Butter Yellow · Straw · Golden Brown
Dark Goldenrod · Antique Gold · Crocus Yellow
Calypso Orange · Poppy Orange

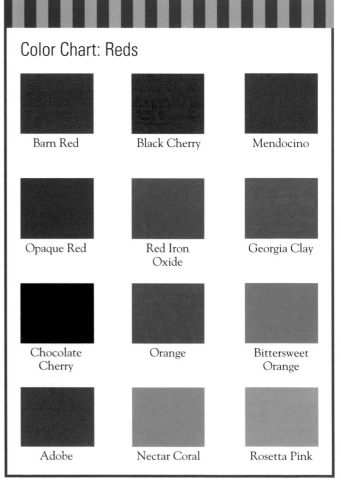

Color Chart: Reds

Barn Red · Black Cherry · Mendocino
Opaque Red · Red Iron Oxide · Georgia Clay
Chocolate Cherry · Orange · Bittersweet Orange
Adobe · Nectar Coral · Rosetta Pink

Color Chart: Blues and Purples

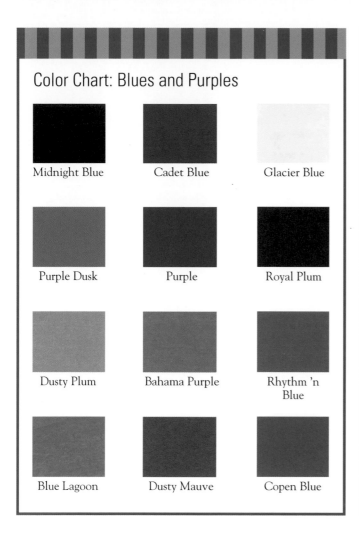

Midnight Blue

Cadet Blue

Glacier Blue

Purple Dusk

Purple

Royal Plum

Dusty Plum

Bahama Purple

Rhythm 'n Blue

Blue Lagoon

Dusty Mauve

Copen Blue

Color Chart: Greens

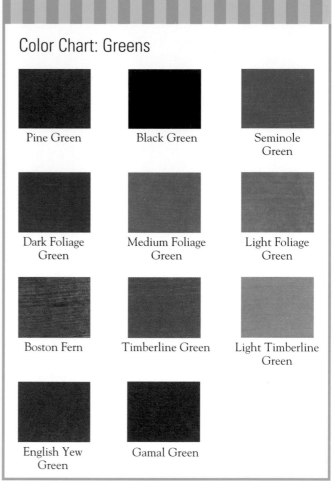

Pine Green

Black Green

Seminole Green

Dark Foliage Green

Medium Foliage Green

Light Foliage Green

Boston Fern

Timberline Green

Light Timberline Green

English Yew Green

Gamal Green

141

Color Chart: Browns

Walnut

Autumn Brown

Candy Bar Brown

Burnt Umber

Trail Tan

Bambi Brown

Burnt Sienna

Spice Brown

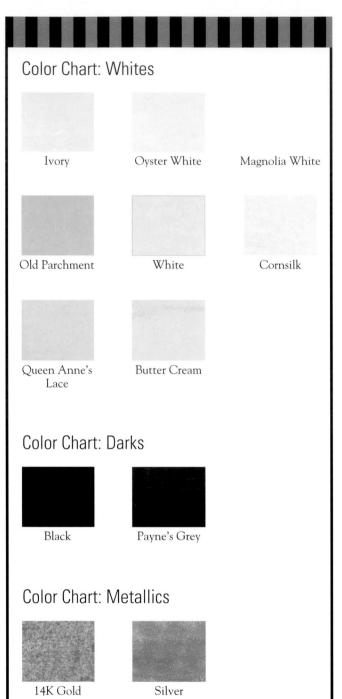

Color Chart: Whites

Ivory

Oyster White

Magnolia White

Old Parchment

White

Cornsilk

Queen Anne's Lace

Butter Cream

Color Chart: Darks

Black

Payne's Grey

Color Chart: Metallics

14K Gold

Silver

WHAT YOU'LL NEED TO KNOW

Terms and Techniques

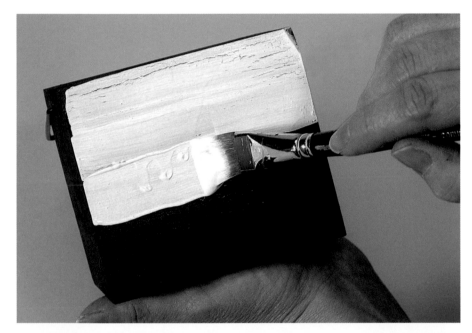

Crackling

1 Basecoat your surface with either a dark color or a light color depending on what look you want. Let this dry about twenty-four hours. Once your first coat has dried, apply the crackle medium of your choice. Please follow the directions on the label.

2 When your crackle medium has dried, begin to apply the top coat. It will almost immediately begin to crackle. Don't brush over the same area twice. You'll lose your desired effect.

Sponging

1 Thin the paint with water to the consistency of ink. Use a plastic or Styrofoam plate, so your paint doesn't run.

2 Apply to the surface by tapping the sponge lightly on the surface.

3 Apply a lighter color on top of the previous sponging in the same manner, but don't cover up the original sponged color. The color used here is Light Timberline Green.

4 Add a contrasting color or a color from your design to liven up the painting and provide harmony. In this case, the color is Bittersweet Orange. As you can see, this technique provides a very subtle background.

Filbert Brush:
Comma Stroke

1 Apply pressure to the brush, pushing the bristles down and out.

2 Slowly begin to lift, turn and pull the brush toward you.

3 You should end up on the chisel edge of the brush to form the tail of the stroke. You can do this same stroke in the opposite direction as well.

Filbert Brush:
Leaf Stroke

1 Apply pressure to the brush, pushing the bristles down and out.

2 Slightly turn the brush as you lift.

3 Lift to the chisel edge to make the tip of the leaf.

Flat Brush: "S" Stroke

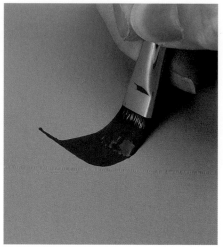

1 Touch the brush down on the chisel edge and slide toward you.

2 Begin to apply pressure, but not all the way to the ferrule.

3 Begin to release pressure as you come back to the chisel edge and slide to create the tail of the stroke.

Flat Brush: Comma Stroke

1 Using a flat brush, set it down at about a 45-degree angle.

2 Apply pressure and pull the stroke toward you.

3 As you pull the brush toward you, lift and turn the brush and slide on the chisel edge to create the tail of the stroke.

Sandy's Sure Stroke Brush: Comma Stroke

1 Touch the tip of the brush down and apply pressure.

2 Pull the brush toward you as you begin to lift the brush.

3 End on the tip of the brush to create the tail of the stroke.

Round Brush: Daisy Stroke

1 Touch the tip of the brush to your surface, but don't add pressure.

2 Pull it slightly and then add pressure creating a dip before the beginning of the comma stroke.

3 Complete the stroke as you did the comma stroke, above, and end on the tip of the brush.

147

Liner Brush: Comma Stroke

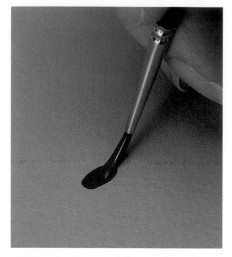  

1 Touch the tip of the brush to the surface and begin to apply pressure, until you're about halfway down to the ferrule.

2 Slide the brush as you begin to lift the brush.

3 Lift to the tip of the brush and slide to create the tail.

Liner Brush: Squiggles or Vines

 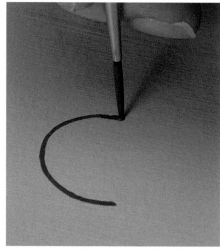 

1 Thin the paint to the consistency of ink. Keep the brush on its tip.

2 Notice how the brush doesn't move. Create the squiggles by moving your whole arm, letting the bristles do the work for you.

3 Complete the stroke when you are satisfied with the squiggle by simply lifting the brush straight off the surface.

Miracle Wedge Brush: Leaf Stroke

1 For foliage and some flowers, load the brush in one color. Dip the tip of the brush in a second color.

2 Touch the tip of the brush down on the surface. Apply pressure almost to the ferrule.

3 Slide the brush toward you and slowly lift to the tip of the brush.

4 As you begin to lift the brush, notice the wonderful streaks this brush leaves behind.

5 This easy leaf stroke can be drawn out a long way to create a long thin leaf, like that of an iris or tulip.

LEAVES & TWIGS

L eaves, twigs and botanical themes are popular for today's home decor items. I love to paint them because they are so simple. With a few shades of green paint and a little imagination, you can paint leaves and botanicals to your heart's content. This is not "rocket science." This is just plain fun painting. So play with the colors and don't be afraid to experiment. You'll come up with all kinds of projects to decorate your home and to give as gifts.

Surfaces

- Mirror frame
- Coffee table

Brushes

- Sandy's Sure Stroke (approximately a no. 4 round)
- nos. 4, 6, 8, 10 filberts
- no. 1 liner
- All-Purpose brush
- Ultra-round
- no. 10 flat

Paint

- Delta Ceramcoat Acrylics

Yellow/Green Combination

Boston Fern

Light Timberline Green

Ivory

Foliage Green Combination

Dark Foliage Green

Medium Foliage Green

Light Foliage Green

Black

Ivory

Pine Green Combination

Pine Green

Seminole Green

Black Green

Ivory

Twigs & Branches

Black

Trail Tan

Walnut

Ivory

How to Double-load a Flat Brush

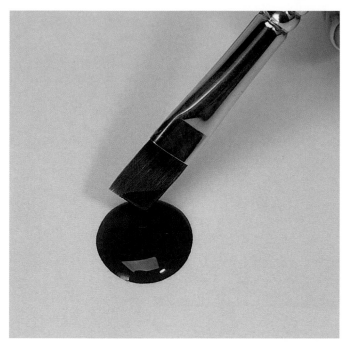

1 Using a no. 10 flat brush, side-load in the darker green, in this case Pine Green. You'll want to dip the corner of the brush on the edge of the paint puddle, so the brush has paint about halfway across the chisel edge and one-third of the way up the side.

2 Now, dip the other corner in the lighter color, in this case Crocus Yellow. Load this corner of the brush exactly the same as the other corner, so the colors meet in the middle.

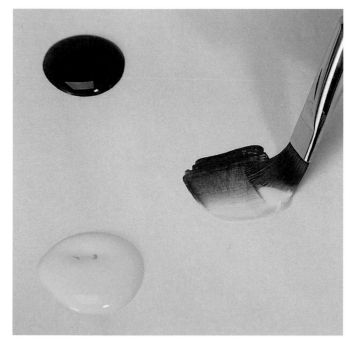

3 Stroke the double-loaded brush on the palette to blend the two colors together.

4 You'll need to stroke both sides of the brush. Your brush is now double-loaded and you're ready to paint the flat brush leaves. The double-loaded brush will allow you to shade and highlight the leaves in one stroke.

Flat Brush Leaves

Long "S" Stroke Leaves

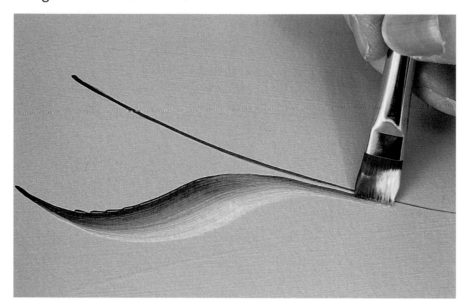

With your double-loaded brush, make an "S" stroke. Start away from the stem on the chisel edge and end on the chisel edge running into the stem. See page 146 for further instructions on making "S" strokes. Use this stroke for tulip, lily and iris leaves.

Short "S" Stroke Leaves

1 With your brush double-loaded in Pine Green and Seminole Green, make short "S" strokes to create veins in the leaves. Any darker and lighter greens will work for this technique. The darker green should face the stem. Make an "S" stroke ending with the chisel edge on the stem.

2 Create the highlight side of the leaf with a double load of Seminole Green and Light Foliage Green. Again the darker color faces the stem. Turn your work to make painting as comfortable as possible.

3 The strokes get smaller as you get closer to the leaf tip. Fill in the entire leaf with these strokes.

The Completed Leaf

Filbert Brush Leaves

Single-Stroke Leaves

1 Double-load the filbert brush with Pine Green and Seminole Green. Any size brush will work and any two greens. Begin on the chisel edge.

2 Apply pressure to the bristles and slide the brush toward you.

3 Lift up onto the chisel edge and slide to create the tip.

4 Connect the leaves to the stem using a liner brush loaded with Pine Green or the darker green you used in the double load.

The Completed Leaf Spray

Filbert Brush Leaves, continued

Two-Stroke Leaves

1 Using a no. 10 filbert brush double-loaded with Pine Green and Seminole Green, pull in the stem. Use the chisel edge of the brush to do so.

2 Start on the chisel edge, just as you did for the single-stroke filbert leaves. Apply pressure to make the fat part of the leaf, then lift up to the chisel edge.

3 For the second stroke, do not flip the brush. Make the same stroke about halfway on the first stroke. Apply pressure to the brush.

4 Slide back up to the chisel edge and into the tip of the first stroke.

5 Using the liner brush loaded with Pine Green, pull from the stem into the leaf following the dark and light line in between the two strokes.

Round Brush Comma Stroke Leaves

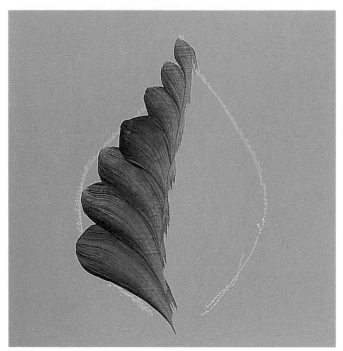

1 Begin at the base of the leaf, using the Sandy's Sure Stroke round brush double-loaded with Pine Green and Seminole Green. With Seminole Green facing the tip of the leaf, make comma strokes with the tail ending in the center vein. For more information on comma strokes see page 147.

2 To create the highlight side of the leaf, double-load the Sandy's Sure Stroke with Light Foliage Green and Seminole Green. Again, make your comma strokes go into the center vein. Turn your work to make painting more comfortable.

3 As you get closer to the tip of the leaf, the comma strokes get smaller, but all pull into the center vein.

The Completed Comma Stroke Leaf

Ultra-Round Long Thin Leaves

1 Load one side of an Ultra-round brush with Pine Green and the other with Light Foliage Green. Start the stroke on the tip of the brush.

2 Apply pressure so the bristles spread out to the width of the leaf and slide.

3 Slowly come back to the tip of the brush as you pull into the stem.

Cluster of Long Thin Leaves

Background Foliage

1 Using the All-Purpose brush, load in the darkest green, in this case Black Green. Pat the brush on the palette to remove excess paint. Pounce in the area you want background foliage. Do not clean the brush.

2 Without cleaning the brush, load with the medium green, in this case Seminole Green. Pat again on the palette to remove some paint. Without covering the previous background, pounce Seminole Green toward the middle of the same area. Do not wash the brush.

3 Pick up Ivory on one side of the brush and Light Foliage Green on the other. Blend by patting these colors together on the palette. Pounce lightly over the same area, but without covering the previous colors. Keep this area light and airy-looking.

Twigs and Branches

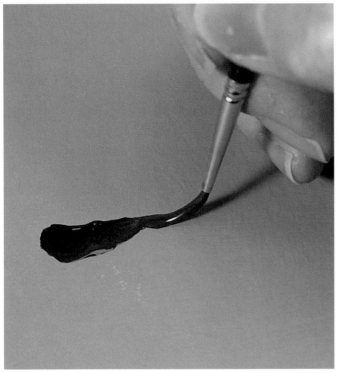

1 Load a no. 1 liner brush with Black on one side and Walnut on the other. Press down on the bristles and wiggle the brush a little as you pull it toward you.

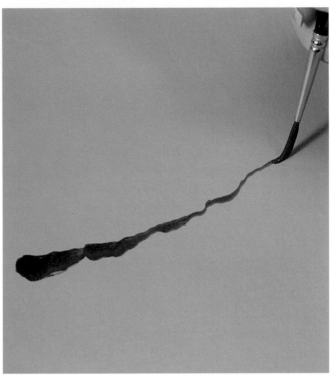

2 As you pull the stroke toward you, begin to lift the brush back to the tip of the bristles.

3 Pull side twigs off the main branch using the same technique. Start on the main branch and pull the brush, wiggling the brush as you pull it toward you.

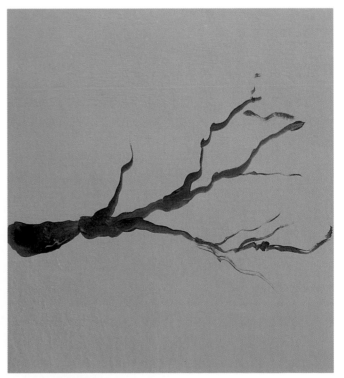

The Completed Branch

More Leaf Ideas...

Have fun and use your imagination. Mix and match these leaves with the fruit and flowers in this book. You'll have endless possibilities for your painting pleasure. Here are a few more ideas to get you started.

Small one-stroke and two-stroke leaves are combined with oranges to make wonderful art for the kitchen.

Long thin "S" stroke leaves are combined with tulips to make a beautiful wall plaque.

A simple mirror frame is turned into a striking ornament for fall.

Background foliage and tiny one-stroke leaves are an easy decoration for this clock.

With parts from your local home center, you can make this lovely coffee table to decorate your home.

FILLER FLOWERS

F iller flowers are wonderful additions to almost any project, or if you're looking for a quick gift, these flowers can be applied to any surface. Mix and match these little lovelies with each other, larger flowers, fruit or all of them for a spectacular work of art. Take a look at the idea section (pages 180-181) to spark your creativity and provide you with endless possibilities for these quick and easy flowers that fit in anywhere.

Patterns

Daisies & tiny five-petal flowers

Coreopsis

Mini-Roses

These patterns may be hand-traced or photocopied for personal use only. They are shown here full size.

Sweet Williams

These patterns may be hand-traced or photocopied for personal use only. They are shown here full size.

Lilacs

One O'clocks

Coreopsis

1 Double-load a no. 8 flat with Black Cherry and Butter Yellow. Don't overblend. Begin the stroke with the Black Cherry toward the center. Wiggle the brush back and forth to create the petal.

2 Wiggle the brush to the other side of the petal and end on the chisel edge.

3 Be sure you turn the brush as you wiggle to follow the petal shapes.

4 Pat the coreopsis center with a small flat brush loaded with Burnt Sienna.

5 Using a no. 1 liner loaded with Butter Yellow, add dots around the center. Wash the brush.

6 Using the same brush loaded with Magnolia White, add a few more dots for variety.

7 Using the liner brush, pat a little Black in the center.

8 Add little two-stroke leaves using Light Foliage Green and Black Green double-loaded on a no. 6 filbert.

170

Sweet William

1 Double-load a no. 8 flat brush with Purple and White. Do not blend too much. You want to keep the white edge strong. Start on the chisel edge.

2 Press down and wiggle, slightly turning the brush. Come back to the chisel edge. Slightly overlap the petals.

3 With the petals completed, it's time to work on the center.

4 Pat a little White in the center of the Sweet William petals using the no. 8 flat. Wash the brush.

5 Pat a bit of Seminole Green around the outer edge of the wet White center. This will keep the white from being so stark.

6 Add dots of Seminole Green using the no. 1 liner brush around the edge of the center.

7 To complete the Sweet William, add the one-stroke leaves with a no. 6 flat brush double-loaded with Light Foliage Green and White.

Fuchsia

1 Add the lines at the bottom of the fuchsia, using a no. 1 liner loaded with Black Cherry.

2 Fill in the bottom of the fuchsia using a no. 6 filbert brush loaded with Purple.

3 Fill in the calyx with Black Cherry using a no. 6 filbert brush.

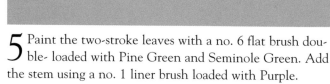

4 Paint the outside petals with Black Cherry using the same filbert brush as you did for the calyx.

5 Paint the two-stroke leaves with a no. 6 flat brush double-loaded with Pine Green and Seminole Green. Add the stem using a no. 1 liner brush loaded with Purple.

172

Aster

1 Load a no. 1 liner brush with Copen Blue. Make long comma strokes from the outer edge of the aster to the center. The tail isn't important because it will be covered.

2 Load the no. 1 liner brush with a brush mix of Copen Blue and Magnolia White. Repeat the comma strokes, but make them a little shorter.

3 Load the no. 1 liner brush with Magnolia White. Make your comma strokes a little shorter.

4 Pat in the center using the Sandy's Sure Stroke round brush loaded with Golden Brown. Don't wash the brush.

5 Shade the outer edge of the center with Candy Bar Brown using the dirty brush. Pat as you did in the last step.

6 Add white dots to the center using a stylus.

Mini-Roses

1 Double-load a ⅜-inch (10mm) angular brush with Payne's Grey and Magnolia White. Stroke an upside down "U".

2 Finish the bowl of the rose with a right-side-up "U" stroke. Make sure the center is rounded with the lightest top edge and bottom edge connecting.

3 Using the same brush double-loaded with the Payne's Grey and Magnolia White, paint the right petal with a comma stroke.

4 Paint the left petal using the same double load and the same stroke in the opposite direction.

5 Paint the right flip stroke petal, like the comma stroke, but smaller.

6 Paint the left flip stroke petal in the same manner.

7 Slide the brush from one side of the center to the other to create the middle petal. The dark side of the brush is toward the center.

8 Add the mini-dashes near the bowl to complete the mini-rose.

Rosebud

1 Double-load the ³⁄₈-inch (10mm) angular brush with Payne's Grey and White. Make the upside-down "U".

2 Using the same brush make the "U" stroke to complete the bud. Make sure the center is round.

3 Paint the calyx using a no. 4 filbert brush double-loaded with Pine Green and Seminole Green. Add pressure to the brush, turn and lift up to the chisel edge.

4 Add the second calyx petal and the stem in the same way. Turn your work to make painting more comfortable.

Lilacs

1 Using a no. 10 flat brush, basecoat the lilac area with Midnight Blue and Purple. Place colors randomly to fill in the area and mix the colors on the surface where they meet.

2 With little push strokes, using the no. 4 filbert brush, create the flower petals in the background. Use Purple and Bahama Purple in the lighter areas and Midnight Blue and Blue Lagoon in the darker areas.

3 For the lighter petal colors, use a mix of the previous colors plus Magnolia White. Add these petals using the dirty brush from the previous steps.

4 Add the lilac centers using a stylus dipped in Straw.

5 Paint the lilac leaves using the no. 6 filbert brush double-loaded with Pine Green and Medium Foliage Green.

6 For the highlight side of the leaf, double-load the same brush with Medium Foliage Green and Light Foliage Green. Make the "S" strokes into the center.

One O'clocks

1 Paint the tiny one-stroke leaves around the area of flowers using a no. 4 filbert brush loaded with Pine Green.

2 Paint the flowers with Purple, Bahama Purple and Glacier Blue, using the Sandy's Sure Stroke brush. Touch down lightly on just the brush tip to make a dab of paint.

3 Dab in the centers with Candy Bar Brown using Sandy's Sure Stroke Brush.

4 Paint dot flower petals on the outside of the cluster using a stylus dipped in Antique Gold.

5 Dot the flower centers with a stylus dipped in Candy Bar Brown.

Johnny Jump-ups

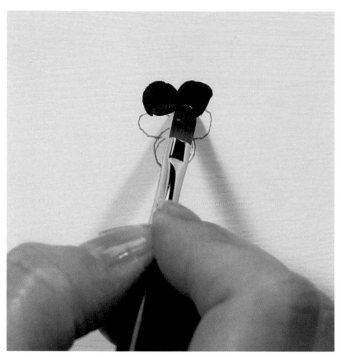

1 Load a no. 4 filbert brush with a brush mix of Royal Plum and Crocus Yellow. Touch the brush down and pull toward the center.

2 Pick up a little Crocus Yellow on the tip of the brush and pull in the side petals.

3 Pick up more Crocus Yellow on the brush and add the center petal in the same manner as you did the others.

4 Add the Crocus Yellow center using a no. 1 liner. The Black lines are added with the same brush.

Forget-me-nots

1 Pat in the background using the All-Purpose brush with a grouping of the greens listed on page 152.

2 Make a cluster of these tiny blossoms made up of "C" strokes using the no. 4 flat brush double-loaded with Midnight Blue and Magnolia White.

3 Add the two-stroke leaves using a no. 4 filbert brush double-loaded with Pine Green and Seminole Green.

4 Add a dot for the center using a stylus dipped in Antique Gold.

More Filler Flower Ideas...

This wonderful sampler board of filler flowers can be used as a trivet for your table, as coasters, or as a wall decoration for your kitchen.

Add similar flowers to wooden jar lids and cooking utensils in colors picked up from your kitchen decor.

Cute trinket boxes make wonderful gifts for friends, kids, just about anyone.

A few filler flowers on the base of a hurricane lamp or on a jar lid can be changed to represent the seasons or holidays.

Mini-roses look great on almost any surface. Dress them up with ribbon and you've got a great gift for friends or family.

FOCAL FLOWERS

F ocal flowers are the large flowers that are at the focal point, or center of interest, of each of my designs. The flowers are generally easy to paint, just like the filler flowers and leaves. The nice thing about these flowers is you can paint them almost any color. Paint them to match your decor, or fill in the design with complementing filler flowers and leaves, and voilá, you've created your own unique design.

A Basket of Spring

Materials

Surface
- Blank Journal

Brushes
- no. 10 filbert
- 1/2-inch angular shader
- no. 1 liner

Dclta Ceramcoat Paint

- Butter Yellow
- Burnt Sienna
- Poppy Orange
- White
- Light Foliage Green
- Dark Foliage Green
- Spice Brown
- Black
- Burnt Umber
- Ivory
- Bambi Brown
- Pine Green

On a trip to the mall, I came across some blank journals in a variety of colors. I knew they would look great with large flowers or fruit designs. When you paint this type of project with several different flowers, paint the background foliage, then paint the largest flowers and finish with the filler flowers and leaves until you're satisfied.

1 Basecoat the basket with Bambi Brown. Pounce some background with the All-Purpose brush with Dark Foliage Green and Pine Green.

2 Add dark shading under the rim and down the left side of the basket with Burnt Umber. Double load a no. 8 flat brush with Bambi Brown and Burnt Umber. Make S strokes on the handle and rim.

3 Use the no. 1 liner brush loaded with Spice Brown and then Burnt Umber to paint the scribble lines on the basket. Add a few more lines with Black. Then add the light lines on the right with Ivory.

Paint the Daffodils

1 Basecoat the daffodil petals with a no. 10 filbert brush loaded with Butter Yellow. You may need two coats.

2 Using a ½-inch (12mm) angular shader sideloaded with Burnt Sienna, add the shading on the trumpet.

3 Pat a little Poppy Orange down the throat of the daffodil using a ½-inch (12mm) angular shader.

4 Using a no. 1 liner brush loaded with White, dab around the edge of the bowl.

5 Overstroke the daffodil petals with a no. 10 filbert double-loaded with Butter Yellow and White.

6 Paint two strokes. Make sure the white side of the brush is facing the left for both strokes.

7 Using a liner brush loaded with thinned Burnt Sienna, pull lines from the bowl's base toward the top.

The Completed Daffodil

Using Sandy's Sure Stroke brush double-loaded with Light Foliage Green and Pine Green, pull in the stems and paint the bumpy leaves. Add a few Black dots in the throat using the no. 1 liner brush.

For instructions on how to paint the basket turn to page 184. For instructions on how to paint the foliage turn to page 162. For instructions on how to paint the daisies turn to page 241.

Basket of Spring

This pattern may be hand-traced or
photocopied for personal use only.
Enlarge at 109% to bring up to full size.

186

Tulips in a Basket

Materials

Surface
- ¾-inch board cut to desired shape

Brushes
- Sandy's Sure Stroke
- Sandy's Sure Stroke Mini
- nos. 4, 6, 8 & 10 filberts
- 18/0 liner
- All-Purpose brush
- ½-inch angular shader
- no. 10 flat

Delta Ceramcoat Paint
- Midnight Blue
- Old Parchment
- Black
- Autumn Brown
- Trail Tan
- Burnt Umber
- Royal Plum
- Queen Anne's Lace
- Magnolia White
- Antique Gold
- Candy Bar Brown
- Ivory
- Pine Green
- Seminole Green
- Dusty Mauve

Supplies
- Delta Crackle Medium

My dad cut this board for me. It is 7¼ x 19 inches. He cut a rounded top on the board and I placed the basket and the three tulips, leaves and filler flowers in the basket until it suited me.

Prepare the Surface

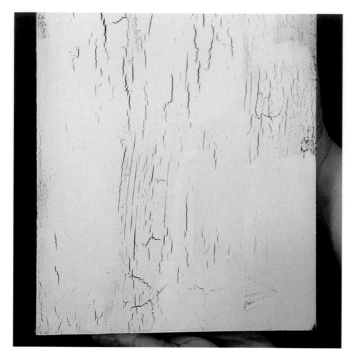

Basecoat the board with two coats of Midnight Blue, using a large flat brush. When the basecoat is completely dry, apply a coat of Delta Crackle Medium, following the directions. When the crackle medium is dry apply a top coat of Old Parchment. Do not go over your strokes again or the paint will smear over the crackle medium. Once this has dried you can apply a basic pattern, if you want to.

Paint the Tulips

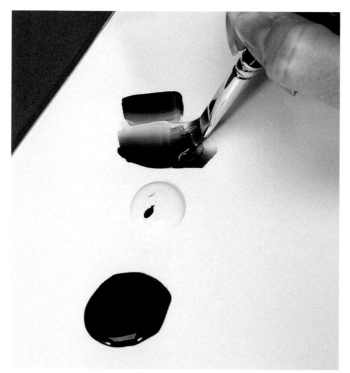

1 Double-load a no. 10 flat brush with Royal Plum and Queen Anne's Lace. Stroke the brush back and forth on your palette to achieve a nice blend. Paint the side petals of the tulips with S strokes.

2 Using Sandy's Sure Stroke brush, load Royal Plum fully on the brush and pull through Queen Anne's Lace on one side of the brush. Face the light color to the ceiling, make a push stroke, pulling the tail of the stroke toward the stem.

188

3 To create the middle strokes, place the Sure Stroke brush down and push the bristles, so they open. Be careful not to push down to the ferrule. Push the brush away from you into the stroke.

4 Once you've pushed the brush into the stroke, finish the stroke by pulling toward you and into the stem to create the tail of the stroke.

5 Finish the center petals of the tulip using the push-pull stroke. Make the strokes smaller as you get close to the stem. Paint the other two tulips in the design the same way.

Paint the Stems, Leaves & Basket

1 Basecoat the basket with Burnt Umber, using a large flat brush. Double-load a flattened Sandy's Sure Stroke brush with Pine Green on one side and Seminole Green on the other. Pull the stems from the tulip into the basket.

2 Using the no. 10 flat brush, double-loaded with Pine Green and Seminole Green, paint long "S" strokes for the leaves. Turn the piece so it is comfortable for you to pull the stroke from the basket out toward the tulip.

3 The tulips and stems are now complete. It's time to work on the basket.

4 Using a no. 1 liner brush loaded with Black, make wiggly lines from one side of the basket to the other. These are random lines and do not need to be precise.

5 Using the same liner brush loaded with Autumn Brown, make more wiggly lines like the ones you did previously. Do not completely cover the basket.

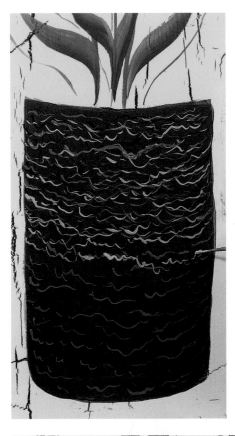

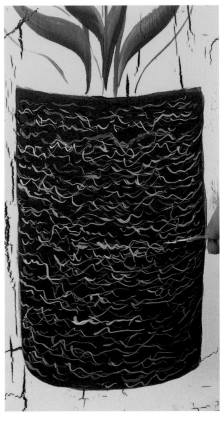

6 Make wiggly lines using the liner brush loaded with Trail Tan.

7 Add wiggly highlights to the basket using the liner brush loaded with Ivory.

8 Complete the basket by using a no. 10 flat brush, double-loaded with Burnt Umber and Autumn Brown, to make a series of "S" strokes across the rim of the basket to form the edge.

Paint the Pink Flowers and Leaves

1 Using a filbert brush loaded with Dusty Mauve, begin placing the filler flowers in randomly. The filler flowers in this lesson are the same as the lilacs on page 176.

2 Using a filbert brush, place small filler leaves and stems. Use a comma stroke with a variety of greens. Do not clean your brush in-between colors.

3 Using your filbert brush loaded with Dusty Mauve plus a little bit of Magnolia White on one side of the brush, make some five petal flowers randomly placed.

4 Using the same dirty brush, make the lightest flowers by adding more white and paint a few of the lightest five petal flowers.

5 Using your liner brush, add Antique Gold dots to form the center of the five petal flowers. Next, add Candy Bar Brown dots to the center.

6 Using Sandy's Sure Stroke Mini brush, place filler flowers and stems. The flower petals are touch and lift strokes using Old Parchment. Paint the stems Pine Green.

7 Using the Sure Stroke Mini brush, add a few more flowers with white. If you use two different colors when you do these small flowers, they will be more interesting.

8 Add the flower centers with a no. 1 liner brush double loaded with Antique Gold and Candy Bar Brown.

193

Tulips in a Basket

This pattern may be hand-traced or photocopied for personal use only. Enlarge at 125% to bring up to full size.

A Sign of Carnations

The carnation, a lovely little summer flower, is used often in arrangements. This house address sign will make sure your home looks like summer all year long.

Materials

Surface
- Wooden Sign Board (available at craft stores)

Brushes
- Sandy's Sure Stroke
- no. 6 filbert

Delta Ceramcoat Paint
- Black Cherry
- Barn Red
- Oyster White
- Medium Foliage Green
- Dark Foliage Green

How to Paint the Petals

Follow this diagram to help you paint the carnation petals. After you have completed the carnation, paint the "bumpy" leaves using a no. 6 filbert brush double loaded with Dark Foliage Green and Medium Foliage Green. Use a push down, release, push down, release stroke and pull to the stem.

This pattern may be hand-traced or photocopied for personal use only. Enlarge at 200% to bring up to full size.

Paint the Carnation

1 Load the Sure Stroke brush with Black Cherry and Barn Red. Press the brush almost to the ferrule and fan out the bristles.

2 Push the brush forward to create the feathery edge.

3 Pull the brush back to the tip and toward the stem. Paint about five petals on the back row.

4 Load the brush with Barn Red and Oyster White. Repeat the push-pull stroke for the mid-layer of about three petals.

6 Add the leaves and stems with Medium and Dark Foliage Green double-loaded on Sandy's Sure Stroke brush.

5 Add more Oyster White to the brush and create the top layer of of about one petal using the push-pull stroke as before.

Lilies

Materials

Surface
- Oval Plaque (available at craft stores)

Brushes
- Miracle Wedge brush
- no. 1 liner

Delta Ceramcoat Paint
- Light Foliage Green
- Pine Green
- Dark Goldenrod
- Straw
- Magnolia White
- Georgia Clay

1 Apply the leaves using a Miracle Wedge brush loaded with Light Foliage Green and tipped in Pine Green. Make a long leaf stroke, starting from the outside and pulling to the stem.

Paint the Lily

2 Triple load a Miracle Wedge brush with Dark Golden-rod, Straw and Magnolia White. Press the bristles down almost to the ferrule to spread them out half the width of the petal.

3 Paint each petal with two or three leaf strokes, starting with the ones underneath and pulling them into the flower center. The next layer of petals goes over the first. All of the flower petals are painted in the same manner.

4 Slowly release the pressure on the brush as you come to the center. Return to the point of the brush as you complete each stroke.

5 Gently wipe the brush on a damp paper towel removing some of the paint. Reload by tipping in Magnolia White.

Paint the Lily, continued

6 As you complete the petals that are behind, wipe the brush and reload, tipping in Magnolia White.

7 Turn your work as needed to make painting more comfortable. Begin layering the petals on top.

8 Apply a third stroke to the petal if needed to fill in the petal. Wipe the paint out of the brush. Start from the outside edge and pull this stroke down the center over the two previous strokes.

9 Paint the center of the lily with a no. 1 liner brush loaded with Light Foliage Green. Pull a curved line stroke from the center out. Clean your brush.

10 Using the no. 1 liner brush, add dots of Georgia Clay to the center. Touch the tip of the brush in Straw and add dots to the end of the stamens.

11 Load the liner brush in Georgia Clay and add tiny dots to the petals.

12 Add a saying with a stamp or create your own lettering. If you're using a stamp, remember to lift straight up, so you don't smear the saying.

Lilies

This pattern may be hand-traced or
photocopied for personal use only.
It is shown here full size.

Poinsettia & Holly

Holiday decorations are a snap when you use this method of creating poinsettias and holly berries. Combine them with fruit and other flowers and you'll have a treat to delight your holiday guests.

Materials

Surface
- Piece of scrap linoleum approx. 2½ x 3 feet

Brushes
- no. 6 flat
- no. 1 liner
- Ultra-round
- stencil dauber

Delta Ceramcoat Paint
- Black Green
- Pine Green
- Light Foliage Green
- Barn Red
- Magnolia White
- Seminole Green
- Butter Yellow
- Dusty Mauve
- Black Cherry
- Chocolate Cherry

Holly Leaves & Berries

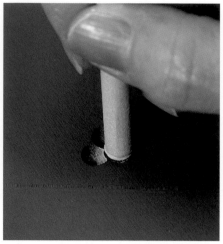

1 Double load a no. 6 flat brush with Black Green and Pine Green. With the darkest color to the outside edge, follow the leaf contour, painting half of the leaf. Load the brush with Pine Green and Light Foliage Green. With the light color to the outside edge, paint the other half. Add the stem and vein with Black Green loaded on a no. 1 liner brush.

2 Paint the berries by tapping one side of the stencil dauber in Barn Red and the other in Magnolia White. Pat the dauber on your palette to slightly blend the colors. Put the dauber in place and add pressure to create a berry.

3 Lift straight up. Paint about three berries per leaf. Reload the stencil dauber if needed.

Poinsettia

1 Using an Ultra-round brush loaded with Barn Red, pull two strokes from the outside tip into the center to complete each petal just like the two-stroke leaves. Paint all the lower petals in the same manner. (See page 158 for further instruction on two-stroke leaves.)

2 With the same dirty brush wiped on a paper towel, pick up Dusty Mauve. Paint the same two-strokes, but make this layer in-between the first layer of petals. Then, in-between the second layer of petals, paint slightly shorter strokes with the dirty brush plus Magnolia White.

3 With a no. 1 liner brush loaded with Black Cherry, paint the veins on the petals. You can use Chocolate Cherry if you want darker veins.

4 Completed veins.

5 Pat in the center with a no. 1 liner brush loaded with Seminole Green.

6 Add dots of Butter Yellow to the green center, using your stylus or liner brush.

7 Add smaller dots of Barn Red on top of the yellow dots using the stylus or liner brush.

8 Completed poinsettia.

Poinsettia & Holly

These patterns may be hand-traced or
photocopied for personal use only.
Enlarge at 200% to bring up to full size.

Zinnia

The zinnia is another very easy flower to design with and paint. You need three values of one color, but you can use blue, purple, orange, yellow or red so your design is in harmony and balanced.

It's fun to use this project as a candle holder on a patio. Simply put sand in the bottom of the container, insert your candle and you're ready for entertaining.

1 Paint two-stroke leaves around where the blossom will be. Load a no. 8 filbert brush with Rhythm 'n Blue. Paint the edge petals with flat strokes.

2 With the dirty brush, add the next layer of petals with Bahama Purple. These strokes are longer on one side to create a slightly "off-center" center.

Zinnia

This pattern may be hand-traced or photocopied for personal use only. Enlarge at 189% to bring up to full size.

3 To your dirty brush, add a little white and paint the next layer of petals. Continue to add white to the brush until you reach the very center of the flower.

4 Pat in the center with Boston Fern loaded on a no. 1 liner brush.

5 Add dots of Black around the outer edge of the green center using the no. 1 liner brush.

6 With Black Green on the liner brush, add the stems and curlicues to complete the Zinnia.

A Mum Welcome

Welcome everyone to your house with your very own Mum welcome sign. It's easy and fun. Best of all, when you're done you'll have another set of flowers that you can incorporate into your own designs.

Basecoat the board with Black Green mixed with Glazing Medium (1:1). Test your color on the back of your surface. It should look like a dark green stain. Paint the edge of the board with Antique Gold and let dry. Mix Burnt Sienna and Glazing Medium (1:1). Brush this over the Antique Gold to give an antique look.

Materials

Surface
- Half-round wooden board

Brushes
- Sandy's Sure Stroke
- no. 4 filbert
- nos. 1 & 2 liner
- scruffy brush

Delta Ceramcoat Paint
- Pine Green
- Seminole Green
- Magnolia White
- Adobe Red
- Nectar Coral
- Rosetta Pink
- Queen Anne's Lace
- Antique Gold
- Candy Bar Brown
- Black
- Bambi Brown
- Autumn Brown

1 Double load Sandy's Sure Stroke brush with Pine Green and Seminole Green. With the Pine Green side facing the base of the leaf, pull comma strokes from the outer edge of the leaf toward the center using the tail of the comma to help form the veins. The comma strokes get shorter as you get closer to the leaf tip.

2 Double load your Sandy's Sure Stroke with Seminole Green and Magnolia White. With the Seminole Green side of the brush facing the base of the leaf, pull comma strokes as you did in the previous step.

3 Using the tip of your round brush, pat Candy Bar Brown into the center area (bowl) of the mum.

4 While the Candy Bar Brown is still wet, pat Black in at the lower edge of the bowl. Blend the colors to shade.

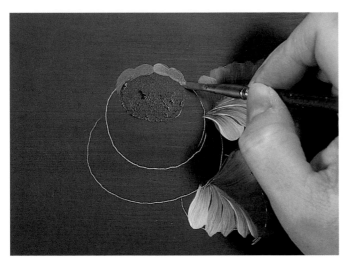

5 Using Sandy's Sure Stroke brush and Adobe Red, pull in the back petals. Start in the center and use bumpy strokes to create the ruffled back edge. Go back to the center and paint the strokes on the opposite side of the flower.

6 With the Sure Stroke brush loaded with Adobe Red, pull in comma strokes. Pull each of the strokes toward the stem.

creative hint:

When you paint any flower, visualize the point where the stem would attach and pull your strokes toward that point. If it helps, you can make a dot at that point and use it as a target to pull your strokes toward.

7 With the Sure Stroke brush loaded with Adobe Red, pull the comma strokes to form the skirt. The side strokes are curved more. Pull all strokes toward the stem.

8 With the Sure Stroke brush loaded with Adobe Red, pull the strokes in the center of the skirt straighter, but still end toward the stem.

9 Load the "dirty" brush with Nectar Coral and pull in a lighter layer of comma strokes on the ball of the mum.

10 Stroke a lighter layer of petals on the skirt using the same "dirty" brush loaded with Nectar Coral. Each layer of strokes will be a little shorter and lighter.

11 Use the "dirty" brush loaded with Rosetta Pink and Queen Anne's Lace to add a few lighter strokes to the ball of the flower.

12 Add a few comma strokes to the skirt using the colors from the previous step.

13 With a no. 1 liner brush, add a few dots to the center of the flower using Antique Gold, White and Black.

Paint the Aster

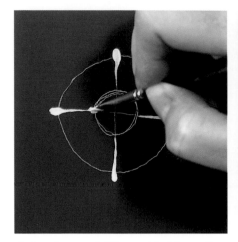

1 Load a no. 4 filbert with Magnolia White. Form the first four petals with the "drop-pull stroke."

2 Apply pressure to the side of the brush to form a tear drop shape. Release the pressure, pulling a thin line toward the center.

3 Continue by placing strokes in the center of each section, until each area is complete.

4 The second layer of strokes is shorter than the first. Place these strokes in-between the first layer of strokes.

5 Use only a few strokes for the third layer to fill in any gaps.

This pattern may be hand-traced or photocopied for personal use only. It is shown here full size.

6 Pat Antique Gold in the center using Sandy's Sure Stroke. Let this dry before continuing.

7 Double-load a scruffy brush with Candy Bar Brown and Antique Gold. With Candy Bar Brown toward the outside edge, pat blend the colors.

8 Add dots to the center edge with the tip of the liner brush loaded with Black.

9 Add a few white dots using the liner brush.

Add Filler Flowers

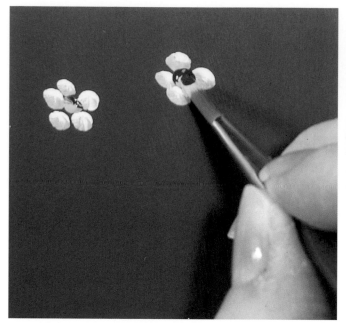

1 Load your Sandy's Sure Stroke with Antique Gold and pull through Magnolia White on one side. With the White facing the right, touch the brush tip to the surface and push slightly toward "one o'clock." Repeat for each petal, usually five petals per flower. Load the brush with Antique Gold and Candy Bar Brown. With the Brown facing the right, slightly push the brush tip toward "one o'clock" to form the center.

2 Pull in the small comma strokes to form the ball of the spoon mum bud using a no. 2 liner loaded with Magnolia White. Be sure to follow the shape of the flower and pull toward the stem. Pull the skirt strokes using the no. 2 liner loaded with Magnolia White. Make sure to follow the shape of the flower and pull toward the stem.

3 To make the spoon mum buds, use the no. 4 filbert brush and the "drop-pull stroke." Pull a few random strokes toward the stem.

4 Use the filbert brush double-loaded with Pine Green and Seminole Green to pull two "S" strokes to form the calyx. Pull in the stem using the no. 1 liner brush.

5 Pull comma strokes to form the ball of the flower using the Sandy's Sure Stroke brush loaded with Adobe Red. Use less pressure to form small strokes.

6 Pull strokes to form the skirt using Sandy's Sure Stroke loaded with Adobe Red. Use the dirty brush loaded with Rosetta Pink to pull the highlight strokes to the ball skirt of the flower.

7 Use a stencil for the lettering, or if you feel brave you can freehand it. Apply the base color, Bambi Brown, with a stencil brush. Then add a little Autumn Brown with the stencil brush. This gives the lettering a little texture and a softer appearance.

FRUITS & BERRIES

F ruit is one of my favorite subjects to paint. It is diverse enough that it can be painted separately or with some of the flowers in this book.

When I think of fruit, I think about my grandmother's kitchen and the ripe fruits ready to be canned. I don't have time or the patience to can fruit, but I do have time to paint my kitchen decor to imitate these luscious goodies. I hope you enjoy these quick and easy projects with surfaces you can find just about anywhere.

Blueberries

1 Basecoat the blueberries using a no. 6 filbert brush loaded with Cadet Blue.

2 With a ¹/₂-inch (12mm) angular brush corner-loaded with Midnight Blue, shade one edge of the berries.

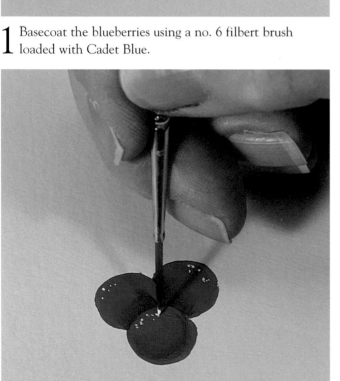

3 Dab little dots of Oyster White with your no. 1 liner brush on the edge opposite the shading.

4 Add a few one-stroke leaves with Light, Medium and Dark Foliage Greens loaded on a no. 6 filbert brush. Add a blossom end using Black. Paint the stems and curlicues using a no. 1 liner brush to complete the blueberries.

Cherries

1 Basecoat the cherries using a stencil dauber and Mendocino Red as your base color. Pick up Black Cherry on one side and pounce on the cherries to shade. Highlight with Magnolia White.

2 Using a no. 4 filbert brush, add the stems, leaves and curlicues using a variety of the Light, Medium and Dark Foliage colors. The yellow dots are added for interest using a stylus and Crocus Yellow.

Strawberries

Blackberries & Raspberries

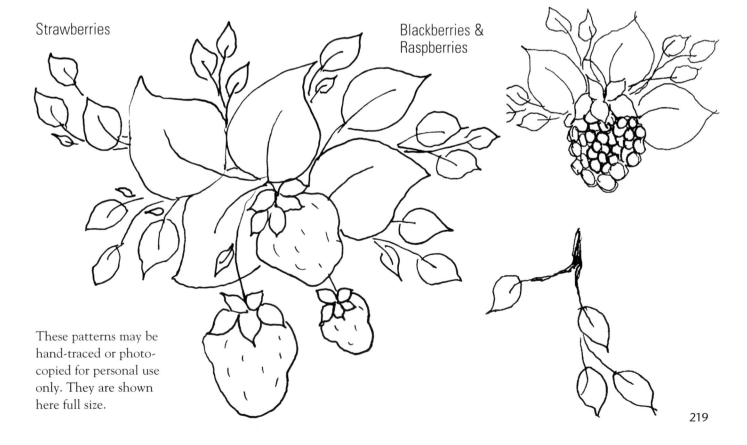

These patterns may be hand-traced or photocopied for personal use only. They are shown here full size.

Strawberries

1 Basecoat the strawberry with Barn Red using a no. 10 filbert brush.

2 Float Chocolate Cherry using a ¹/₂-inch (12mm) angular brush on the left side of the berry for shading. Float Orange on the right half of the berry using a ¹/₂-inch (12mm) angle brush to create the highlight.

3 Paint the sepals with a no. 4 filbert brush double-loaded with Seminole Green and Pine Green.

4 Paint the seeds using no. 1 liner brush loaded with Black.

5 Highlight the seeds with Butter Yellow on the right half of the seed using a no. 1 liner brush.

Blackberries & Raspberries

1 Basecoat half the raspberry with Black Cherry and half with Dusty Mauve using a no. 4 filbert brush. Pat the colors together in the middle to create a gradation of values.

2 With a hard-packed Q-tip, pick up White. Pat some of the color off on your palette. Stamp down around the berry to make the seed pockets. This step must be done in wet paint.

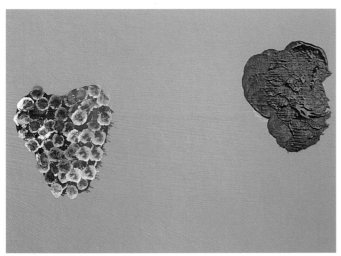

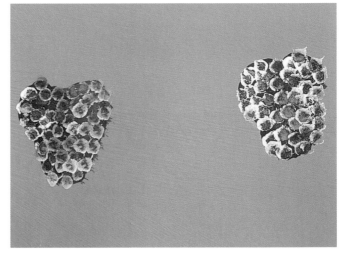

3 Basecoat the blackberries with Midnight Blue on the left and Purple on the right with a no. 4 filbert brush.

4 While the paint is still wet, pat a hard-packed Q-tip in White as you did for the raspberry. Make the seed pockets with the loaded Q-tip. Don't make too many pockets.

5 Paint the one-stroke leaves with a no. 6 filbert brush double-loaded with Black Green and Seminole Green. Use a no. 1 liner brush to paint the stems.

221

Pear

1 Basecoat the pear with Butter Yellow. Using a ½-inch (12mm) angular shader double-loaded with Orange and Butter Yellow, float orange on the left half of the pear to create a shadow.

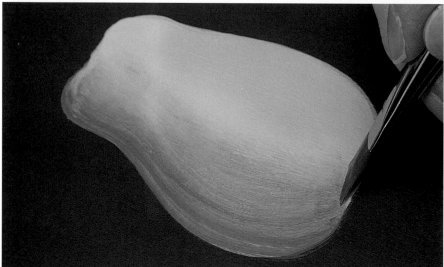

2 Walk the orange toward the center of the pear using the double-loaded ½-inch (12mm) angular shader.

Pear

This pattern may be hand-traced or photocopied for personal use only. Enlarge at 125% to bring it up to full size.

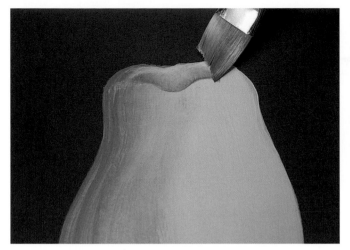

3 Corner-load the ½-inch (12mm) angular shader with Burnt Sienna. Paint the indent at the top of the pear.

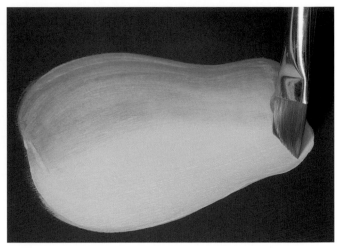

4 Float Light Foliage Green on the right half of the pear using the ½-inch (12mm) angular shader. Walk the color toward the center of the pear.

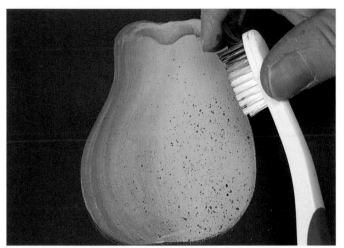

5 Using an old toothbrush loaded with thinned Black Cherry, flyspeck the pear, especially the right half.

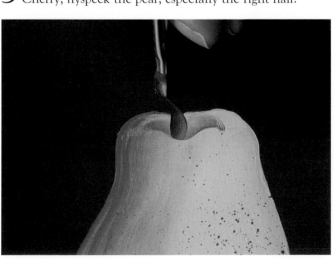

6 Paint the pear stem with a no. 4 flat brush double-loaded with Bambi Brown and Candy Bar Brown.

7 Paint the leaves with a no. 10 flat brush double-loaded with Boston Fern and Timberline Green. Using the no. 1 liner brush loaded with Timberline Green, paint the veins and curlicues.

223

Apple

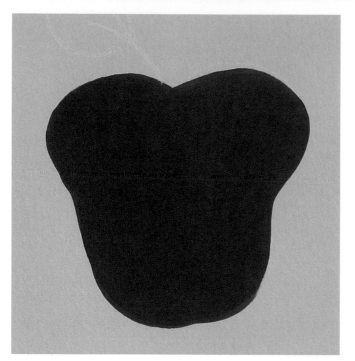

1 Basecoat the apple with Barn Red.

2 Using a ½-inch (12mm) angular shader, float Chocolate Cherry on the top of the apple to create the stem end.

Apple

This pattern may be hand-traced or photocopied for personal use only. It is shown here full size.

3 Float a little Orange on the side opposite the shading to create a highlight.

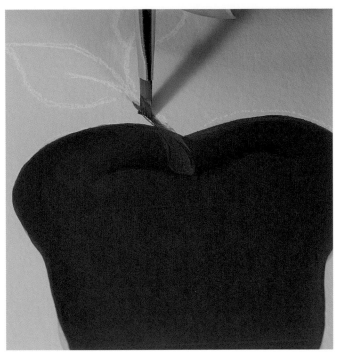

4 With a no. 4 flat brush double-loaded with Burnt Umber and Bambi Brown, pull a little stem out from the apple.

5 Add leaves with Dark and Medium Foliage Greens.

Apple Variation

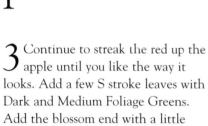

1 Basecoat the apple with Butter Yellow.

2 Using the filbert rake brush and thinned Barn Red, pull up from the apple's bottom end. Paint the streaks following the contours of the apple.

3 Continue to streak the red up the apple until you like the way it looks. Add a few S stroke leaves with Dark and Medium Foliage Greens. Add the blossom end with a little Black loaded on a no. 1 liner brush.

Orange

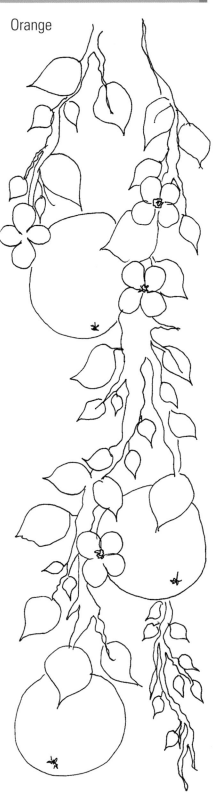

Orange

1 Basecoat the orange with Butter Yellow using a no. 10 filbert brush.

2 Add a wash of Bittersweet Orange over the entire orange.

3 With a scruffy brush, or stippler, pat on more Bittersweet Orange. This will add the dimply texture.

This pattern may be hand-traced or photocopied for personal use only. Enlarge at 200% to bring up to full size.

227

4 Add leaves with Dark Foliage Green and Medium Foliage Green double-loaded on a no. 10 filbert brush.

5 Paint the five-petal flower in Oyster White loaded on a no. 10 filbert brush.

6 With a no. 1 liner brush, add the flower center with Bittersweet Orange and Burnt Sienna.

7 Add the stem with Dark Foliage Green.

Grapes

1 Basecoat the stool with Oyster White. Let the sea sponge sit in water for about thirty minutes while the paint dries.

2 Squeeze a sponge full of clean water on your palette. With a very damp sponge, but not dripping wet, pick up Purple Dusk. Sponge lightly on the surface of the stool. Let dry completely.

3 Apply Midnight Blue in the same manner, using the same plate and sponge. Sponge lightly, but more toward the edges than in the center. Let this dry completely.

4 Using a sponge, apply paint to the leaf press (or rubber stamp). Use Pine Green and Antique Gold. Apply the Antique Gold randomly on the press (or stamp) as shown.

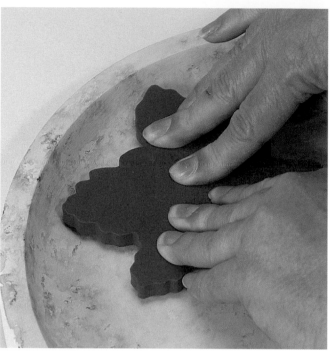

5 Press the stamp onto the surface. Make sure you apply it straight down and with firm pressure. You want to be sure the stamp doesn't slide on the surface.

6 Be sure to lift straight up. Repeat these steps as many times as needed until you're satisfied with the results.

7 Completed grape leaves.

8 Using a stencil dauber loaded with Midnight Blue, paint the back layer of grapes. Apply them randomly in the center.

9 Double-load the stencil dauber with Midnight Blue and Purple Dusk. Pounce on the palette to blend colors.

10 Fill in areas to begin defining the individual grape clusters.

11 With the same mix as in the previous step, add a little Butter Cream to the light side of the dauber. Begin adding more grapes with the highlight side toward the outside of the cluster. Add some highlights to the grapes in the previous steps.

12 Double-load Burnt Umber and Pine Green on a no. 1 liner brush. Paint the tendrils. The two colors will create the shading and highlighting.

This wonderful grape stool will add a little Old World flavor to your kitchen or den.

Blackberries on a wooden spatula will make a wonderful gift or a decoration for yourself. The spatula can be found just about anywhere making this a quick and inexpensive project.

What a wonderfully fruity kitchen you'll have with a few of these fantastic canisters and spatulas or spoons. In an afternoon, you could decorate your entire kitchen.

Add a little fruit to your floor with this wonderful floorcloth made from a scrap piece of linoleum. Paint the back and your floorcloth won't slip and slide like regular canvas floorcloths. Make sure you apply two coats of Gesso to the backside of the linoleum (the painting side) before you begin to paint.

I Love You!

Add a message to a plaque or message center and send a little love to a special person.

235

PULL IT ALL TOGETHER

Many years ago when I took my first decorative painting class, I painted daisies. Since that time I have painted daisies in many styles, some very quick and easy and some that seemed to take forever. Finally, I discovered that if I undercoated and painted wet-on-wet, I could get a look I liked and still paint quick daisies. Daisies are so fresh and can be used with almost any fruit or flower to form a pretty design. If you take time to practice, you'll find many uses for daisies in your own designs.

Daisy Basket Lid

This pattern may be hand-traced or photocopied for personal use only. Enlarge at 148% to bring it up to full size.

Materials

Surface
- Round basket from Pesky Bear

Brushes
- nos. 4, 6, 8 filberts
- nos. 0, 1 liner
- All-Purpose brush
- scruffy brush
- ½-inch angular shader
- Sandy's Sure Stroke

Colors
- Glacier Blue
- Cadet Blue
- Midnight Blue
- Walnut
- Magnolia White
- Straw
- Candy Bar Brown
- Black
- Black Green
- Dark Foliage Green
- Medium Foliage Green
- Light Foliage Green
- Old Parchment

Additional Supplies
- Old toothbrush
- Wood Sealer
- Sandpaper
- Tack cloth
- White chalk pencil

Prepare Your Surface

1 Sand any rough areas on the basket lid.

creative hint:
If a piece is not extremely rough, sand it after it's been sealed. This will save you from doing an extra step.

2 Prepare your basecoat by mixing your wood sealer with Old Parchment (1:1).

3 Basecoat the surface with the paint and sealer mix. Let the first coat dry thoroughly. Then sand the surface and wipe the dust off with a tack cloth. Apply the second coat. Some colors require a third coat, but Old Parchment covers well in just two.

Paint the Background Foliage

1 Using the All-Purpose brush, pounce in the background foliage. Use all the greens on your palette, starting with the darkest color. The foliage color choices can be found on page 152. You'll need a variety of greens to correspond with the leaves.

2 After the background foliage has dried, transfer the pattern. The ovals represent the size and shape of the daisies and daisy centers. This will help you maintain a good layout for your design and allow you to be spontaneous as well.

3 Using a no. 8 filbert brush, place a few large leaves around the daisies. These can be one- or two-stroke leaves depending on the room available. The darkest green color is used for the larger leaves.

Paint the Daisies

1 Using a round brush (I use Sandy's Sure Stroke, or no. 4 round), thin Dark Foliage Green with water to make a wash, transparent, but not runny. If the paint is too thick, the base stroke daisy petals will be very dark. If the paint is too thin, it will run when you try to paint the petals.

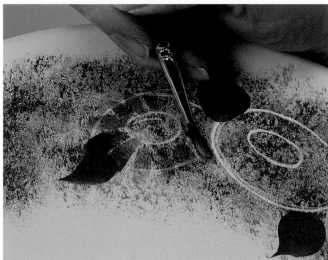

2 When placing your understrokes, you'll need to work quickly, in order to overstoke into the wet paint. Using a comma stroke, paint the understroke, starting at the outside circle and stroking toward the inner circle. These strokes will be covered up with Magnolia White later.

3 Begin the daisy petals by painting the two side front petals first and work toward center front. The petals on the sides should be curved toward the center of the flower. The strokes should get longer and straighter closer to the front. Then, paint the side petals and work toward the back. The back petals get shorter as they get closer to back center. You can vary the number of petals a daisy has. It simply depends on the size of the daisy, the size of the brush, and the amount of pressure you apply when making the strokes.

4 Let your daisy petals dry before proceeding.

Paint the Daisy Center

1 With your round brush, pat a basecoat of Straw in the center of each daisy. Let this dry.

> **creative hint:**
> Patting the surface instead of painting the basecoat gives a bumpy texture as opposed to a smooth texture.

2 Using an old scruffy brush, double-load the brush with Straw and Candy Bar Brown. Then, pat the end of the bristles on your palette to blend. Starting with the Candy Bar Brown side at the back edge of the daisy center, pat the shading around the left side, walking the colors in toward the center and out. This will help blend the colors. Let this dry.

3 Using the old scruffy brush loaded with a little bit of Magnolia White, pat in a highlight on the right side of center. This gives you a little hint of a highlight.

4 Using the bristle end of a no. 1 liner brush tipped in Black, make dots randomly around the outside edge of the daisy center. You can add a few dots using other colors from your design to add a little variety.

The completed daisies.

Paint the Branches

1 Using a no. 1 liner brush loaded with Black on one side and Walnut on the other, randomly place your branches with a wiggly stroke. Apply a varied amount of pressure to your brush to get a variety of branch sizes.

2 With a white chalk pencil, place the blueberries randomly throughout the design in clusters of three.

Paint the Berries

1 Basecoat the blueberries using a no. 4 filbert brush loaded with Cadet Blue.

2 Shade the blueberries using a ½-inch (12mm) angular shader. Float Midnight Blue on the bottom of the berries and where they're underneath another berry.

3 Highlight the blueberries with a ½-inch (12mm) angular shader. Float Glacier Blue in the upper left corner to indicate a highlight.

4 Place a small dot for the blossom end of the blueberry using a no. 1 liner brush loaded with Black. Then, paint small wispy lines going away from the center to form a star shape. This is the actual blossom.

Paint the Filler Flowers

1 Paint the filler flowers using Glacier Blue and the no. 4 filbert brush. Make filler flowers by placing the brush down flat and twisting onto the side edge, pulling slightly toward the center to form a point on each of the petals. I usually make four to five petals for each flower.

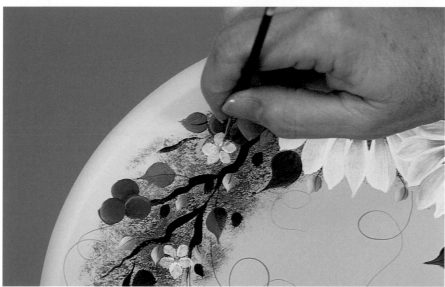

2 Paint the filler flower centers by making four or five small dots with the handle end of the brush dipped in Straw.

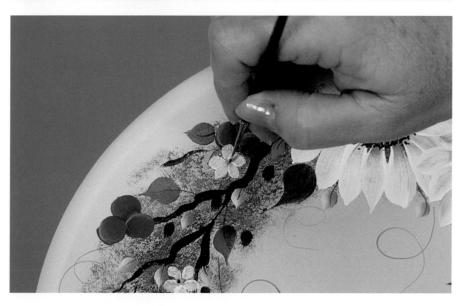

3 Shade the filler flower centers with the handle end of the brush dipped into Candy Bar Brown. Add 1 or 2 dots quickly after the first coat, so you're painting wet-into-wet.

Finishing Touches

1 Paint the tendrils using a no. 0 liner brush loaded with Dark Foliage Green.

2 Using a stiff-bristled brush or toothbrush and Midnight Blue thinned with water, spatter in the basecoat areas. You can do the flyspecking before or after you have completed the painting.

3 Paint little filler leaves on the handle with the same greens you used on the basket lid using a no. 4 filbert brush.

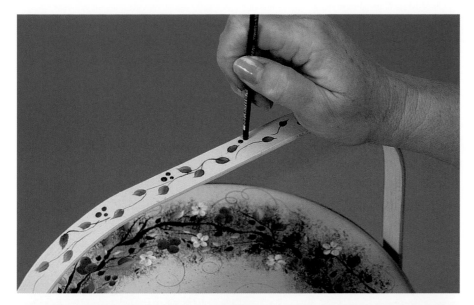

4 Add blueberries to the basket handle using the same brush's handle dipped in Midnight Blue. Randomly, make the dots in sets of three.

5 Using Dark Foliage Green and a no. 1 liner brush, connect the leaves and dots on the handle with vines and stems. Using a variety of filbert brush sizes (4-6-8), begin filling in the design with leaves painted Black Green, Dark Foliage Green, Medium Foliage Green, Light Foliage Green and Glacier Blue. Add interest to your design by using any combination of these colors double-loaded on your brush to create a variety of filler leaves.

The completed daisy basket

Combine daisies, leaves and fruit for striking combinations.

4

DESIGN YOUR OWN

You Can Do It!

So, you've always wanted to design your own pieces, but it always seemed too intimidating? Here is how I combine fruit with flowers and pick colors. Before you know it, you'll be painting your own quick and easy originals.

Let's Doodle...

When you're trying to put a project together, sit down with a pencil and a blank sheet of paper and just doodle. Start by making a rough sketch of the surface. (When I say rough, I mean rough. I still find it difficult to draw things accurately.)

Place a basket or container in the design first. Then put in the focal flowers. These can just be large ovals or circles if you like. Decide where you are going to need filler and what you would like to see there—maybe a color or maybe a flower or leaf. Just draw a blob or a triangle to hold that place. Use simple shapes to lay out your design.

I use a chalk pencil to help me keep these smaller items as well as fruits and berries to the correct size. If I don't do this, I tend to make my berries bigger than the focal flowers.

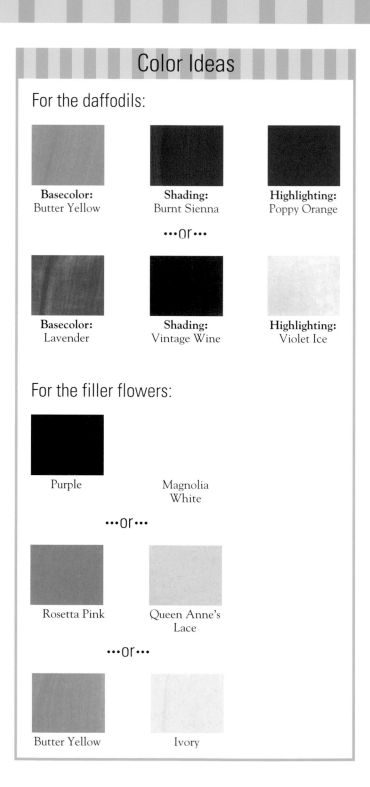

Color Ideas

For the daffodils:

Basecolor: Butter Yellow

Shading: Burnt Sienna

Highlighting: Poppy Orange

•••or•••

Basecolor: Lavender

Shading: Vintage Wine

Highlighting: Violet Ice

For the filler flowers:

Purple

Magnolia White

•••or•••

Rosetta Pink

Queen Anne's Lace

•••or•••

Butter Yellow

Ivory

Refine Your Design

Once you're pretty happy with your general design, go back and refine it. Make the circles, ovals and triangles look a little more like flowers or fruit. You still don't have to draw the filler leaves or flowers. Perhaps you would feel more comfortable drawing the flowers to the side.

Add the Color

Okay, so you made it through the drawing part, now what? It's time to choose the colors. This is one of the most fun areas of designing your own pieces.

This is easy. Choose the colors you like. I prefer deep, rich colors, but if you prefer pastels, go with it. Remember you can change any of the flower colors in this book to match your decor or your preference.

I'm always asked questions in classes about the shading and highlighting colors. This has been made easy by the major paint manufacturers. They can provide a shading and highlighting guide that lists every color in their line and what the shading and highlighting colors are for your favorite colors.

Don't forget you can visit your local department store to stare at their towels and linens to get color ideas. They know the latest trends in home decorating, so use their expertise.

You can get this brochure by writing to Delta Technical Coatings; 2550 Pellissier Place; Whittier, CA 90601 or call 1-800-423-4135. Their web address is www.deltacrafts.com.

Resource List

Products

Eagle Brush, Inc. - Brushes
431 Commerce Park Drive SE
Suite 100&101
Marietta, Georgia 30060
770-419-4855
800-832-4532

Loew-Cornell, Inc. - Brushes
563 Chestnut Ave.
Teaneck, NJ 07666-2490
201-836-7070
web site: www.loew-cornell.com
E-mail: loew-cornell@loew-cornell.com

In Argentina:
Cleo International Especials
Arenales 2532 (1425)
Buenos Aires, Argentina
54-1148242009

In Australia:
Bauernmalerei Folk & Dec. Art
P. O. Box 616
Narrabeen Australia NSW 2101
61-2-9979422

In Brazil:
Arte Versata
Sep/Sul-Eq 705/905-Bloco C
Centro Empresarial Mont Blanc
Brazilia/DF 70.390-055

In Japan:
Dean's Inc
M-1 Bldg 2F
1-1-4 Nigashi Nihonbashi Chuo-ku
Tokyo, Japan
81-3-3861-2555

Royal Brush Manufacturing, Inc.
6707 Broadway
Merrillville, IN 46410
219-660-4170

Daler-Rowney/Robert Simmons
2 Corporate Dr.
Canbury, NJ 08512-9584
609-655-5252

Delta Technical Coatings, Inc. - Delta Ceramcoat Acrylic Paint
2550 Pellissier Place
Whittier, California 90601
562-695-7969

J.W. Etc. - Prep and Finishing Products
2205 First Street #103
Simi Valley, California 93065
805-526-5066

Walnut Hollow - Memory Album Cover #3703
1409 State Road 23
Dodgeville, Wisconsin 53533-2112
608-935-2341

Pesky Bear
5059 Roszyk Hill Road
Machias, New York 14101
Phone/fax 716-942-3250

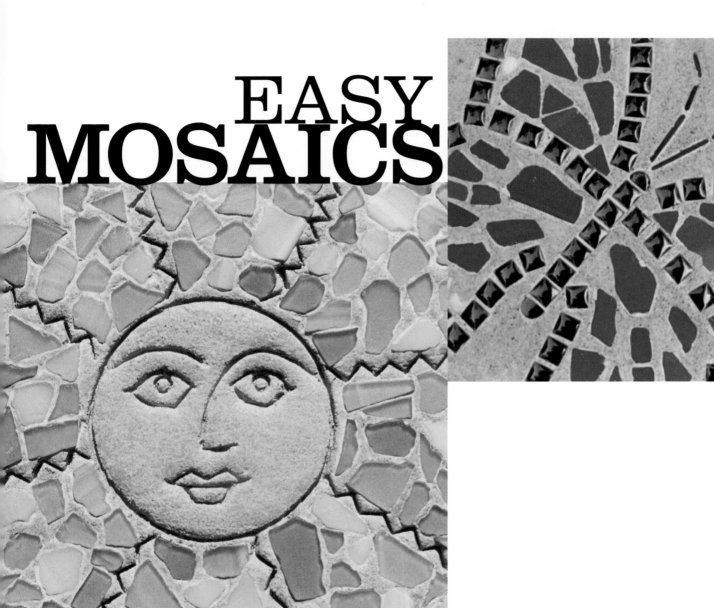

EASY
MOSAICS

for your home and garden
sarah donnelly

table of
contents

256 Introduction

258 Getting Started

Tools **258** - Tesserae **260** - Crazy Paving **262** - Molds **263** - Smashing Technique **264** - Planning Your Mosaic **266** - Making the Templates **267** - Using the Design Template **268** - Preparing the Mold with a Mounting Device **271** - Concrete **272** - Preparing the Mix **273** - Adding Colorant **277** - Transferring Mosaic Pieces to the Wet Mix **278** - Embedding Mosaic Pieces **279** - Using an Embedding Block **281** - Contact Paper Transfer and Embedding Method **282** - Smoothing the Surface **285** - Incising Lines **286** - Setting the Stone Aside to Harden **287** - Unmolding a Stone with a Mounting Device **288** - Cleaning and Unmolding the Stone **289** - Elevating and Curing the Stone **290** - Caring for Your Stone **291** - Quick Fixes **292**

Fruit Path -------------------------------------- 294
River Rock Garden Path ------------------------- 302
Reflective Heart Wall Stone --------------------- 308
Maple Leaf -------------------------------------- 312
Chicken --- 316
Petroglyph -------------------------------------- 322
Frog Wall Stone --------------------------------- 326
Fleur de Lis Tabletop --------------------------- 332
Garden Gloves ----------------------------------- 336
House Number Sign ------------------------------- 340
Lizard --- 346
Pot of Geraniums -------------------------------- 352
Pique Assiette Boot Brush ----------------------- 356
Forget-Me-Not Wall Flower ----------------------- 360
Sundial --- 364
Garden Stakes and Paperweights ----------------- 370

374 Gallery

376 Resources

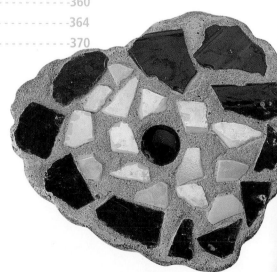

Introduction

You probably cringe at the sound of breaking glass, but it's music to my ears because it means a new mosaic is about to begin. My interest in mosaic-making has grown over many years from a passing fancy to a passionate fascination. When I began exploring mosaic art, I discovered that many mosaics can be complicated and messy to make, requiring large investments in special tools and many hours of patient work. I yearned for a fun, inventive, foolproof method that I could do in one rainy afternoon. So this is how my book of easy mosaic projects came into being!

If you are making your first mosaic, these projects were created with you in mind. If you've already made some mosaics, stay put because as the book progresses, the projects become more challenging and creative. All of the projects are flat and portable: stepping stones, wall plaques, patio tabletops, house signs and garden stakes. Some are useful; others are decorative. The designs are clear, bold and playful. The instructions are detailed but not complicated, and the sequence and nature of the steps stay the same throughout the book.

The materials and tools are common and easy to find. It's hard to go wrong with broken materials such as glass and ceramics. Concrete is truly amazing. It is easy to mold to different shapes and sizes; it anchors a wide variety of mosaic materials; and mistakes are easy to fix. Once you've gathered your supplies, you can do any of these projects in two to three hours. Basic how-to's are covered in detail in the Getting Started section of the book. Individual projects will refer you to specific page numbers for in-depth, step-by-step instructions.

If you know how to bake a cake, you will catch on very quickly. If not, it will take more time—approximately one minute more! In fact, these projects have a lot in common with baking a cake. First, you lay out and organize your mosaic design on paper. Then blend a small amount of concrete mix and water—like cake mix—and empty it into a mold—like a cake pan. Then smooth the surface—like frosting—position a stencil on top, and finally transfer, arrange and push in your mosaic pieces—like adding candles and candy sprinkles. It's a piece of cake!

Although I can't claim sole credit for inventing this method, I have explored it to its limits and have created some wonderful projects for you to try. To make the process as simple as possible, I've eliminated several steps that other mosaic techniques require.

✳ My method does not demand the cutting and nipping of glass pieces. That technique requires special tools, time and patience, and it can be frustrating to master. As you gain experience and confidence you may want to try cutting your own pieces, but even beginners can achieve satisfying results utilizing broken glass or ceramic pieces for every project in this book.

✳ My method provides patterns so you don't have to worry about your drawing skills.

✳ My method utilizes a mold filled with wet stepping stone mix rather than a base onto which mosaic pieces must be glued before they are grouted. Consequently, each project is self-grouting: you simply push pieces directly into the wet mix and you do not have to wait for any glue to dry.

✳ My method is direct: there are no backward images to confuse you. What you see is what you get.

As you advance through the projects in this book, you will learn important concepts and valuable skills, such as how to create a unified design by controlling the space between the pieces and how to balance the contrast between foreground and background. You will discover techniques and ideas that you might want to explore further. As you follow the various steps from start to finish you will become more proficient while you're developing greater patience and flexibility. After you've completed a few projects, I encourage you to experiment. Don't limit yourself to the shapes and sizes described in this book. Think big: make a tabletop. Think small: make a paperweight. Be bold: embed odds and ends directly into the wet mix. Once you get started making these fun and easy mosaics, I predict the sound of breaking glass will become music to your ears, too!

Tools

Most of the tools you will need may be found around the house or garage. The most useful special items to invest in are a couple of unusual molds, specially formulated concrete mix, color pigment and a dust mask.

1 Stepping stone molds and tart pans are some of the molds you can use. Manufactured molds come in a variety of shapes: round, square, hexagon, octagon, butterfly and flower.

2 Milestones Products makes a specially formulated, light-gray concrete called StoneCraft Mix. It has a very smooth texture and is workable for about one hour. It comes in two sizes: 7 and 3½ pounds (3.2 and 6.3kg). A perfectly good alternative is vinyl concrete patcher made by Quikrete and other manufacturers. It follows similar mixing proportions but dries a somewhat darker gray. It is available in 6- and 20-pound (2.7 and 9kg) pails, and in 40-pound (18kg) bags at home improvement stores and lumberyards. It is easier to use one brand of concrete so that you can become accustomed to its properties. Don't combine different brands of dry mix.

3 Powdered pigment for coloring concrete is available at craft stores, potter's supply stores and home improvement centers. Liquid pigment is also available.

4 A dust mask is essential to wear when mixing dry concrete or cleaning up broken glass. I recommend investing in one that is a notch above the cheapest.

5 Rubber gloves protect hands from wet concrete mix and sharp, broken glass and tile.

6 Goggles or eye protection must be worn when breaking glass and during the stone clean-up step.

7 An apron protects your clothes.

8 A rigid board is used for moving a newly-poured stone in a mold.

9 A round-bottomed 18" (46cm) diameter plastic bowl is ideal for mixing concrete. The smaller bowl is used for soaking ceramic tiles.

10 A large measuring cup is used to measure water for making the stepping stone mix.

11 A water spray bottle is needed for misting your stone while it cures.

12 A wooden paddle or garden spade is used for blending concrete and water.

13 A plastic putty knife, wall scraper or even an old credit card may be used for smoothing the surface of the wet concrete mix.

14 Duct tape and corrugated cardboard scraps are used for making an indentation in the back of a stone for hanging.

15 A fine-grain sanding block or sandpaper is used to smooth sharp edges of broken glass and ceramic tile.

16 Ruler

17 Scissors

18 A craft or utility knife and several sharp blades are required for cutting out the patterns to make the Mold Templates.

19 Felt-tip pen

20 A pencil with an eraser is used for moving and embedding tiny mosaic pieces and for making dots in the wet mix.

21 Large tweezers are useful for picking up tiny tesserae.

22 A hammer covered with a sock can be used to break glass. A rubber mallet also works.

23 A hacksaw is used for one project to cut a terra-cotta pot.

24 Plastic bags are used for containing breaking glass and covering wet concrete.

25 Rags or a towel

26 A foam paintbrush or sponge is used to clean mosaic pieces and smooth the wet concrete surface.

27 A paper clip is used for cleaning hardened concrete from the mosaic pieces.

28 A screwdriver is used to scrape the edges of the hardened stone.

29 Transparent vinyl contact paper may be used for saving and transferring mosaic layouts.

30 A tray of fine sand may be used for laying out pebble and rock mosaic designs.

31 A small paintbrush and dishwashing liquid, petroleum jelly or cooking oil spray are used for coating molds which might otherwise adhere to the concrete. Commercial release agents are also available at home improvement stores.

32 A 5-gallon (3.8l) bucket with water is used for rinsing wet concrete mix from your tools and bowl so you won't clog your sink drain.

33 Paper is used for tracing the mold when you are doing a project that does not use a photocopied pattern.

34 An awl is used to punch holes through a paper pattern for transferring leaf stems and other linear design elements to the wet mix.

35 A toothbrush, scouring pad and sponge are used fto clean hardened mix from the mosaic pieces after the stone has cured.

Tesserae

Tesserae are the pieces which make up your mosaic design. You should be familiar with the characteristics of various types of tesserae because some materials are better for certain uses. For example, mosaics made of porous materials are more susceptible to cracking in cold weather. Keep these features in mind when considering the design, use and location of your mosaic creation.

Glass

* Vitreous glass tiles, also known as Venetian tesserae, come in uniform sizes and are very versatile. The opaque tiles are smooth on one side and ridged on the other for better bonding. Practical and economical, they are strong, non-porous, and stain- and weather-resistant. The color selection is good and they are easy to break or cut. Buy them loose or on 12" x 12" (30cm x 30cm) sheets.

* Stained glass or art glass has both smooth and textured surfaces with irregularities: bubbles, swirls and waves. The opaque glass is more practical for mosaic purposes because the gray concrete will not show through. Since this glass is very thin, it must be fully embedded in the mix in order to remain in place. Most packaged broken glass has been tumbled to dull the sharp edges.

* Smalti, or Byzantine tesserae, are made in Italy specifically for mosaic applications. Large, hand-poured glass slabs are hand-cut into small irregular cubes. The surfaces are highly reflective, faceted and pitted, making them semi-porous. Smalti come in an amazing selection of intense opaque and transparent colors as well as reflective metallic gold. Since it takes practice to make accurate cuts, it's better to use the cubes whole. They are beautiful and expensive.

* Tumbled glass is shiny glass that has been machine smoothed so it becomes matte or frosted. This process also breaks the pieces into sizes that are just right for the projects in this book. (If the pieces are large, the chance of fractures increases.) Most "sea glass" is actually broken recycled bottles that have been tumbled.

* Glass nuggets look like half-melted marbles, flat on one side, rounded on the other. They come in several sizes and many colors. They are used in this book for eyes, grapes, raspberries and other round accents.

* A broken mirror isn't bad luck for a mosaic artist, because just a few pieces can add a lot of sparkle to any mosaic design. Before using, seal the reverse side with two light coats of acrylic spray or other sealant to prevent the silvering from deteriorating when it comes in contact with the caustic wet concrete.

Broken china and pottery

Save those chipped bowls and shattered plates! You can embed an entire broken plate or use pieces of patterned china as accents. I recommend sanding the sharp edges, especially if you're using the pieces in a stepping stone.

Ceramic tile

Ceramic tile is available in many different finishes, from rough and rustic to highly polished. Ceramic tiles are produced in uniform sizes and shapes and are inexpensive. Buy them loose or on sheets. Tile is easily cut with nippers or broken with a hammer. Some types of tiles to try in your mosaic designs are:

* Glazed floor and wall tile has a thin highly reflective glaze on one side. It may be porous and isn't reversible.

* Unglazed tile has a nonreflective matte finish and is reversible. It's strong, easy to cut and may be porous.

* Porcelain is high-fired ceramic that comes glazed and unglazed. It's the least porous and toughest of all tiles and is usually waterproof and weather-resistant.

Stones and shells

Pebbles, shells and rock (such as granite and marble) are manufactured by Mother Nature to be irregular, imperfect and unique. There is a wide variety of shapes, sizes and finishes: from natural matte to highly polished. They are available in a beautiful but limited natural color range or are coated with bright paint or clear acrylic. Hard stones are very durable and resistant to water and weather. Manufactured stone tiles and cubes of marble are easy to break but difficult to cut.

Found objects

"Junque" is cheap, free and fun. You can use broken bottles, keys, buttons, beads, trinkets and brass charms — almost anything not made of plastic or rubber (which don't adhere to concrete). Sort through your drawers for unique items and have fun experimenting!

1 translucent stained glass

2 opaque stained glass

3 stained glass with iridized surface

4 translucent smalti

5 opaque smalti

6 gold smalti

7 glass nuggets

8 vitreous glass tiles

9 pressed glass star

10 beach glass or sea glass

11 chunky glass, tumbled

12 glass rods

13 glass beads

14 fused-glass heart ornament

15 mirror tiles

16 glazed ceramic wall and floor tiles

17 unglazed earthenware tiles

18 decorative porcelain tiles

19 china and pottery

20 polished and unpolished river rocks

21 painted gravel

22 white marble

23 granite

24 seashells

25 keys

26 coins

27 costume jewelry

28 buttons

29 toys

30 drawer pull

31 spoon

32 assorted found objects

33 broken chandelier crystal

34 metal house numbers

35 terra-cotta frog

36 alphabet press set

37 decorative scrolls and border stamps

38 oversized rubber stamp

39 cookie cutters

40 craft stick

Crazy Paving

The layout of the individual pieces of a mosaic give the design its energy. Many mosaics are made up of a simple, repetitious pattern. Imagine a brick wall, row upon row of rectangular bricks all evenly spaced. This is a predictable and calm pattern. Other familiar patterns include circles, overlapping fans, basket weave, and herringbone, which are graceful and have more motion and fluidity than the wall. Every mosaicist learns that the **joint**, the mortar-filled space between the bricks, is just as important as the bricks themselves. These spaces move your eyes in a desired direction and rhythm.

The projects in this book use only one pattern: **crazy paving,** also known as **opus palladianum**, which is a busy arrangement of broken, irregularly shaped pieces of glass, ceramic and stone. What sets it apart from other more traditional patterns is its broken lines, unpredictable fractures, and its seeming chaos. It is a high-energy, fun, and sometimes dizzying pattern.

Crazy paving is extremely versatile. It easily lends itself to portraying a variety of forms. The designs in this book are simple, bold shapes that when expressed as a crazy-pave mosaic will remain interesting and easy to recognize. Each design is unique, yet repeatable many times over. No two crazy-pave mosaics will ever look the same due to the unique arrangement of broken shards and pieces.

Most of these designs consist of a crazy-paved shape within a plain gray background. The image stands out clearly against the unadorned concrete. The background and foreground aren't competing for attention so the eye has an easier time "reading" the image.

Crazy paving is the perfect mosaic pattern for beginners. The irregular arrangement of tesserae allows for inconsistencies but it is fun and challenging for the more experienced mosaicist. Laying out a design is quick and easy because it is less complicated and intricate than other paving patterns. The technique is easy to learn because less time is spent on precision and detail.

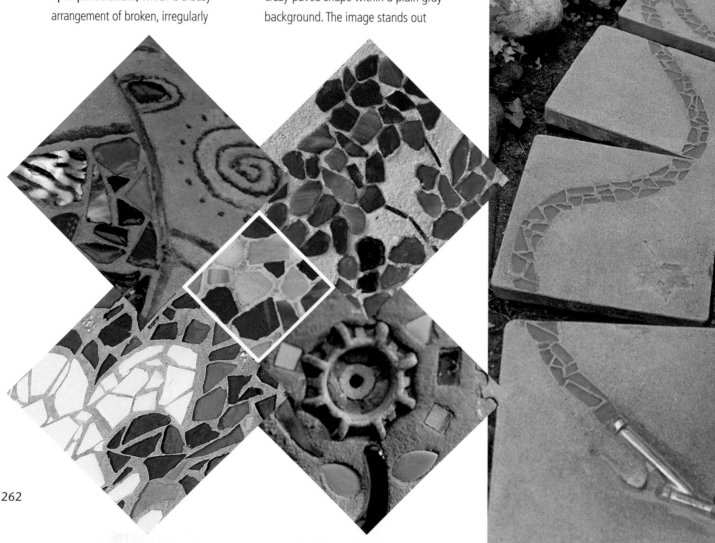

Molds

In the following projects, you will cast a concrete stone by filling a shallow mold with thick wet concrete, adding your mosaic pieces and leaving it to harden. There are three kinds of molds: manufactured, makeshift, and made-from-scratch. Craft stores carry a variety of shapes and sizes of molds that are specifically designed for casting stones. Some molds are flexible vinyl which can last through many castings. Others are more expensive heavy-duty, rigid plastic which can be used almost indefinitely.

When hunting for makeshift molds, you should consider the material and the angle of the sides. The material I prefer is flexible plastic because it releases hardened concrete very easily and it's reusable. Molds can also be made of rigid plastic, wood, plaster, or corrugated cardboard (which must be coated with a thin layer of release agent). Spray cans of mold release are sold at home improvement centers or you can use dishwashing liquid, cooking oil spray or petroleum jelly. You can also line these molds with heavy plastic sheeting or garbage bags, but any wrinkles in the plastic will show up on your stone.

A makeshift mold is a container that came into this world intended for another use. For example, assorted sizes of round, vinyl plant saucers can be used as molds for mosaic stones of various sizes. If you want to make a five-paver garden path, you can buy five inexpensive plant saucers and mold your stones all at once. We buy and throw away potential molds every day. Blister display packaging is made of plastic that wet concrete easily forms to and hardened concrete easily releases from. Many food products are protected or served in plastic containers which serve as perfect casting molds: deli and bakery containers, microwave food trays, margarine tubs, party trays and lids. Other unusual plastic mold substitutes are soap and candle molds, dog food bowls, garbage can lids and plant flats lined with plastic.

You should look for containers with sides that angle outward. Even if you coat a straight-sided metal with mold release, your hardened stone may not come out. However, your stone will pop right out of a coated metal pie pan that has angled sides.

Here are a few suggestions for non-plastic molds: metal pie pans, tart and springform pans; waxed paper cups and foil roasting pans. A cardboard pizza box without a plastic liner makes a rustic-looking stone: just fill it with concrete mix, push in your mosaic pieces, let it harden, then tear off the box. Any embedded cardboard fragments will disintegrate when exposed to the elements.

If you're handy with tools, you may want to make your own molds "from scratch." Build a plywood frame or make a freeform shape with a flexible garden border and stakes shoved into the ground; pack wet sand into a cardboard box and carve out a shape; or simply dig a shallow hole in the dirt and empty your wet concrete mix into it.

If you have a choice, it's best to select molds that have smooth bottoms. This will allow you to try the indirect method of creating a mosaic. Instead of filling the mold with wet mix and placing the tesserae on the top surface (the direct method that's described in this book), the bottom of the mold is lined with contact paper, sticky side up. Tesserae are arranged on the contact paper with the design reversed. Then wet mix, usually fast-setting concrete, is poured into the mold. When the stone is hard, it is removed from the mold and the contact paper is peeled off to reveal the design. This method creates a mosaic with a smooth, shiny top surface. Although the instructions in this book are for the direct method, you may use the designs in this book with either method.

In the project instructions "prepare the mold" means for you to apply mold release if needed, or attach the wall mount to the bottom of the mold (more about this later), or rinse out a previously used mold.

tip

1. Beveled sides are a must.

2. Flexible plastic and rubber molds do not need mold release.

3. Metal and rigid plastic molds require a coat of mold release.

Smashing Technique

What is the purpose of breaking perfectly good, usable bowls, tiles, plates and sheets of glass? It's fun and it's a good excuse to make a truly unique mosaic. Look for old china and tile at flea markets, secondhand stores and yard sales. Look around your house for cracked or chipped china that may be more useful smashed to create a mosaic design.

A hammer is the perfect tool for pounding in nails, but it's too dense and

MATERIALS

safety glasses

rubber gloves

dust mask

plate to be broken

rubber mallet or hammer covered with old socks fastened with rubber bands

old towel

heavyweight transparent plastic bag

pointed for glass-smashing purposes. The hardened steel head shatters the glass or china in one place, sending straight cracks radiating in all directions. The result is often pointed, elongated and very sharp shards. Fine china may even turn into dust when hit with a claw hammer.

A rubber mallet is a perfect smashing tool because it will break glass just as easily as a hammer, but the pieces will be more irregular and interesting in size and shape. If you don't have a rubber mallet handy, you can wrap a hammer head with one or two old socks and use a rubber band to hold them on.

Smash on a surface you do not value, preferably the newspaper-padded concrete floor of your garage or basement. If you want to smash plates in your kitchen, protect the floor with a

piece of plywood or a thick towel. And while we're talking about protection, don't forget to protect your eyes from airborne glass shards.

How hard you must hit the glass to break it depends on the type of glass. Bone china will be easier to break than stoneware or ceramic bathroom tile. Sometimes an object will break perfectly and completely with one stroke. Other times it may refuse to break after five or ten whacks, and you hesitate to hit it any harder lest you smash it to smithereens. Try propping the stubborn piece against a brick or another piece of broken pottery; it will more readily break into usable pieces.

If you want to break a tile or plate and reassemble it "whole" in your mosaic design, apply strips of strong tape to one side before you smash it.

1 ➤ Wrap. Put on goggles and gloves. Center the plate on the towel, then wrap it up.

2 ➤ Ready. Place the towel in the plastic bag and fold the open end under, sealing the bag.

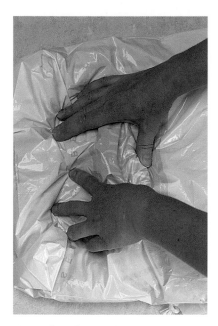

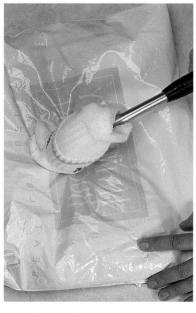

5 ➤ Voilà! Broken bits! It may take two or more blows to break the plate into usable pieces, about 2"x 2" (5cm x 5cm) and smaller.

3 ➤ Aim. Check for the placement of the plate in the bag.

4 ➤ Smash! Take one light swing at it. Peek in the bag to see what kind of damage you did. Handle sharp pieces with gloved hands and extreme care.

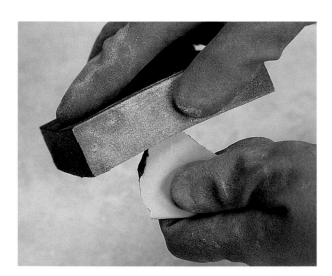

6 ➤ Sand off the sharp edges. You may use the pieces as they are or, to make them safer and easier to work with, you may want to sand down all of the edges. This is time-consuming, but a good idea. If you plan to walk on your stepping stone barefoot, you will definitely want to blunt the edges because some will be exposed in the finished mosaic.

Put on the dust mask and safety glasses when you sweep up broken leftovers. Fine particles of glass and clay will be airborne and undetectable.

tip

Save any leftover broken bits in glass jars. They will be easy to identify, safe to handle and beautiful to see.

Planning Your Mosaic

Here are some things to consider when you design and gather the materials for your mosaic:

Will the stone be functional or decorative?

Do you want to hang it on a wall?

Will it be indoors or outdoors? Will it be exposed to weather extremes or in a protected area? Would it be convenient to remove it and bring it indoors during freezing weather?

Do you want to leave space to write a name or date, or make a hand print?

Is it part of a series (a path, for example) or does it stand on its own?

What colors of tesserae and concrete do you want?

These and other points will be covered as we go. Look through the projects and choose one you like. If this is your first mosaic, consider trying one of the simpler designs: the apple, pear, bananas, mirrored heart, river rock path or the maple leaf. Buy or find a mold in a size and shape you like.

It's important to choose colors that you like. Craft stores carry mosaic pieces in a variety of shapes, sizes and colors. If you are unable to find the exact color of mosaic pieces shown in a photograph, you'll need to improvise. You may have a chipped plate in the perfect color that you don't mind sacrificing to make your work of art. A store that sells stained glass may have just what you're looking for, and you can usually buy a small portion of a large sheet which will break into more than enough pieces for your project. Boxes of small pieces of scrap glass are often available at reduced prices. The Internet also offers easy access to the world of mosaic materials. Estimate what you'll need, then buy a little more just to be safe. Going back later to match a ceramic or glass color is difficult or impossible.

The red in this simple border design contrasts beautifully with the green foliage that surrounds the plaque.

Making the Templates

Templates are your guide to laying out your mosaic design. Most of the projects in this book call for two templates: a Design Template and a Mold Template.

The Design Template is for your initial layout of tesserae. It's where you arrange the pieces that will create your mosaic design. Use the template to practice outlining shapes, to experiment with spacing and to make your final arrangement of pieces.

The Mold Template determines the position of your design within the edges of the mold. After the mix has been poured into the mold and smoothed, this template is placed on the surface of the wet mix. The cut-out shape makes a window which you use for transferring and positioning all the mosaic pieces in your design.

1 ➤ Enlarge the pattern. All of the patterns in this book have been reduced in size. Use a copier to enlarge the pattern to fit your mold, using 11" x 17" (28cm x 43cm) paper if possible. Bring your mold or a tracing of it with you to the copy machine so you can check the fit of the enlarged pattern. Try to keep the outlines of the pattern ½" (1cm) but no closer than ¼" (6mm) from the edges of the mold. You may have to experiment with different percentages to get the right size. The advantage of this technique is that you can use the patterns in this book with molds of many shapes and sizes. When the enlargement is correct, make a second copy.

2 ➤ Position the mold and trace it. Set your mold base-side down on the enlarged pattern over the design. This will be easier if you have a clear plastic mold and can see the pattern through the mold. Check to see that the design outline is ½" (1cm) from the edge of the mold, and trace around the base of the mold. It's OK if the mold runs off the edge of the paper copy. You need only a partial mold outline to properly position the template on the mix surface. Use scissors to cut along the mold outline.

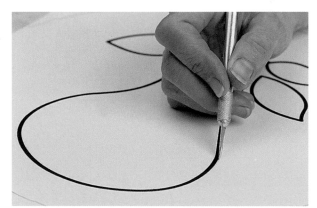

3 ➤ Cut out the design. Use a craft knife or small scissors to cut out the design outline. Cut on the outside of the line, making as large an opening as possible. You can lift out the design shapes and use them for your Design Template if you didn't make two copies of your pattern initially. The template with the cut-out areas is your Mold Template, which is the one you will place on the wet mix surface when you're ready to transfer your tesserae.

Using the Design Template

Before you lay out your design, it is helpful to organize your tesserae in trays or shoe box lids, using one tray per color. For some designs, sorting pieces by size and shape is also a good idea. A white-lined tray for translucent glass shows truer colors, although a gray background shows how the glass will look when placed on the concrete.

If you lay out your mosaic in the following order, you will save some time and reduce your frustration. Start by finding and placing key mosaic pieces: points, corners, narrow bands, and tight spaces. Next, outline the shape. Finally, fill in the rest of the shape.

When you have your colors organized, begin to arrange the mosaic pieces on the Design Template. Practice putting pieces together like a jigsaw puzzle, leaving ⅛" (3mm) between the pieces. For some people, this step will take great patience. However, for many of us, this is a relaxing, creative, engrossing activity. Take your time and keep in mind that when you transfer the pieces to the surface of the wet mix, their positions will change slightly. Don't worry, you will have the chance to fine-tune the placement of the pieces before you embed them.

MATERIALS

Design Template

tesserae

trays to hold and sort mosaic pieces

1 ➤ Select the key pieces. Tesserae come in many shapes, but generally broken glass or ceramic pieces have straight, gently curved, and angular edges. Your eyes will learn to pick out certain shapes and curves. Key pieces such as points should be selected and positioned first.

2 ➤ Position the key pieces. Try to break down each design into several smaller shapes or parts. Then find key pieces to highlight and define each shape. For example, triangular pieces are perfect for pointed leaf tips, feathers, beaks, toes, animal ears, bent knee joints and tight corners on numerals.

tip

Lay out translucent tesserae on concrete-gray colored paper for a realistic preview.

3 ➤ Select round shapes. Experiment with various round shapes for eyes or spots: glass beads, buttons, glass nuggets, marbles or thumbtacks. Avoid plastic beads and items made of rubber, which do not adhere to the concrete.

4 ➤ Outline the shapes. The outlines of your design include all kinds of bends and twists. Making a good outline is especially critical because we are using the crazy pave pattern. The outline needs to be bold and clean to organize the fractured and busy pattern of lines within. Simple shapes with smooth outlines are usually the most effective.

Some curves are long and gradual.

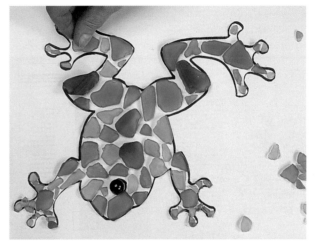

Others are short with tight bends. Try to match the curve of the line as best as you can because you may see it clearly now, but when you take away the paper template, it may look very different. Your placement of pieces has to re-create that line as closely as possible so that anyone can easily "read" the image.

Using the Design Template

> continued

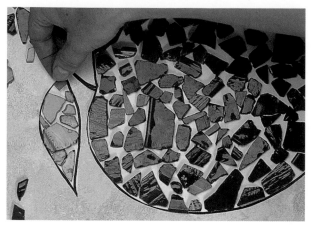

5 ➤ Fill in the middle. As you fill in the shape, pay attention to the spaces between the pieces, which are called **joints.** Spacing affects the "readability" of an image because the design is created by broken pieces. The closer the spacing of the pieces, the easier it is to see the image as a unified whole. Larger spacing between the pieces emphasizes the shapes of the individual pieces, making it more difficult to see the image as a single shape. However, don't space the pieces too closely; allow enough space for the wet mix to come up and anchor each individual tessera. Generally, I try to allow ⅛" (3mm) between pieces.

6 ➤ Adjust the spacing. The shape of the tesserae affects the spacing. Flat tesserae should be spaced evenly thoughout a design.

Round or irregularly-shaped tesserae such as rocks or glass nuggets are difficult to space evenly. The rocks may look fine on the paper template, but when the pieces are partially submerged in the mix, they will shrink and the joints between them will widen. The image will not "read" very well. To solve this problem, rocks, nuggets and other rounded tesserae should be placed so they touch each other. Lay out rounded tesserae in a box of sand so that you can see how they'll appear after they are embedded.

Preparing the Mold with a Mounting Device

If you are planning to make a stone that will hang (on a wall, fence, or door) complete these steps before preparing the mix. This is an inexpensive way to create a rectangular indentation in the back of your stone to accommodate one or more nails or screws. The indentation should be ¼" to ⅜" (6mm-9mm) deep and wide enough for two nails or screws, since a 12" (30cm) stone weighs over 7 pounds (3.2kg) and may require heavy-duty screws set in anchors in your wall. When you hang your stone you will be able to adjust the plaque from side to side to center and straighten it. Any project may be turned into a wall plaque by adding this mounting device.

MATERIALS

2" x 2" (5cm x 5cm) piece of corrugated cardboard

3" x 2" (8cm x 5cm) piece of duct tape

1 ➤ Bend the cardboard. Set the mold on a rigid board. Bend the piece of cardboard in half.

2 ➤ Wrap the cardboard with tape. Wrap the folded cardboard with the piece of duct tape sticky-side out.

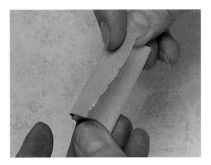

3 ➤ Secure the ends of the tape. Overlap the ends of the tape so it sticks to itself and flattens the bent cardboard piece. The sticky cardboard mounting device should now be about 2" x 1" x ¼" (5cm x 2.5cm x 6mm) and ready to position.

4 ➤ Position the mounting device. Place the mounting device centered in your mold, about 1½" (38mm) from the top edge.

When you unmold your stone, the tape will stick to the mold and you will have to peel it away as your stone releases. Use a stick or screwdriver to remove the cardboard and duct tape from the stone. The stone will have a depression to accommodate two screws or nails for hanging the plaque.

tip

Use the plastic hanging tab of the mold as a marker for the top of a round or square stone. If there is no tab, stick a small piece of tape on the edge to mark the top. When you place your tesserae, you'll know which edge is the top of your wall plaque.

Concrete

Concrete is an amazing material. It can be formed into just about any shape: a plain concrete block, a sidewalk, a park bench, garden statuary, foundation walls, bridge footings or even skyscrapers. All of these objects begin as a soft, malleable mixture which is placed in a mold. Within a short time the mixture hardens into a strong and durable material: concrete. It used to be considered a building material only. Now it's being used everywhere, outdoors and indoors, as a functional and decorative surface for kitchen counters, bathroom floors, front door columns; and for this book, wall plaques, house signs, tabletops, garden stakes, paperweights and stepping stones.

First, I want to discuss terminology. Is it cement or concrete? Cement, concrete, grout, mix and mortar are often used interchangeably to refer to the material used to fill in around tesserae, but in fact they refer to different types of mixtures. Each was created for a specific purpose, but they all have one thing in common: each contains cement, a very fine powder of crushed rocks. I learned to keep the terms straight by remembering that cement is to concrete (and all the others) what flour is to a cake. It's an ingredient.

The projects in this book use **concrete** or **mix** that is specially formulated for making smooth-textured, long-lasting, gray stepping stones. It also works for making other objects, as you will see. It comes in convenient 3½- and 7-pound (1.6kg and 3.2kg) bags, a very manageable size and quantity compared to the large and heavy bags of concrete mix sold at home improvement centers. Stepping stone mix is sold at craft stores and garden centers. Most concrete is gray, but white is also available and colorant may be added to make any other desired color.

Mixing concrete is an inexact science, but it is very easy to do. It is a forgiving medium with very few absolutes; most mistakes can easily be corrected. And it's less messy than you may think, so don't be afraid to experiment and have fun!

Some conditions which influence the strength and durability of concrete are the amount of water used in the mix, temperature and humidity, and the hardening or **curing** conditions. Concrete should last for a very long time when mixed in ideal circumstances: moderate temperature, no direct sun or high wind, mixed with as little water as possible, and kept moist while hardening. Use my measurements as a starting point; no two mixtures will ever be the same. As you make more stones, you'll develop a feel for the conditions that affect the mix on any given day.

If you are not using a premeasured bag of mix, estimate the amount of dry mix you will need by measureing the amount of water it takes to fill the mold. You will need roughly the same amount of dry mix, but add an extra cup just to be safe. For every 5 cups (1.6kg) of dry mix, start with 1 cup (236ml) of water. Different manufacturers' proportions may vary.

Your workspace can be in your kitchen or garage on a level surface at a comfortable height for working. (Although you may want to prepare the mix outdoors.) Protect the work surface with plastic or newspaper, put on an apron and gather your tools and materials for the next step: preparing the mix.

Here are two molds with the correct amount of dry mix needed for each. The packets at the bottom of the photo are powdered pigments that can be added to color the concrete.

Preparing the Mix

When you are told to "prepare the mix" in the instructions for the projects, keep in mind the Tips (below) and follow the steps on pages 274–276.

tips

➤ Always wear a dust mask and rubber gloves when mixing concrete.

➤ The less water used initially, the stronger the final stone. Start with less water than called for, especially if you have only one small bag of mix.

➤ Use drinkable water only; impurities may weaken the stone.

➤ Use mix specifically formulated for stepping stones, or an equivalent product. Do not use generic concrete mixes, which usually contain coarse gravel. Do not use fast-setting concrete.

➤ Measured amounts are approximate; use them as a starting point. Have extra dry mix on hand to make adjustments.

➤ Prepare you mix in a temperate location: 55-75°F (13-24°C).

➤ Use a mold material which allows the hardened stone to release easily: rubber or flexible plastic

➤ Other mold materials (metals, cardboard, rigid plastic or wood) may need to be coated with a release agent. Use a commercially available release agent, dishwashing liquid, cooking oil spray or petroleum jelly.

➤ Do not use straight-sided pans. Use molds with sides which are angled outward, even slightly.

➤ Use a rigid board to lift a flexible mold once it has been filled with wet mix to avoid creating an unseen crack.

➤ The fewer and shallower the impressions you make in the stone (writing, stamping, mounting device, etc.), the stronger it will be.

➤ Do not embed any more pieces after the stone begins to harden or set up, about one hour after adding water. If the surface cracks, spray it once with water, smooth it, and set it aside to harden.

➤ Allow the molded stone to harden at a moderate temperature and in a level, undisturbed place away from sunlight.

➤ Spray the curing stone liberally with water daily for the first seven days.

➤ Wait 48 hours before removing your stone from the mold.

➤ Wait at least fourteen days before stepping on a stone.

➤ Do not put concrete or mix down any drains; it may harden and clog the pipes. Instead, rinse your bowl and tools in a bucket of water. Let the water settle overnight, drain off the clear water into your yard and dispose of the gray concrete sludge in the garbage.

➤ Store concrete mix in a dry place in an airtight container or plastic bag.

MATERIALS

dust mask

rubber gloves

one bag of dry stepping stone mix

scissors

mixing bowl

measuring cup

teaspoon

water

mixing tool, garden trowel or spade

mold

rigid board 16" x 16" (41cm x 41cm)

smoothing tool: 3" (75mm) plastic putty knife or trowel

5-gallon (3.8l) bucket half filled with water to clean tools

optional: one-hour timer

Preparing the Mix

> continued

1 ➤ Empty the dry mix into a bowl. Try to mix concrete outdoors whenever possible. Put on a dust mask and gloves. Cut open the bag of mix and gently pour it into the mixing bowl. Keep the dust to a minimum by pouring and mixing slowly. If you want to color your mix, turn to page 277 for directions.

2 ➤ Add water. Add exactly 2 cups (472ml) of water, a few teaspoons (5-10ml) less if you are in a humid or damp climate (follow the manufacturer's instructions if the amount given is different from this).

The amount of water added to the dry mix determines the durability and strength of the finished stone. **Use the least amount of water possible to reach a workable consistency.** This amount will vary with the brand of mix you're using, the air and water temperatures, and the humidity. If the mixture is so thin that it can be poured, it will make a weaker, less durable stone. A wet, sloppy mix will delay hardening and will be too watery to hold embedded objects. If the mixture is too dry, it will be hard to work with, but this is easy to correct. It's best to begin with a mixture that appears to be a bit too dry.

3 ➤ Mix well. Using the mixing tool, thoroughly combine the dry mix with the water. This photo shows a desirable consistency. The mixture looks coarse and a little crumbly.

4 ➤ Test the consistency. Pick up a handful in your gloved hand and press together firmly. Does it stay in one lump without any cracks or crumbling? If so, it's mixed correctly. Go to Step 5. If it crumbles easily when poked, add more water.

TOO DRY!

This mixture needs just a little more water. Trust me: 1 teaspoon (5ml) of water will go a long way, especially when you are about to reach the "just right" point. Blend very well and test again before adding another teaspoonful. If it's a hot day, you may need more water, but add just a little at a time.

TOO WET!

This mixture is soupy, runny and unusable. You should add a small amount of dry mix and stir well. Keep adding and stirring until your mixture is "just right."

JUST RIGHT!

If you've mixed it correctly, the mix should hold together in your hand—and in the bowl—in one lump or mass. It should be fairly smooth and plastic, like thick cookie batter.

5 ➤ Empty the mixture into the mold. Put your mold on a rigid board and empty the mix into the mold, which should "plop" into the mold in one lump. Remove your mask and check the time. You have about 45 to 60 minutes, weather and temperature permitting—usually plenty of time to finish a project. If it's dry and hot, you may have only 45 minutes. If it's wet and cool, you'll have more time to work. I like to set a timer for 35 minutes, so when it rings I know I have ten or twenty minutes left before the mix starts to harden.

6 ➤ Spread out the mix. Use your mixing tool to quickly and rather unevenly spread out the mix in the mold, especially into the corners and rippled edges if your mold has them. You'll have a chance to level the surface in Step 8.

Preparing the Mix
continued

7 ➤ Smooth and compact the mix. Now use the putty knife to tamp down the mix and smooth the surface. Go over it several times, turning the mold to get the tool into the corners if your mold has them. Last, smooth the entire edge.

8 ➤ Jiggle the mold. Hold opposite sides of the mold and move the mold one or two inches (25-50mm) back and forth, three or four times in a continuous motion. Rotate the mold 45° and do it again. Rotate and repeat once more. Notice how the mix unifies and the surface smooths out. Jiggle the mold as little as possible, only until the surface is level and the texture evens out. If you jiggle it too much, the mix will start to separate; finer particles will rise to the top, and water will pool on the surface. Don't worry about popping all the bubbles that will arise and don't try to make a perfectly smooth surface now; it will get lumpy when you push in the mosaic pieces. You'll have the chance to smooth it again after embedding your tesserae.

9 ➤ Clean your tools. Rinse out the bowl and tools in a large bucket (never in a sink; see Tips on page 273). Now you have three choices: practice embedding some tesserae; practice incising lines; or put your Mold Template on the mix surface and start transferring tesserae for your first project.

   The lime in concrete is caustic and will dry out your skin. It may help to rinse your hands with vinegar to restore the pH balance.

tip

An advantage to this direct, self-grouting technique is that changes can be made and mistakes fixed midway through the project. If you don't like something, remove it, smooth it over and start again. If this is your first stone, take just a couple of minutes after preparing the mix to practice embedding mosaic pieces (see pages 279–280). Try different materials: pieces of glass and tile, a couple of pebbles, a curved piece of a broken cup. Make a line or letter with a craft stick or your finger (see pages 286–287); make a hand print. Then remove all the bits, rinse them off in the bucket of water, smooth the surface and start on your chosen project.

Adding Colorant

Changing a gray stone to a different color is really fun and exciting. It will dramatically affect the look, readability and unity of your mosaic design. The color of the concrete can be changed by adding dry or liquid colorants. Here, I use a packet of powdered pigment. A little goes a long way, so read the instructions carefully. The color of the pigment is much more intense and concentrated than the finished, mixed color. Not all pigments are made for coloring concrete, so be sure to check the manufacturer's instructions. Go for good quality, and match brands with your specific concrete mix. Colorants are available at home improvement centers and most tile and potter's supply stores.

1 ➤ **Add pigment to the dry mix.** Wearing your dust mask and gloves, slowly add the dry colorant to the dry mix before you add water. The powder is **very** messy; it spreads everywhere if touched, and it may stain your clothes.

2 ➤ **Stir.** Slowly stir the two powders together. The mixture may look just as gray as it did before you added the colorant, but don't add more pigment.

Go to page 274 Step 2 for mixing directions. The color develops after water is added, and it will appear darker than the finished stone will look. As the stone cures, the color will lighten.

tip

Lay out tesserae on colored paper that matches your concrete color: gray, terra-cotta, sandstone, light blue or whatever color you have chosen. Experiment to see how the different concrete colors can change the overall look and readability of your design.

Transferring Mosaic Pieces to the Wet Mix

Using a Mold Template

1 ➤ Place the Mold Template. Position the Mold Template on the wet mix surface so that it is flat and smooth. Adjust the location of the design outline within the frame of the mold.

2 ➤ Transfer key pieces. Start transferring pieces to the mix surface, but don't push them in yet. First, the key pieces: points, tips, angles and tight corners.

3 ➤ Outline the figure. Next, transfer the pieces that outline the design. Follow the outline carefully, but work quickly; you can fine-tune the positions in a few minutes.

4 ➤ Fill in the center. Fill in the figure rather quickly. Once all the pieces are moved to the mix, you can adjust the positioning or add more pieces. Keep the pieces inside the cut edge of the Mold Template so you can remove it without disturbing your layout.

When the pieces are in place, step back and look at the arrangement. Is the outline smooth? Is the spacing consistent and close? Make any final adjustments using tweezers to move the pieces. Next you'll embed them.

Transferring with no Template

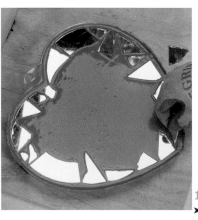

1
➤

Outline, then fill in. If your design is abstract and covers the entire surface, you won't need a Mold Template. Transfer the border pieces from the Design Template; then fill in the center. If you have several large pieces, or pieces which must be placed precisely, position them first before placing the border pieces.

MATERIALS

Mold Template, cut out

final mosaic layout on Design Template

prepared mix in mold

tesserae

rubber gloves

Embedding Mosaic Pieces

You may begin embedding pieces before or after you remove the Mold Template. If you leave the template in place, it serves as a clear guide for the outline. If you take it off, it's easier to see how the image as a whole "reads," and where changes may be needed. You can decide what to do. The template is reusable if you wipe it off and lay it flat to dry.

The sequence of embedding tesserae is usually determined by the design and the materials. If the design includes an outline, a border around the mold or key pieces, embed them first. As you push them straight down into the mix, be careful that these pieces do not shift position. If interior pieces move. you may adjust them. Be sure that each piece of an outline flows into the next, creating a smooth, even line.

The next priority of the embedding order depends on the thickness of the pieces. If the pieces are of varying thickness, embed the thickest piece, followed by thinner and thinner pieces. (Very thin, flat pieces such as coins or bicycle gears and sprockets need to be pushed in more deeply than other pieces to ensure proper bonding and stability.) If pieces are of equal thickness and the design has no important outlines, you may embed them in any sequence.

No matter what order you press in the pieces, you will have to go over all the pieces several times because as you shove one piece into the wet mix another will undoubtedly pop up.

MATERIALS

rubber gloves

pencil with eraser

tweezers

water spray bottle

prepared mix in mold with tesserae on the surface

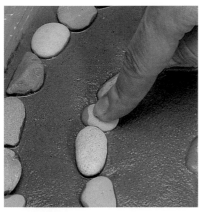

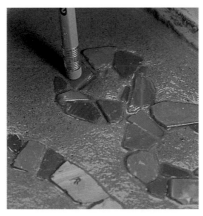

To embed, push straight down at the center of a piece. If it's a flat piece of glass or tile, press until it is flush with the surface of the mix. You want to force the mix to rise up and surround each piece, filling in all the joints without covering the piece. If the piece is pushed in too far, it may sink and disappear or create a crater-like depression (see page 293). If it isn't pushed in enough, it may fall out after the stone has hardened. If a piece is tilted, it will have exposed edges (sharp or not) which can get caught and pop out easily. Overall, it's better to embed pieces a little too deeply rather than not deeply enough.

When you have especially tiny pieces to push in, put the eraser head of a pencil on the piece and push it straight down. A pencil or tweezers may be helpful for moving pieces around and fine-tuning their positions.

If your mosaic piece is rounded, three-dimensional or just unusual (rocks, broken cups, jewelry), it needs to be embedded at least two-thirds of the way in. This is to ensure that the mix comes up and surrounds it so it will stay firmly embedded.

Although I am not wearing them in these photographs, I recommend wearing rubber gloves while embedding to keep the mix from drying out your skin.

Embedding Mosaic Pieces
> continued

The Law of Mosaic Embedding says, "What goes down must come up (and vice versa)." When you push a mosaic piece down, the mix must come up somewhere else; when you do this to many pieces, the surface will get rough and wavy. This does not mean that you can't make a level, even surface that is good enough to walk on. You can! It just will take some practice. If the surface is a bit uneven, I like to think of it as rippled, textured and much more interesting.

The mosaic material affects the embedding process. Glass, metal, nonporous materials and pieces with straight edges embed very nicely. More difficult to embed are many types of ceramics and rocks because they are porous. When you push them into the wet mix they absorb water from the mix. The surrounding concrete sinks with the piece as you push down, creating a depression. To minimize this effect, soak tile and ceramic pieces in water before embedding. Submerge them until the bubbles stop rising. You can soak them all at once, then do your layout, or soak each piece as you go. Be sure to wipe excess water from the piece before embedding; otherwise the tiny puddle may leave a white powdery stain on the surface that is not desirable and not easy to remove.

Often it can be surprisingly difficult to push certain objects into the mix. Large pebbles, thick hardware and large pieces of tile are the most difficult to embed. Gently seesaw the piece as you're pushing down on it and tap or vibrate it as you push it into the mix. Always embed the thickest pieces first.

When the mix starts to set up or harden, the pieces will become very difficult to push in. That is your signal to quickly finish embedding the pieces.

If the surface cracks when you push a piece in, you may spray the surface with water and try again — but only once. If the mix keeps cracking, your hour is probably over and you should stop working.

Using An Embedding Block

Another embedding method involves using a heavy, flat block to embed your tesserae after partially embedding them with your fingers or pencil ereaser. The block levels the tesserae, pushes in hard-to-embed pieces, and usually speeds up the embedding process. My favorite block is a heavy, smooth block of granite, about 6" x 4" x 1" (15cm x 10cm x 25mm), a comfortable size to hold in one hand. You can use a wood block, as in the photographs, or some other heavy, flat weight (but not a brick; it's too heavy). Begin by using it to embed projects that have flat, even pieces. When you're accustomed to using the block, you can use it to embed projects with uneven pieces.

MATERIALS

rubber gloves

prepared mix in mold with tesserae partially embedded

embedding block

After you've laid out the tesserae on the wet mix and are satisfied with the placement, partially embed them with your fingers. Place the block in the middle of the stone on top of the pieces. Lift it about an inch (25mm) and drop it flat onto the surface. Move the block slightly then lift and drop again. Work your way out from the center, overlapping each time. The pieces will become embedded uniformly and (depending on the material) fairly quickly, so monitor your progress often. Go over the entire surface lightly a few times rather than heavily once or twice, to fully and evenly embed all the mosaic pieces.

I recommend using the embedding block on pebble, stone and glass nuggets because it levels out bumpy, irregular stones. Vibrating or tapping the block while holding it down also helps embed those especially stubborn items. One note of caution: It's easy to over-embed irregularly shaped items, so check your progress often.

The embedding block will probably spread wet mix over your tesserae. If this occurs, sponge off the surface (see Smoothing the Surface on page 285) before you set the stone aside to harden.

tip

Don't use the embedding block on chunky glass tesserae such as in the frog project. The pieces will become covered with wet mix, which will settle into the tiny depressions in the glass. After the mix hardens, it will be nearly impossible to clean off.

Contact Paper Transfer and Embedding Method

There may be times when you lay out a design and get interrupted, or you may want to set a layout aside until another day. You can finish the layout as precisely as possible, use the contact paper as shown below, and instead of trimming off the excess contact paper, replace the paper backing on the contact paper. Your pieces will remain in place.

This technique can also be used to lay out and embed a small design; large projects or designs with lumpy pieces will not work. This is a great technique because it embeds the pieces exactly the way you positioned them in the first place. It is especially useful for small designs with many tiny, uniformly flat pieces.

Clear contact paper is not paper at all, but vinyl; so don't be confused when I refer to it as "paper" in the instructions. You should test the adhesion of your contact paper before using it for this technique. Less expensive brands of paper may not hold the pieces firmly, causing them to fall off, which will prove to be very frustrating.

MATERIALS

tesserae

Design Template

transparent adhesive-backed vinyl or contact paper, 10"x 10" (25cm x 25cm)

scissors

rubber gloves

tweezers

mold filled with wet mix

optional: embedding block

1 ➤ Lay out pieces. Lay out your tesserae on the Design Template. Rearrange them until you are satisfied with the design. The way you lay it out now is how it will look on the finished stone.

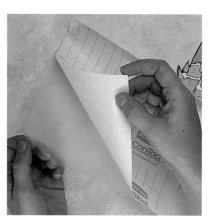

2 ➤ Cut the contact paper to size. Cut a sheet of transparent contact paper large enough to cover the design and leave a 1" (25mm) border all the way around it. Remove the paper backing. Fold over each of the corners to create four places to hold that won't stick to your fingers when you position the paper.

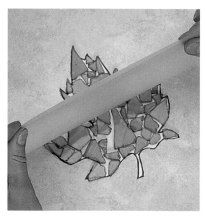

3 ➤ Center the contact paper on the design. With the sticky side out, bend the contact paper in half. Line up the bend with an imaginary horizontal line going through the center of the design. Be careful and confident — you have only one chance. The trick is to lay the contact paper on top of the tesserae without disturbing them. Otherwise, they will shift and stick in the wrong position. Do this and the next two steps in one fluid motion, if possible.

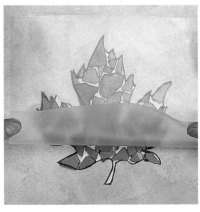

4 ➤ Roll the paper over the pieces. Lower the paper until the bend touches the tesserae. Keep lowering it, rolling the two halves down evenly and lightly onto all the pieces.

5 ➤ Let go. Lower the paper until it is flat on the pieces. Then let go of the paper.

6 ➤ Press each piece. With one finger, touch each of the pieces, making sure that they adhere to the contact paper.

7 ➤ Turn it over. Lift the contact paper and carefully turn it over on the table.

8 ➤ Trim the contact paper. Use scissors to trim the excess paper, staying as close to the outline of the design as possible. If you replace the paper backing, you can more easily move or store your layout. Or you can go ahead and prepare your mold, mix up some concrete and embed the pieces as the next step describes.

9 ➤ Lay the contact paper on the wet mix. When the wet mix is smooth in the mold, you can transfer the pieces. Place the contact paper on the tabletop with the tesserae on the bottom. Pick it up, bending it in half. Hold it above the prepared mix, then lower it onto the mix surface, rolling the two halves evenly. Position it within the mold edges, resting the pieces and vinyl on the mix surface. If necessary, reposition the sheet now.

Contact Paper Transfer and Embedding Method
continued

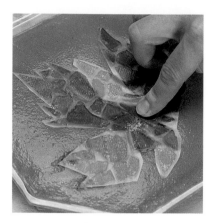

10 ➤ Embed the pieces. Push in the pieces one at time, starting at the center of the design and working your way out.

11 ➤ Use the embedding block. You may instead choose to embed the pieces using the embedding block as described on page 281.

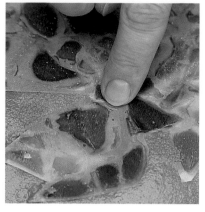

12 ➤ Level the surface. Notice how the wet mix rises between each piece and spreads between all the pieces and the contact paper. This is what you want. The tesserae will look pretty gray and messy, but will clean up easily.

Use your fingertips to smooth out the contact paper so all the pieces look wet and embedded. It's OK if the pieces and the contact paper sink into the mix a bit. Jiggle the mold and turn it, jiggle and turn, and watch the surface level out. Then wait five to ten minutes for the mix to dissolve the contact paper adhesive.

13 ➤ Peel off the contact paper. Use tweezers to slowly peel away the contact paper, which should easily release from the glass. If the paper sticks, lightly spray water on the seam between it and the glass. Soak up extra water with a paper towel.

14 ➤ Embed the stem. Embed any pieces you didn't include in the original layout, such as this stem. Now it's time to clean and smooth the surface.

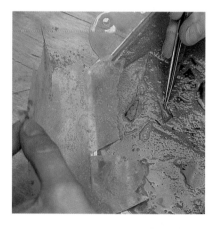

If a small tessera sticks to the contact paper, use the tweezers to replace it.

Smoothing the Surface

When you make a particularly smudged up, messy surface (as the block and contact paper methods are known to do) clean it up before the mix sets—no later than one hour after combining the concrete mix and water.

All your projects should be jiggled, as shown at the bottom of this page. Sponging, however, is optional. Sponge only if you have a particularly messy surface.

MATERIALS

sponge or foam paint brush

bowl of water

rubber gloves

Sponging

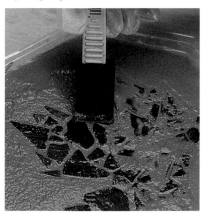

1 ➤ Wet the sponge. Fill a bowl with water and put on gloves. Wet the sponge and squeeze out most of the water.

2 ➤ Wipe the surface. Lightly wipe the dampened sponge over the entire surface to smooth it and even out the texture. Rinse the sponge often. This adds a very small amount of water to the top layer of the mix which will easily fill any cracks and even out the surface. For your last few strokes, absorb this excess water by rinsing the sponge and squeezing it dry. Spots or pools of water left on the surface may stain or discolor the hardened stone. Now proceed to the next step: jiggling.

Jiggling

3 ➤ Jiggle the mold. Do this step before you make any lines, hand prints or writing in the wet mix. This is your last chance to make a level, smooth surface, if that is what you want.

Make sure the pieces are properly embedded. Now jiggle the mold. It's the same technique you used to smooth out the mix when you prepared it at the outset, but not as vigorously. Hold opposite sides of the mold and jiggle it one to two inches (25-50mm), back and forth, two times in a continuous motion. Notice how the mix unifies and the surface smooths. Rotate the mold and repeat, jiggling as little as possible, just enough to even out the surface.

Too much vibration may cause water to rise to the surface. Use a paper towel to soak up water that may stain or discolor the hardened stone. If jiggling the mold creates a gap around a piece, use a gloved fingertip to smooth over the mix and refill the space. If the jiggling completely submerges a piece, see page 293 for directions on fixing this problem.

If the jiggling seems too risky but the surface needs smoothing, try vibrating the table or tapping the sides of the mold, as shown in the photograph. This may take a little longer, but it will smooth the surface without submerging any precarious pieces.

Incising Lines

Besides decorating your stone with pieces of glass, tile, stone and found objects, you can also embellish it by making impressions: marks, grooves, figures, notches, symbols, lines, prints and furrows, just to name a few. There are countless ways to do this; here are a few of my favorites to get you started.

There is a lot you can do with a plain craft stick or kitchen utensil. You'll get many ideas by experimenting right after you put the mix in the mold before you transfer your tesserae. This is a good time to practice lettering your family name or "Welcome." Write words in different styles and sizes. Use a craft stick with an up-and-down dabbing motion (don't drag the stick), pressing into the surface about ¼" (6mm). If you soak the wooden stick in water, the wet mix won't stick to it. The tool should make a crisp, dry line in the mix. If the line looks wet or keeps filling with water, wait ten or fifteen minutes and try again. A little excess water may be absorbed with a cotton swab.

Other tools to try are cookie cutters, chisel-shaped tools such as a screwdriver or wood chisel (which makes letters that look like calligraphy), pencil tips (for dots) and large rubber stamps with simple, deeply-etched designs. An empty tin can or the lid of a saucepan can be used to stamp a perfect circle. One of my favorite lettering tools is a set of plastic stamps designed for cake decorating. The stamps are pressed into cake frosting as a guide for thin lines of icing. A sign made with these letters is shown on page 266.

MATERIALS

wet mix in a mold

craft stick

miscellaneous kitchen utensils

cookie cutters

pencil

large, thick rubber stamps

cake lettering stamps

The chicken and petroglyph projects have outlines incised around the mosaicked forms. This border highlights the image and adds depth and contrast. Plan for the placement of lines or impressions when you do your initial design. Estimate the amount of space needed and leave it blank until you've embedded all the tesserae. The time to make this line is after the final smoothing and jiggling. Try to make a smooth and flowing line ¼" (6mm) from the tesserae. Do not jiggle the mold again because the lines will disappear!

Impressions by their very nature create fault lines in your hardened stone. The rule is the deeper the incision, the weaker the overall stone. Keep this in mind when considering the stone's function. Wall plaques and decorative garden art are great projects for this technique. A stepping stone with a long line or an outline is at risk for cracking under pressure when someone walks on it. For a strong stepping stone, keep the lines short, such as dashes, dots and letters.

Setting the Stone Aside to Harden

After you've finished embedding, smoothing and possibly incising, move your creation to an out-of-the-way place to harden for two days (48 hours). While the mix is wet, it is important to move the stone by picking up the rigid board underneath the mold. Any bends or creases in the wet mix may create concealed cracks which will set as weakened fault lines. After 48 hours, you can move the stone without the board.

Set the stone in a level place out of direct sunlight and in a moderate temperature for 48 hours. Cover it loosely with plastic, making sure the plastic doesn't touch the wet mix surface or it may leave a permanent stain. Spray the stone with water after 24 hours.

Unmolding a Stone With a Mounting Device

After hardening for 48 hours, your stone may be removed from the mold. This is usually a simple task: turn the mold over and pop the stone out onto a padded surface, such as a folded towel. If you put a wall mounting device on the back of the stone, however, it will stick to the mold and you will have to use greater effort and care.

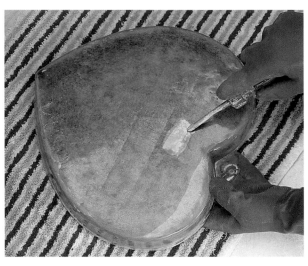

1 ➤ Invert the mold. Lay the stone face down on an old towel. If your mold is transparent, you will be able to see the tape through the back of the mold.

2 ➤ Loosen and remove the mold. Carefully pull the edges of the mold away from the stone all the way around, then start removing the mold. The tape will stick, so the mold must be pried away, Be careful not to damage the stone or crack the mold.

3 ➤ Remove the tape. Remove the tape with the screwdriver tip to reveal the nail hole. Carefully scrape and smooth the opening with the tip of the screwdriver. One or two heavy nails or screws are usually enough to hold a seven- to ten-pound (3.2-4.5kg) stone securely. Depending on the composition of your wall, you may have to add anchors or use masonry screws.

Cleaning and Unmolding the Stone

If you wait much longer than 48 hours to do this, you'll have a difficult if not impossible time cleaning the surface. Set aside 20 to 30 minutes for this series of steps.

MATERIALS

rubber gloves

plastic sheet or newspaper

toothbrush

scouring pad

small bowl of water

safety glasses

paper clip, nail, or other pointed tool

old towel

dust mask

screwdriver

5-gallon (3.8l) bucket

garden hose and water source

1 ➤ Gently scrub the surface. About 48 hours after you set you stone aside to harden, you will need to clean the mix from the tesserae. Now you may lift the mold without the board. Inspect the mosaic surface to see if any of the pieces have a film or layer of concrete over them. If so, put on gloves and dip a toothbrush or scouring pad in water. Gently scrub the entire surface, both the concrete and the tesserae, until the excess concrete lifts off. Use as much water as you need. The concrete is still "green," which means that it is hard but it can still crumble, so go slowly and gently. Most glass and tile surfaces are pretty tough and can handle scouring for a short time. Use your judgment about scouring painted china and other delicate surfaces.

2 ➤ Define edges with paper clip. Use safety glasses because this process may cause chips of concrete to fly up. Scrape dried mix from the edges of the tesserae with the sharp tip of a straightened paper clip or other pointed tool. Clearly defined edges make a world of difference in the finished look of your mosaic design. Clean up incised lines, if necessary.

Drain excess water into a large bucket, not down the drain.

3 ➤ Remove the mold. Lay the stone face down on an old towel. Carefully separate the stone from the edges of the mold. Remove the mold from the stone.

4 ➤ Scrape the edges. Keep your safety glasses on and put on a dust mask. Hold an old screwdriver at a 45° angle to scrape and smooth the crusty lip of the stone all the way around. This edge can be very sharp when it comes out of the mold, so be careful.

5 ➤ Rinse the stone and set it aside to cure. Remove your glasses and mask. The easiest way to rinse off the stone is to spray it outdoors with a garden hose. You can also pour clean water over the stone, holding it over a large bucket or pan. Don't pour the water from the bucket down any drain; pour it outdoors and rinse the bucket clean.

Your project is now complete! Set it aside to finish hardening.

Elevating and Curing the Stone

If concrete dries too fast, it shrinks, causing it to lose its strength and compromising its durability. Cracks may form in the concrete and tesserae may pop out. This is why we slow down the drying and hardening process, commonly called curing, by covering the concrete loosely with plastic and watering it frequently. (If plastic touches the concrete, it can cause permanent stains.) For the stone to cure evenly, air must circulate freely around it, so the stone should be elevated on a rack or resting on several pencils.

After you have cleaned, unmolded and rinsed off your stone, set it on a nonporous rack or on several pencils, out of sunlight and loosely covered with plastic. Spray it with water every 24 hours for five more days, then use a soft cloth to polish individual mosaic pieces. Wait seven more days before applying pressure. The stone continues to cure for another 28 days.

tip

Shells, stones, frosted glass and marble may be enhanced with a coating of oil or wax after your project has cured.

Caring For Your Stone

Several conditions influence the strength and durability of concrete: humidity and temperature during mixing, the amount of water used in the mix, and the curing conditions. Concrete mixed with as little water as possible in ideal circumstances (moderate temperature, no direct sun or high wind) and kept moist while curing should last for a very long time. To reduce the chances of cracks, a stepping stone path should be embedded flush with the ground and placed on a firm and even 2" (5cm) bed of crushed gravel or sand.

The concrete surface will change with time. You may leave it to age naturally or you may clean it occasionally. White powdery stains may appear on the surface of the hardened concrete that are difficult or impossible to remove, but you may try to scrub them off with a stiff brush and household detergent and water or trisodium phosphate. De-icer or rock salt will cause the concrete to deteriorate, so keep these off your stone.

Many people want to protect their stone from the weather and stains by waterproofing it. Sealing a mosaic concrete stone is a topic of controversy, and I cannot make any guarantees about fully protecting your stone. Even if you seal it fully and properly, damage may still occur; water may seep in, stains may set. When water freezes it expands, so wet cured concrete can crack in freezing weather. Many types of concrete sealant are available at hardware stores. The sealant is for the concrete only—the stone bottom, sides and the joints between the tesserae on the top. If you cover the tesserae with sealant, you run the risk of changing their appearance. Wait 28 days before sealing your stone, after it has fully cured.

I recommend that you bring your mosaic creations indoors during extreme weather, or place them in a protected spot such as on a covered porch or on a sunroom wall. I live in the Pacific Northwest where it rarely freezes, and if a summer day reaches 85°, it's considered a heat wave. I can leave my stones out all year long unsealed. In other parts of the world, "Mother Nature" can be even tougher than concrete!

Tesserae may crack, loosen or pop out of the concrete bed for several reasons. They may not have been fully embedded in the first place; they may have been too thin to get a grip; plastic or rubber pieces didn't bond with the concrete; or the concrete cured too quickly. You may glue pieces back in place, but you must find the right kind of glue for the specific material you're replacing. For example, gluing glass to concrete requires one kind of glue, but gluing metal to concrete may require another. Weldbond is a strong and reliable glue for many things. Read the glue label to be certain it can handle the job.

Finally, although concrete is almost indestructible, these cast projects will break if dropped. Treat them with care, as you would any work of art, and you will enjoy them for a very long time.

Quick Fixes

Occasionally, you may have an unexpected problem while making your mosaic stone. If you learn about the most common problems and how to handle them before these events occur, you'll be better able to expect the unexpected! All of these problems have happened to me at one time or another, so I have learned to make the best of these situations.

As I said before, concrete is a very forgiving medium while it is still wet and plastic. You can prove this to yourself after you have poured and smoothed the mix for a project. Poke a couple of holes or make a gash with the putty knife, then see how easy it is to smooth it, jiggle it and start all over again.

Because it's common for beginners to create a mix using too much water, before you make your first stone, set aside a small amount of dry mix in a covered plastic container that you can sprinkle in your mix if you accidentally add too much water. You can also mix some of this with a little water to patch holes and depressions that may occur in a hardened stone, although it may not exactly match the new stone's color.

You will find it helpful to set aside a spoonful of wet mix at the start of projects that include tile, broken cups, rocks and pieces with uneven edges or irregular shapes. When embedded, these items usually leave large craters in the mix. After you finish embedding, you can use this extra mix to fill holes and patch gaps rather than stealing mix from another part of the stone, which is a good technique for patching smaller craters.

Excess Water

Occasionally you may find excess water rising to the surface of the mix. Sometimes this happens because the stone has been jiggled too much. Other times, it happens because too much water was added in the first place, as is the case here. I like to get rid of excess water so that I can clearly see the outline of each piece, and to avoid having permanent stains left on the stone after it has hardened. For small spots, use a cotton swab. For larger wet areas, lightly lay a piece of paper towel on top of the wet area. Peel off the paper towel and continue with your project.

Cracks in the Wet Mix

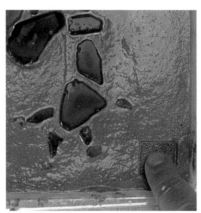

If the mix cracks in a radiating pattern when you make an impression or push in a mosaic piece, it means the concrete is drying out.

If one hour is not yet up, spray the surface lightly once or twice with water. If necessary, smooth or erase the impression with a wet, gloved finger and start again. Work quickly.

If one hour is up, it's too late. The concrete is hardening and you risk permanently setting cracks in the stone. Stop what you're doing. Spray the surface lightly with water, smooth and erase the impression with a wet, gloved finger, and set the stone aside to cure.

Sharp or Exposed Glass Edges

If there are sharp edges protruding above the surface of the hardened stone, you can sand them down with fine-grit sandpaper or a sanding block after the stone has cured.

Mosaic Piece Embedded too Deeply

You've just finished embedding all the pieces, cleaned up the surface and given your mold a final jiggle. As you're adjusting the position of one last piece, it suddenly sinks into the wet mix. Now what?

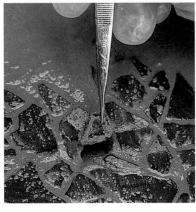

1 ➤ Remove the piece. Use tweezers to carefully retrieve the sunken piece. Try not to disturb the surrounding area. Wipe off the piece and set it aside.

2 ➤ Take some mix. Now you're going to take some mix from the edge of the stone where it won't be missed. It is very important that the mix still be in a wet, plastic state so that it will easily blend in. Use the opposite end of the tweezers to skim off a small amount of mix near the edge of the mold.

3 ➤ Patch the hole. Patch the hole with the extra mix until it is slightly over-filled. Scoop mix from a different edge if you need more. Tamp and smooth the patch with a gloved finger. Lightly skim the surface with the putty knife to smooth out the areas. Jiggle the mold a few times, being careful not to let other pieces sink in.

4 ➤ Smooth the patch. Use a damp sponge to lightly smooth the patched area until it is level with the rest of the surface.

5 ➤ Replace the piece. Use the tweezers to replace the piece and embed it. Smooth the area with a sponge and jiggle if needed.

293

Fruit Path

> Adorn your garden or yard with a colorful pathway of mosaic fruit stepping stones. These five designs are bold and easy to make. If this is your first time making a mosaic stone, I recommend glass tesserae, stained glass fragments or vitreous glass tiles. You will be introduced to several basic techniques with the apple design; the pear and bananas are made in a similar way. The designs for the grapes and raspberries add another mosaic element, glass nuggets; and a new tool, the embedding block, for leveling a bumpy surface.

For variations, consider changing the colors: a pale green apple, purple grapes and a red or yellow pear. Another idea is to add wall mounting devices (see page 21) and hang the plaques as a group in the kitchen or back hallway. You can even "think small" and use these designs to make paperweights for your desk or coasters for the patio. If you "think large," you could make a fruit tabletop.

MATERIALS

round stepping stone mold
12" x 12" x 1½"
(30cm x 30cm x 38mm)

pencil with eraser

craft knife

scissors

stained glass: opaque red and translucent dark green for the apple; opaque light green and translucent dark green for the pear; opaque yellow and translucent dark brown for bananas; transparent dark green for grapes; translucent dark green for raspberries

medium-size round glass nuggets: 45 transparent light green for grapes; 42 transparent red for raspberries

rigid board for each stone

dust mask

rubber gloves

7 lbs. (3.2kg) stepping stone concrete mix for each stone

mixing bowl

mixing tool

2 cups (472ml) water for each stone

3" (75mm) putty knife

sponge and small bowl of water

embedding block for grapes and raspberries

Apple

1 ➤ Enlarge the pattern. Use a copy machine to enlarge the apple pattern from page 301 to fit your mold. For a 12" (30cm) mold, enlarge the pattern 200%, then enlarge the copy 200%. Make a second copy of the enlarged pattern.

2 ➤ Make templates. Use a craft knife to cut out the apple shape from one pattern and trim the outside edge to fit your mold; this is your Mold Template. The cut-out shape is your Design Template, or you can use the extra pattern. See page 267 for more information on templates.

3 ➤ Outline the apple. Arrange red glass tesserae on the Design Template, starting with the outline and staying within the line. See pages 18-20 for more information on laying out your design.

4 ➤ Fill in the apple. Finish arranging the red pieces, filling in the entire apple.

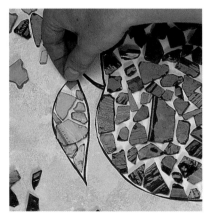

5 ➤ Add leaf tips. Start by finding the key pieces for the leaf: one pointed piece to fit in each of the two corners.

6 ➤ Finish the leaf. Outline the leaf and fill it in. Set aside three or four small pieces of green glass for the stem, but do not put them in place yet.

7 ➤ Prepare the mold and mix. Place the mold on a board. Put on a dust mask and gloves and prepare the mix as described on pages 273-276. Check the time or set a timer for one hour. You have 45 minutes to one hour to complete the process.

8 ➤ Place the Mold Template on the wet mix surface. Be sure it is centered.

9 ➤ Transfer the outline and key pieces. Transfer the pieces to the mix surface in the same order that you laid out the design, starting with the outline and key pieces. Be careful to keep pieces inside the paper edge. Refer to page 278 for a full description of this process.

10 ➤ Fill in. Now fill in the apple and the leaf, arranging and rearranging pieces until they are evenly spaced. Don't push the pieces into the mix yet; just leave them lying on the surface.

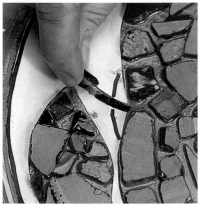

11 ➤ Make the apple stem. Get the green glass you set aside earlier and embed it on edge. See the Tip on page 298 for details.

12 ➤ Remove the template. Slowly peel off the paper template. Stand back and squint to see if any changes are needed: Is the outline smooth and readable as an apple? Are there any holes in the mosaic layout that need filling? If you need to make other changes, make them now.

13 ➤ Embed the tesserae. Begin embedding the pieces, as described on pages 279-281. Begin at the center of the apple and work your way out. Push straight down. You'll need to go over all the pieces several times until every piece is fully embedded: not too deep (submerged), not too high (resting on the surface), but just right (flush with the mix). The surface will be uneven.

14 ➤ Make final changes and jiggle. Stand back, look at the stone and squint. Fill in any gray spaces or gaps with glass pieces. Make sure all pieces are evenly embedded. Gently jiggle the mold as described on page 285.

15 ➤ Set the stone aside to harden for 48 hours. Cover the stone loosely with plastic. Use the board to pick up the stone and move it to a safe location. Spray it with water after 24 hours.

16 ➤ Clean up the stone. When 48 hours are up, gently scrub excess concrete from the tesserae as described on page 289. Remove the stone from the mold and round off the edges. Rinse the stone well.

17 ➤ Elevate the stone and let it cure. Let the stone cure, elevated on a rack or on pencils for five more days. Cover it loosely with plastic to cure slowly, which make a sturdier stone. Spray it with water every 24 hours. After five days, the stone may be used, as long as no pressure is applied to it for an additional seven days.

Pear

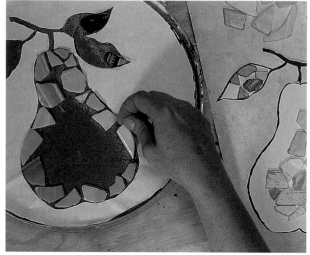

The directions for the pear are similar to those for the apple, but the pear has both concave and convex curves. Arrange light green tesserae on the Design Template to outline the pear, then fill it in, staying inside the line. Try to follow the curves with similarly curved tesserae.

Place key pieces for the leaves: find six dark green pointed pieces to fit into the leaf tips, then fill in the centers. Select eight to ten small dark green pieces to use later for the stem, but don't place them yet.

Position the Mold Template, then transfer the mosaic pieces to the wet mix surface in the same order.

When you make the stem, start next to the pear and leaves and work your way out.

Before you embed a piece, you may want to reposition it slightly. I have a large pair of tweezers that come in handy for this, but you could also use either end of a pencil.

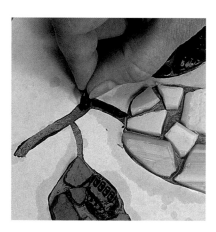

tip

When you need a thin, uniform line, embed glass pieces "on edge." Look for pieces of broken glass that are long and narrow, or triangular, rather than round or square. Choose a piece that has one long edge that is especially straight, which is the edge you want showing on the top side. Pick a piece that is about ½" (1cm) wide that will not go all the way through to the bottom of the mold. Start embedding the first stem piece on edge next to the fruit. Embed the second piece so it touches the first, and so on, working your way away from the fruit until the stem is the correct length. Embed the top edges flush with the mix surface.

Bananas

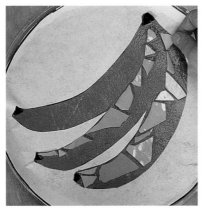

The long, curved shape of the bananas requires a slightly different layout technique from that of the apple and pear. Start with the left outline of each fruit, then the right outline, then fill in the center. Try to use slightly curved glass edges to follow the outlines of each banana. Find four small pieces of dark brown glass with squared-off ends; then place one at the top and one at the end of each banana.

Grapes

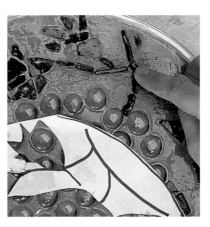

When you cut out the Mold Template for the grapes, the stems may be too narrow to cut; so you may choose to leave them uncut and embed those pieces after the template has been removed.

Arrange 45 light green glass nuggets on the Design Template, placing them so that they touch. If the nuggets are oval, line them up vertically. Next, position the leaf points, then the leaf outlines. Fill in the leaf centers.

To embed the glass, use your fingertips, the embedding block, or a combination of the two. If you want a bumpy surface, embed the glass nuggets at least two-thirds of the way. For a more level surface, use the embedding block over the entire surface. See page 281 for more details on using an embedding block.

If you did not cut out the stems on the Design Template, lay it back on the mix below the stems. Use a craft stick or pencil point to draw the stems. Make a line or series of dots using an up-and-down dabbing motion. First indicate the main stem, then an off-shoot line to the grapes and finally a line to each leaf. Use the line for placing and embedding the green glass on edge.

Raspberries

When you arrange red glass nuggets on the Design Template for each berry, arrange fourteen nuggets touching each other in four parallel rows: 3-4-4-3, then push them together until the shape rounds out and fits inside the outline. Place the large leaf points, outline the leaves, then fill them in. Select nine to twelve triangular, similarly-sized pieces of green glass to be used as small leaves. Choose eight to ten small green pieces for the stems and set them aside.

Transfer the pieces as you did for the grapes. Make sure the glass nuggets are touching. To save time, I didn't cut the small leaves and stems out of the Design Template.

If you want a slightly bumpy surface, embed the glass nuggets at least two-thirds of the way using just your fingertips. Then push in the green glass pieces. For a more level surface, use the embedding block for the entire surface. See page 281 for more details on using the block. For embedding very small pieces, a pencil eraser head is very helpful.

The stems for the raspberries are done the same way as the stems for the grapes. Using a craft stick or pencil point with an up-and-down dabbing motion, make a light line or series of dots connecting the middle berry and the clump of leaves, then the two off-shoot lines to the other berries. Use the lines as guides for placing and embedding the green glass on edge for the stems.

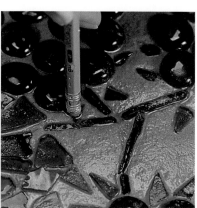

To enlarge these patterns for a 12" (30 cm) mold, use a copy machine to enlarge them 200%. Then enlarge the copies 200%.

River Rock Garden Path

> Often, the simpler the design, the more elegant and versatile it is — plus it is easier and faster to make! The geometric designs of this project may be combined in many ways to create various patterns as shown on page 306. To find out what is most pleasing to you, make copies of the small patterns, cut them out and arrange them on a table until you find a pattern that pleases you and fits the number of stones you need for your path. A path may be two or more stones wide, and your molds may be square, hexagonal or round. Rocks in all shapes, sizes and colors may be found at garden stores or your local creek. In this project you will see how easy it is to change the color of your concrete to coordinate with the color of your stones.

MATERIALS

square stepping stone mold
12" x 12" x 1½"
(30cm x 30cm x 38mm)

pencil with eraser

craft knife or scissors

Indonesian river rocks, about 1 lb.
(454g), average size 1" (25mm) long

rigid board

dust mask

rubber gloves

7 lbs. (3.2kg) stepping stone
concrete mix

2 oz. (28g) packet of
sandstone-colored dry pigment

mixing bowl

mixing tool

2 cups (472ml) water

3" (75mm) putty knife

embedding block

1 ➤ Enlarge the pattern. Use a copy machine to enlarge the pattern to fit your mold. Make two copies of the enlarged pattern.

2 ➤ Make the templates. Follow the directions on page 267 for cutting out your templates. For this project, cut on the outside of the line or a bit farther out to accommodate the rocks. (Too big an opening is better than too small. You'll see why when you remove the template after the rocks are in place.) This pattern with the cut-out area is your Mold Template. The extra enlarged pattern is your Design Template.

3 ➤ Lay out rocks on the Design Template. Try to select rocks of similar width. With this pattern, I suggest starting in the middle and working your way out, positioning longer rocks with the direction of the spiral line. Space them end-to-end and touching, so that the spiral (or other design) will "read" as one continuous line.

Another method of laying out irregularly-shaped tesserae is to lay the Mold Template in a shallow box of sand. Push the pieces into the sand to lay out the design, as in the Lizard project on page 346.

4 ➤ Prepare the mold and the mix. If you wish to add colorant to your stone, see page 277 for instructions. Place the mold on a board. Put on your dust mask and gloves and prepare the mix as described on pages 273-276. Set aside a heaping spoonful of wet mix in a small plastic container before emptying the rest into the mold. You may need this extra mix for patching depressions. Check the time or set a timer for one hour. Your mix will start setting up 45 to 60 minutes after it has been mixed with water. This should be plenty of time for you to complete the simple rock design.

5 ➤ Place the Mold Template on the mix. Position the Mold Template on the wet mix surface and smooth it down. Always check the template at this point to be sure it is positioned the way you want it. The mosaic design edges should be a minimum of ¼" (6mm) from the edges of the mold.

6 ➤ Transfer the rocks. Transfer the river rocks, beginning at the center of the design and working your way out. The rocks should be touching because after they are embedded the curved surface will cause them to appear as if they were spaced farther apart. This happens any time you use rounded mosaic pieces.

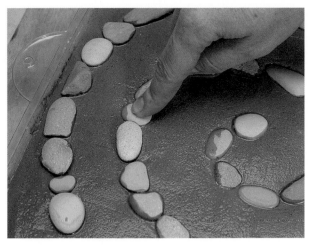

7 ➤ Remove the template. Slowly peel off the paper template. If rocks overlap the paper, carefully lift the paper around them. Stand back to see if any adjustments are needed. If so, do that now.

8 ➤ Begin embedding the rocks. Start in the center of the design and begin pushing in the rocks with your fingertips. Push straight down. A little seesaw action will help embed the longer pieces. Embed the rocks at least two-thirds of the way.

You may stop embedding now if you like this bumpy surface. Skip to step 10 to complete your stone. Here the partially embedded rocks make the stone rougher to walk on, but they show off the varied rock shapes and create a continuous line.

9 ➤ Level the surface. You can choose to make a more level surface by using the embedding block as described on page 281. This step will evenly embed your rounded rocks. The only drawback to this choice is that your rocks will be more deeply submerged in the wet mix, making the spaces between them larger and the result may be that your design loses some of its feeling of continuity.

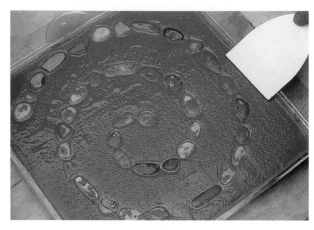

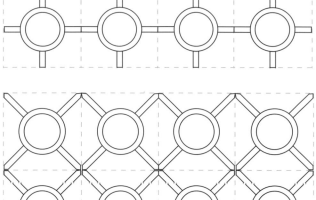

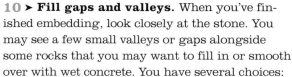

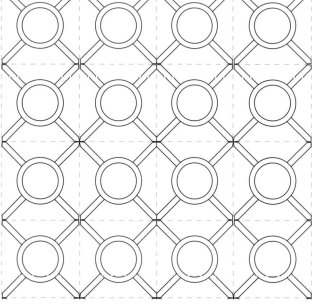

10 ➤ Fill gaps and valleys. When you've finished embedding, look closely at the stone. You may see a few small valleys or gaps alongside some rocks that you may want to fill in or smooth over with wet concrete. You have several choices:

* Use a sponge to fill in and smooth the surface as described on page 285.
* Patch the areas using the mix you set aside. See page 293.
* Take a bit of wet mix from the edge of the stone if you have just a small area to fill.
* Just leave it alone. (This option is my favorite.) The hills and valleys make a more textured and varied surface.

After you've smoothed the surface, gently jiggle the mold as described on page 285.

11 ➤ Set the stone aside to harden for 48 hours. See page 287 for details. Cover the stone loosely with plastic, and use the board to transfer it to a safe location. Spray it with water after 24 hours.

12 ➤ Clean up the stone. After 48 hours, gently scrub excess concrete from the rocks as described on page 289. Remove the stone from the mold and round off the edges. Rinse the stone well.

13 ➤ Elevate the stone and let it cure. Let the stone cure elevated on a rack or on pencils, for five more days. Cover it loosely with plastic so that it cures slowly, making a sturdier stone. Spray it with water every 24 hours. After five days the stone will be ready for use, as long as no pressure is applied to it for an additional seven days.

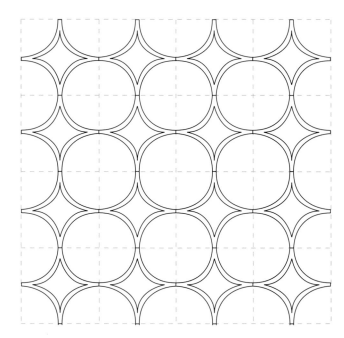

The designs on the following page can be combined in many ways to create patterns when the stones are set in a line to make a path or set next to each other to create a paved area in your yard.

To enlarge these patterns
for a 12" (30cm) mold, use
a copy machine to enlarge
them 200%. Then take the
enlarged copies and enlarge
them 200%.

Reflective Heart Wall Stone

> A broken mirror isn't bad luck for a mosaicist! Mirror pieces can be used to add sparkle to any mosaic design as an accent or used overall as in this heart-shaped wall plaque. Because this is a decorative stone, I was able to use several oversized mosaic pieces larger than the 2" x 2" (5cm x 5cm) maximum glass size for stepping stones.

Designs which cover the entire surface of the stone are quick and fun to make. There are two ways to proceed: make only one template by tracing the mold onto a piece of paper, or be spontaneous and daring and use no template at all! Simply empty the wet mix into the mold and start arranging and embedding.

I used black dry pigment to darken the concrete. You may want to try a different color, such as red or blue, to coordinate with the colors in the room where your plaque will hang. You could also make a set of small coaster-size stones decorated with mosaic mirror bits to scatter in your garden beds (see the last project in the book for using deli containers as small molds). Mirror tiles could be used to outline a stepping stone. And of course, this heart mold can be used with other mosaic materials, such as broken china or tumbled glass.

MATERIALS

heart-shaped stepping stone mold
12" x 12" x 1½"
(30cm x 30cm x 38mm)

paper

pencil with eraser

broken mirror pieces

acrylic spray

rigid board

mounting device:
2"x 2" (5cm x 5cm) cardboard square
3"x 2" (8cm x 5cm) piece of duct tape

dust mask

rubber gloves

7 lbs. (3.2kg)
stepping stone concrete mix

optional: 2 oz. (58g) package
black dry pigment

mixing bowl

mixing tool

2 cups (472ml) water

3" (75mm) putty knife

1 ➤ Seal the mirror pieces. Spray the backs of the pieces of mirror with two light coats of acrylic spray. This prevents the silvering from being damaged by the wet concrete. If your mirror is not yet broken in pieces, follow the instructions on pages 262-263.

2 ➤ Make one template. If you want to use a template, trace the mold you're using onto a piece of paper to create the Design Template. You will not need a Mold Template for this project.

3 ➤ Lay out the mirror pieces on the template. Arrange the broken mirror pieces on the template, wearing gloves to protect against cuts. Begin with the key pieces at the point and V-shape, then start outlining the outer edge. Follow the gradual curve of the border with slightly curved pieces. Then fill in the center.

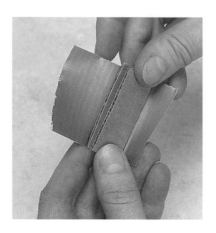

4 ➤ Prepare the mold and the mix. If you're making a wall plaque, follow the directions on page 271 for making a mounting device. Place the mold on a board and prepare the mix as described on pages 273-276. I added black dry pigment to the mix as described on page 277 for more contrast with the mirror pieces.

Check the time or set a timer for one hour.

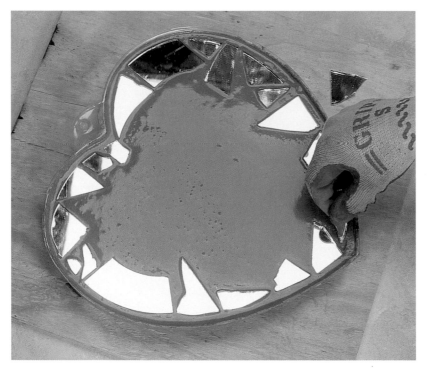

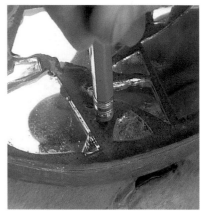

7 ➤ Embed the pieces. When the pieces are where you want them, begin embedding them. Push straight down.

In cases when your fingers are too big for especially tiny pieces, use the eraser end of a pencil to push the piece straight down into the mix. The rubber keeps the pencil from slipping.

5 ➤ Position key pieces. Transfer mirror pieces to the wet mix surface, starting with the point and V-shape.

6 ➤ Place outline pieces. Next, outline the heart shape placing pieces an even distance from the edge all the way around. Let the pieces just rest on the mix surface for now. Fill in the rest of the shape, arranging and rearranging as you please. I like to use a variety of sizes and shapes for a more interesting design.

8 ➤ Fill in spaces. When you've finished embedding all the pieces, stand back and look at the spacing — is it fairly consistent? Add pieces to any gray spaces or gaps that need them.

9 ➤ Jiggle the mold. Gently jiggle the mold, leveling and smoothing the surface and pieces.

10 ➤ Set the stone aside to harden. Cover the stone loosely with plastic and set it aside for 48 hours. Spray it with water after 24 hours. Be sure the plastic is loose; if it touches the cement it may leave a stain.

11 ➤ Clean up the stone. After 48 hours, gently scrub excess concrete from the mirror pieces. As you remove the stone from the mold, the duct tape will stick to the bottom of the mold and will have to be loosened as the stone releases, as described on page 288. Round off the edges as described on page 289. Rinse the stone well.

12 ➤ Elevate the stone and let it cure. Let the stone cure, elevated on a rack or on pencils, for five more days. Cover it loosely with plastic so that it cures slowly, which makes a sturdier stone. Spray it with water every 24 hours. After five days, the stone will be ready for hanging.

tip

Use a tray to hold and sort your tesserae. It will be easier to put them away and to keep colors separate.

Maple Leaf

➤ This is one of my favorite designs. I have made several of these 8" (20cm) stones, each one in a different color of glass. I have them outside propped up on my kitchen steps. If you choose to make these stones the size shown here, you will need to use smaller tesserae. Small triangular key pieces help create the distinctive maple leaf shape. Because of its small size, this project lends itself well to the contact paper transfer method (see page 282). You could make this design with multicolored instead of solid-colored maple leaves. Another idea is to photocopy and enlarge leaves from other types of trees and make a stepping stone path with one of each type of leaf.

octagonal stepping stone mold
8" x 8" x 2" (20cm x 20cm x 5cm)

pencil with eraser

scissors

craft knife

tumbled frosted red-orange
stained glass

rigid board

dust mask

rubber gloves

3½ lbs. (1.6kg)
stepping stone concrete mix

mixing bowl

mixing tool

1 cup (236ml) water

3" (75mm) putty knife

1 ➤ Enlarge the pattern. Use a copy machine to enlarge the maple leaf pattern to fit your mold. Make two copies or just use the cut-out leaf from the Mold Template as your Design Template.

2 ➤ Make the templates. Place your mold on the paper template, centering it over the design. Trace the mold with a pencil. Use scissors to cut out along the traced line. With a craft knife, cut out the leaf design. This is your Mold Template.

3 ➤ Lay out key pieces on the design template. Maple leaves have many toothy points on the edges. Look for triangular glass pieces to be the key pieces, which you should place first.

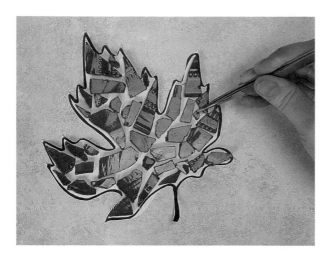

4 ➤ Outline the leaf and fill it in. Arrange the tesserae on the Design Template, starting with the three large leaf points. Add the other points; then outline the shape, staying within the line. Finish arranging pieces by filling in the leaf.

5 ➤ Prepare the mold and the mix. Place your mold on a board. Put on a dust mask and gloves and prepare the mix as described on pages 273-276. Check the time or set a timer for one hour.

6 ➤ Place the mold template on the wet mix surface. Be sure the design is centered. Smooth down the template.

7 ➤ Transfer key pieces. Start transferring your tesserae, starting with the three main leaf points.

8 ➤ Transfer the outline pieces and fill in. Outline the rest of the leaf. Be careful to keep pieces inside the edge of the paper cutout. Finish filling in the rest of the design.

tip

The small scale of this pattern lends itself well to the contact paper transferring and embedding method. Follow the directions on pages 282-284 if you want to use this method.

9 ➤ Make the stem. Select three to four small, narrow pieces of glass each with one long, straight edge. With the straight edge up, embed the first piece adjacent to the leaf, creating a glass line as the leaf stem. Continue the line with a second piece of glass on edge touching the first piece, and so on until the stem is complete.

10 ➤ Remove the template. Carefully peel away the template. Step back and look at the outline of the design and the spacing of the pieces. You may see a few gray spaces that still need a piece of glass. Add those pieces now.

11 ➤ Embed the glass. When you have all the pieces where you want them, begin embedding. Push straight down. See pages 279-284 for more information on embedding.

12 ➤ Jiggle the mold. Gently jiggle the mold to level the surface. Follow the directions on page 285.

13 ➤ Set the stone aside to harden for 48 hours. Pick up the board to move the stone to a safe location. Cover the stone loosely with plastic and spray it with water after 24 hours.

14 ➤ Clean up the stone. After 48 hours, gently scrub excess concrete from the tesserae as described on page 289. Remove the stone from the mold and round off the edges. Rinse the stone well.

15 ➤ Elevate the stone and let it cure. Let the stone cure, elevated on a rack or on pencils, for five more days. Cover it loosely with plastic so that it cures slowly, which makes a sturdier stone. Spray it with water every 24 hours. After five days the stone will be ready for use, as long as no pressure is applied to it for an additional seven days.

To enlarge this pattern for an 8" (20cm) octagonal mold, use a copy machine to enlarge it 200%.

Chicken

> Chickens and roosters are popular motifs, especially for kitchen decor. I decided to get the chicken out of the kitchen and into the garden by putting her on a stepping stone. Even though this is a very detailed project, it's not complicated if you break the design into several smaller shapes. You won't need much yellow or red glass for this design, but have extra on hand so you have plenty to break, sort through, then break again, to create a variety of tiny pointed pieces to use.

I thought of a few variations, and I'm sure that you can think of others. Instead of white glass, use white tile or gravel. Make another stone reversing the image so you have a pair of chickens facing each other. If you make the chicken smaller, you can add your house number using contrasting glass pieces and hang it on your house or place it near the curb.

MATERIALS

round stepping stone mold
12" x 1½" (30cm x 38mm)

pencil with eraser

scissors

craft knife

opaque white, translucent red and
translucent yellow stained glass

1 pea-size black glass bead

rigid board

dust mask

rubber gloves

7 lbs. (3.2kg)
stepping stone concrete mix

mixing bowl

mixing tool

2 cups (472ml) water

3" (75mm) putty knife

craft stick

tweezers

1 ➤ **Enlarge the pattern.** Use a copy machine to enlarge the chicken pattern on page 321. For a 12" (30cm) mold, enlarge it 200%.

2 ➤ **Make the templates.** Place your mold on the enlarged pattern, centering it over the design. Trace the mold with pencil and cut along the line with scissors. Use a craft knife to cut out the chicken. This is your Mold Template. Use an extra copy of the pattern for your Design Template, or use the cut-out chicken shape.

3 ➤ Lay out the tesserae on the template. With practice, you'll discover the order you prefer for laying out your pieces. For beginners, I suggest the following sequence:

* Set aside eight to ten small white pieces for the chicken head.
* Select and place the key pieces on the Design Template, beginning with the red pieces on the head and the yellow beak and legs.
* Place four to five oval or rectangular white wing pieces of similar size across the center of the figure.
* Put several small pointed white pieces up and down the chicken's ruffled tail end.
* Follow the outline of the figure from its neck down.
* Now arrange the small white head pieces you set aside earlier. Be sure to surround the space for the eye with white, however small the pieces. Don't put the eye in now, because it will roll off the table.
* Finally, fill in the rest of the figure, leaving a space of ⅜" (9mm) below the wings for an incised wing line.

4 ➤ Prepare the mold and mix. Place the mold on a board. Put on a dust mask and gloves and prepare the mix as described on pages 273-276. Check the time or set a timer for one hour.

5 ➤ Practice making lines. If this is your first time incising lines in the mix, practice making a few lines now. Use a craft stick or a metal tool. When you've practiced for a few minutes, smooth and jiggle the mold to erase the practice lines.

6 ➤ Place the mold template on the wet mix surface. Position the Mold Template on the wet mix surface and smooth it down.

7 ➤ Lay out the tesserae on the mix. Transfer the tesserae in the same order as in Step 3, beginning with the combs, beak and feet. Now you can put in that eye.

8 ➤ Transfer the wings. Next, position the wing pieces in the middle of the chicken's body.

9 ➤ Transfer the outlines. Lay in the ruffled tail and the outline from the neck down.

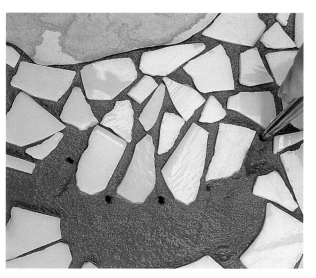

10 ➤ Fill in the head. Take a few minutes to arrange the tiny white pieces for the head. Tweezers are helpful for this small scale work. Then fill in everywhere but below the wing.

11 ➤ Rough in the wing line. Using the tweezers or a pencil point, make a few small dots below the wings pieces to mark the ends of the scallops of the wing line.

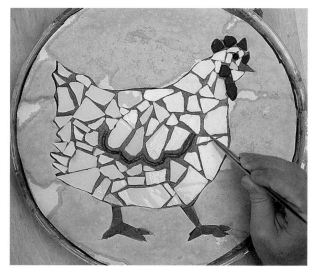

12 ➤ Draw the wing line. Use a craft stick to make a shallow line. Instead of dragging the tool through the wet mix, connect the dots using an up-and-down dabbing motion. Keep ⅛" to ¼" (3mm to 6mm) away from the glass. It doesn't have to be perfect now; you'll go over it again at the very end.

13 ➤ Fill in. Finish filling in the chicken figure with white glass. Is the spacing fairly consistent? If any rearranging or fine-tuning is needed, do it now.

14 ➤ Remove the template. Carefully peel away the template. Some glass pieces may overlap the paper; if so, carefully lift the paper around them. Stand back and take a look. Is the tail outline ruffled? Is the rest of the outline smooth? Finalize the placement of pieces.

15 ➤ Embed the pieces. Begin embedding pieces, pushing straight down. It's OK if the wing line becomes blurred; you'll come back to it later. The pencil eraser head is helpful for pushing in tiny pieces. Embed all the glass.

16 ➤ Smooth and jiggle the mold. Gently jiggle and tap the mold now, smoothing and leveling the glass pieces and the surface. This is the last chance to smooth because after you make lines in the mix, the mold can't be vibrated without erasing the lines.

17 ➤ Incise the outline and wing line. With your craft stick, incise a line all the way around the chicken. Use a dabbing, up-and-down motion, pushing the tool about ¼" (6mm) into the mix. Make the impression a consistent distance from the figure's outline, ⅛" to ¼" (3mm to 6mm) away from the glass. Keep the line simple and smooth. It should look crisp and dry. If it doesn't, wait ten minutes and try again.

18 ➤ Add tail feathers. To soften the tail line, make eight to ten ¼" (6mm) lines at different angles extending from the figure.

19 ➤ Redraw the wing line. If it's been less than an hour since you added water to your dry mix, go over the wing line you made earlier. You may need go over all the lines two or three times to even them out. Do not try to make or clean up any incised lines after the concrete starts to harden; it may damage or crumble the stone. If you must, wait until 48 hours have passed and go over your lines with the tip of a bent paper clip. This is still risky because chipping or flaking is possible.

20 ➤ Set the stone aside to harden for 48 hours. Use the board to set the stone aside to cure for 48 hours. Cover the stone loosely with plastic and spray it with water after 24 hours.

21 ➤ Clean up the stone. After 48 hours, follow the directions on page 289 to clean the stone.

22 ➤ Elevate the stone and let it cure. Let the stone cure, elevated on a rack or on pencils, for five more days. Cover it loosely with plastic so that it cures slowly, which makes a sturdier stone. Spray it with water every 24 hours. After five days, the stone will be ready for use, as long as no pressure is applied to it for an additional seven days.

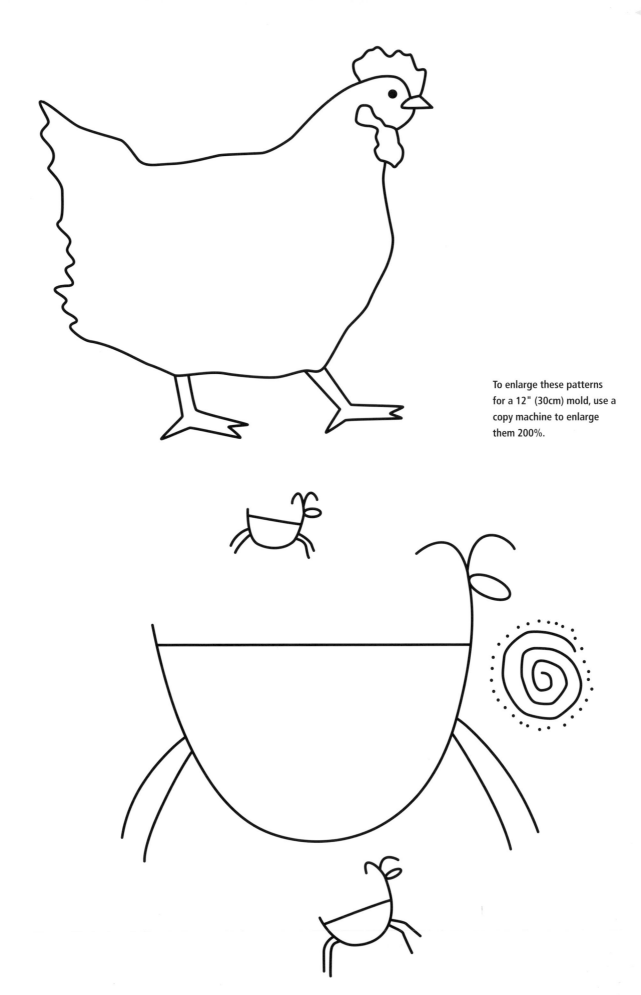

To enlarge these patterns for a 12" (30cm) mold, use a copy machine to enlarge them 200%.

Petroglyph ➤

I like the simplicity of this bowl-shaped sheep. The tesserae are fragments from other projects. You can create your own combination of leftover bits and pieces from your projects. This project will further explore the technque of incising lines to add detail to a mosaic.

In keeping with the origin and spirit of the image, I added terra-cotta pigment to the mix. If this appeals to you, I recommend exploring Aboriginal art, prehistoric cave paintings, and Native American pottery and sand paintings.

For a variation of this project, you could make a sand-cast mold, shaped and carved to look like a red rock fragment. Pack wet sand or dirt into a box, dig out a shape, pour in the wet mix and embed your tesserae.

MATERIALS

round stepping stone mold
12" x 1½" (30cm x 38mm)

pencil with eraser

scissors

craft knife

stained glass tesserae (mostly irides-cent, rippled glass): light and dark teal green, dark aqua, light and dark amber, light lavender and light blue

rigid board

dust mask

rubber gloves

7 lbs. (3.2kg)
stepping stone concrete mix

2 oz. (58g) packet
terra-cotta colored dry pigment

mixing bowl

mixing tool

2 cups (472ml) water

3" (75mm) putty knife

optional: craft stick or writing tool, tweezers, ruler

1 ➤ Enlarge the Pattern. Use a copy machine to enlarge the petro-glyph pattern on page 321. For this design it would be easier to make an extra copy of the pattern to use as the Design Template than to use the cut-out parts from the Mold Template.

2 ➤ Make the templates. Place the mold on the paper template, centering it over the design. Trace the mold with a pencil then cut along the line. Use a craft knife to cut out the figure to make your Mold Template. You can choose how much detail to cut out; I cut out every detail, but you could cut out only the largest figure. Then after embedding the tesserae for the large sheep and removing the tem-plate, you would approximate the position of the two small figures and the spiral line.

3 ➤ Arrange tesserae on the Design Template.
First place the key pieces, which are the two upper corners of the figure. Then outline along the top with long straight-edged pieces, and along the belly with slightly curved pieces. Finally, fill in the figure. Alternate sizes, colors and shapes of glass pieces. Put just one or two pieces in each of the two tiny figures.

4 ➤ Prepare the mold and the mix. Place the mold on a board. Put on a dust mask and gloves and prepare the mix described on pages 273-276. If you want to add colorant, follow the directions on page 277. Check the time or set a timer for one hour. If you haven't incised lines, see the "tip" below.

5 ➤ Place the Mold Template on the wet mix surface. Be sure the design is centered in the mold.

6 ➤ Transfer all tesserae. Transfer the tesserae in the same order you placed them on the Design Template: key pieces, outline, then fill in. Do not embed them yet. If you keep the pieces inside the cut paper edge, it will make removing the template much easier.

7 ➤ Incise the lines. If you did not cut out the lines for the legs and antlers, you must remove the template for this step. Otherwise, use the cut-out lines for positioning the incised lines. Follow the template lines with a craft stick, pencil, or toothpick. Use an up-and-down motion to incise dots or lines. Keep them ⅛" (3mm) away from the edge of the glass. Don't try to make perfect or deep lines yet.

tip

If this is your first time incising lines, practice making lines immediately after smoothing the mix in the mold. When you are finished practicing, re-smooth and jiggle the mold until all the marks have disappeared.

8 ➤ Remove the template. If you haven't done this already, slowly peel off the paper template. Some glass pieces may overlap the paper. If so, carefully lift the paper around them. Stand back and squint to see if any adjustments are needed. If so, do it now.

9 ➤ Embed the glass. When you have all the pieces placed, begin embedding them. Push straight down. Be sure that the outline pieces don't shift.

10 ➤ Jiggle the mold. Gently jiggle the mold now, smoothing and leveling the tesserae and the surface as described on page 285. The lines will fill in a bit, and you should stop before they disappear. After you make the final outlines and marks, don't jiggle the mold at all or the lines will disappear.

11 ➤ Incise the lines again. Go over all the rough lines you made earlier and add any others you would like, pushing the tool about ¼" (6mm) into the mix and using a dabbing motion. Again, keep the outline ⅛" (3mm) away from the glass. The lines should look dry and crisp. If the lines are soggy or fill in with water, wait ten minutes and try again. You may need to go over the lines two or three times. Make the border of dots around the spiral with a pointed tool.

Do not try to make or clean up any incised lines after the one-hour time limit is up—it may damage or crumble the stone. If you need to do this, wait 48 hours and use the tip of a bent paper clip. This is still risky; chipping or flaking is very possible.

12 ➤ Add the border. If the hour is not yet up, make the border impressions. Hold the stick at a 45° angle and make a shallow impression every 1" to 1½" (25mm to 38mm) about ½" (12mm) from the edge of the stone.

13 ➤ Set the stone aside to harden. Do not smooth or jiggle the mold. Set your stone aside to harden for 48 hours; spray it with water after 24 hours.

14 ➤ Clean up the stone. After 48 hours, follow the directions on page 289 to clean up the stone. Rinse it well.

15 ➤ Elevate the stone and let it cure. Follow directions on page 290 for this step. After five days the stone will be ready, if no pressure is applied to it for seven more days.

Frog Wall Stone

This beautiful, multihued teal green glass is sold in a pet supply stores as aquarium gravel. It's an assortment of recycled and tumbled "chunky" glass: odds and ends, some curved, some flat, some lumps and chunks. Notice how the glass color changes when it's put on a gray concrete background: bright colors dim to midrange, and midrange colors fade almost to black. That's due to the translucency of this glass. Conversely, opaque glass is not affected by the color of the bedding material. Craft stores carry "sea glass," which is tumbled recycled glass that comes in both translucent and opaque colors. Beachcombers can find real sea glass washed up on the shore.

Variations of this project include using flat glass, which makes this an easier project. Also, since frogs come in shades of brown (or are those toads?) you can substitute highly polished rocks for the glass.

square stepping stone mold
12" x 12" x 1½"
(30cm x 30cm x 38mm)

pencil with eraser

scissors

craft knife

teal green chunky glass
(I used Seaglass brand aquarium glass)

4 teal green vitreous glass tiles,
¾" x ¾" (2cm x 2cm)

1 black glass marble

rigid board

mounting device:
2"x 2" (5cm x 5cm) cardboard square,
3"x 2" (8cm x 5cm) piece of duct tape

dust mask

rubber gloves

7 lbs. (3.2kg)
stepping stone concrete mix

mixing bowl

mixing tool

2 cups (472ml) water

3" (75mm) putty knife

1 ➤ **Enlarge the pattern.** Use a copy machine to enlarge the frog pattern on page 331. For a 12" (30cm) mold, enlarge it 125%.

2 ➤ **Make the templates.** Place your mold on the enlarged pattern, centering it over the design. Trace the mold with a pencil. Use scissors to cut on the line. Use a craft knife to cut out the frog. This is your Mold Template. Use the cut-out frog or an extra enlarged pattern for your Design Template.

3 ➤ **Sort the tesserae.** The glass used in this project is not all one thickness; it is chunky, curved, thick and thin. Sorting this chunky type of glass by size will make it easier for you to find just the right piece. And since the frog is almost symmetrical, look for matching pairs of tesserae while you're sorting.

4 ➤ Lay out key pieces. Start by laying out the key pieces on the Design Template. Find pieces for the four feet; then find pieces about the size of corn kernels for the toe tips. Next find three pairs of matching tesserae for the six joints. Take time to find shapes that match the bend of the joints. Finally, finish filling in the legs.

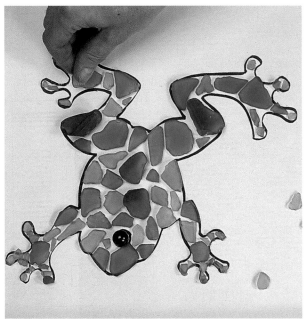

5 ➤ Complete the outline and fill in the frog. Outline and fill in the rest of the figure.

6 ➤ Prepare the mold with a mounting device. If your frog is to be a wall plaque, refer to page 271 for instructions on making an indentation on the back to accommodate a nail or screw.

7 ➤ Prepare the mix. Place the mold on a board. Put on a dust mask and gloves and prepare the mix as described on pages 273-276. Check the time or set a timer for one hour.

t i p

If you use chunky glass, try to keep the glass clean as you work, and do not use a sponge to smooth the surface at the end.

These two tips will save you lots of time when you clean up your stone later.

8 ➤ Transfer the tesserae. Position the Mold Template on the wet mix surface and smooth it down. Transfer the tesserae in the same order as you laid them out: first the feet, joints, and legs.

9 ➤ Embed the tesserae (optional). As you become more confident working with mosaics and concrete, you may want to embed the pieces as you arrange them on the mix.

10 ➤ Finish layout on the mix. Finish laying out the rest of the figure on the mix surface. Fill in the limbs, outline the figure, and fill in the rest of the body. Finally, embed the marble eye.

11 ➤ Finish embedding. Make adjustments if necessary, and embed the rest of the pieces. Embed the pieces with the template still in place so you can follow the outline more easily. After embedding, you can still add a couple of pieces to fill in any spaces. Carefully peel away the template. If any glass pieces overlap the paper, carefully lift the paper around them.

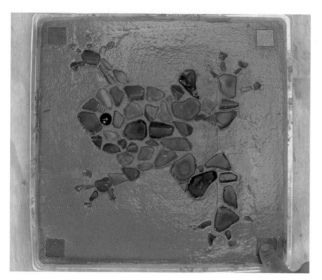

12 ➤ Add the border pieces. Position and embed the square tiles in the corners, about ¼" to ½" (6mm to 10mm) in from the edges.

13 ➤ Jiggle the mold. Gently jiggle the mold now, smoothing and leveling the surface. When the tesserae are very irregular and lumpy, don't sponge the surface. Cleaning the stone later would be very time-consuming, because you would have to scrape and uncover almost every mosaic piece.

14 ➤ Set the stone aside to harden for 48 hours. Cover the stone loosely with plastic and use the board to pick it up to set aside for 48 hours. Spray with water after 24 hours.

15 ➤ Clean up the stone. After 48 hours, follow the directions page 289 for cleaning and unmolding. Rinse well.

16 ➤ Elevate the stone and let it cure. Let the stone cure, elevated on a rack or on pencils, for five more days. Cover it loosely with plastic so that it cures slowly, making a sturdier stone. Spray it with water every 24 hours. After five days the stone will be ready for use, as long as no pressure is applied to it for an additional seven days.

To enlarge this pattern for a 12" (30cm) mold,
use a copy machine to enlarge it 125%.

Fleur de Lis Tabletop

The fleur de lis, or "flower of the lily," has many symbolic meanings, among them purity, the Holy Trinity and the royal badge of France. It is a very elegant and simple design. In this project the entire surface is covered with tesserae. Because the table legs required a tabletop 15½" (40cm) across, this is the largest project in the book. Any of the designs in this book could be enlarged to this scale. When you make a large project, you must plan carefully, work quickly after filling the mold with mix and keep a close eye on the time. The mold I used was a deli tray lid from the grocery store. The scalloped edge provides a decorative touch.

This project uses two new mosaic materials, ceramic tile and smalti. Although smalti is expensive, it is well worth adding a few pieces to the background for extra sparkle (see page 260 for more about smalti). Broken or unglazed ceramic tile pieces are easier to push into the mix if they're soaked in water beforehand. Ceramic often breaks unevenly and the broken edges may have over- or under-hangs that interfere with placing two pieces close to one another. If you haven't worked with ceramic tile before, try a smaller project first or practice embedding a few pieces after preparing the mix.

The timeless fleur de lis lends itself to many variations. You might make a smaller version and add a wall mount for hanging, or make a series of fleur de lis stepping stones with either solid or multicolored backgrounds. The white fleur de lis could be made from broken white china or even white pebbles.

MATERIALS

large round mold
(I used a plastic party tray lid with a fluted edge, 15½" x 2" or 40cm x 5cm)

pencil with eraser

scissors

craft knife

small bowl of water for soaking the tile

broken white ceramic tile

translucent stained glass in assorted blues and blue-greens

assorted gold smalti

rigid board

dust mask

rubber gloves

14 lbs. (6.4kg) stepping stone concrete mix

mixing bowl

mixing tool

about 4 cups (945ml) water

3" (75mm) putty knife

small covered plastic dish

sponge and bowl of water

embedding block

optional: tweezers or craft stick

1 ➤ Enlarge the pattern. Use a copy machine to make two copies of the pattern on page 335 to fit your mold. You may have to make enlargements of two halves of the pattern, then tape them together.

2 ➤ Make the templates. One enlarged pattern should be on paper large enough to trace the entire mold for your Design Template. Trace the bottom of your mold onto the other enlarged pattern and use scissors to cut it out on the line (it doesn't have to be the whole outline). Use a craft knife to cut out the fleur de lis shape. This will be your Mold Template.

3 ➤ Soak the tile. Porous materials are easier to push into the mix if you briefly soak them in water. Either soak all the pieces at once and then do your layout, or soak each piece as you go. Wipe excess water from the pieces before laying them on the mix, because the water may leave a white powdery stain on the concrete that's hard to remove.

4 ➤ Arrange the white pieces on the design template. Arrange the pieces on the template starting with the points, corners, and rounded ends. Then fill in the horizontal band and outline the upper and lower fleur de lis. Try to follow the flow of the curves. Using several smaller pieces will make this easier than using one or two large pieces. Finish by filling in the entire design.

5 ➤ Outline the design and fill in the background. Place blue glass around the outline of the fleur de lis shape. Start with corners, tight curves, points and narrow spaces. Next, place pieces for the outside edge, following the gentle curve and staying ⅛" (1cm) from the edge. Maintain a consistent space between the tesserae, about ¼" (6mm).

Then fill in the background with blue glass and gold pieces. The gold smalti usually are used gold side up, but are beautiful with the gold side down as well.

6 ➤ Prepare the mold and the mix. Due to the large mold, you may want to mix the concrete in two batches. Place the mold on a large, rigid board. Put on a dust mask and gloves and prepare the mix as described on pages 273-276. Set aside some mix in a covered plastic container for later. Empty the first batch in the mold, then mix and add the second batch on top of it. Tamp it well with your putty knife.

Check the time. This is a large stone and you will be covering the entire surface, so the process may take longer than with other projects. The mix will harden after an hour, as usual.

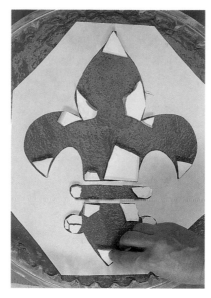

7 ➤ Transfer key pieces. Place the Mold Template on the wet mix surface and transfer the pieces in the same order as you laid them out: first the points, corners and rounded ends. Don't embed yet.

8 ➤ Finish the outline. Fill in the horizontal band and outline the upper and lower fleur de lis, following the flow of the curves. Finish filling in the entire fleur de lis. Be careful to keep pieces inside the paper edge.

9 ➤ Peel off the template. Carefully peel away the template and check to see that the outline is smooth and symmetrical. You may see a few gray spaces that need filling in with tile. Add those pieces now.

10 ➤ Embed the tile. Begin by using your fingers to partially push in all the tile pieces, especially the large ones. Be careful that the outline pieces don't shift as you push them in.

Next, use the block to evenly embed all the tile pieces. I prefer to use the embedding block method here for two reasons: First, tile can be difficult to push into the mix because it absorbs water from the mix; and second, the block will evenly embed all the pieces, making a smooth surface and covering up sharp tile edges.

11 ➤ Fill depressions. All tile edges should be submerged in the mix. Use a craft stick and the mix that you set aside to fill in areas that need more concrete. It's OK to get wet mix on the tile surface; you can clean it up later.

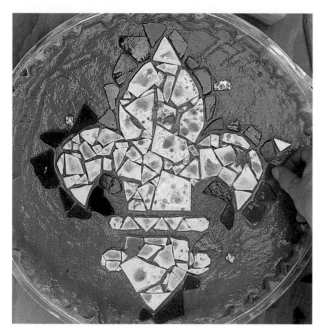

12 ➤ Transfer the background pieces. Check your time. It may be getting difficult to push in the pieces, so work quickly!

Next, outline the entire fleur de lis shape with the blue glass. Transfer the glass from your Design Template starting with corners, tight curves, points and narrow spaces. Then outline the mold with blue glass, following the gentle curve and staying ½" (1cm) from the edge.

13 ➤ Fill in the background. Fill in the background with blue and gold glass. When you're satisfied with the arrangement, embed the pieces using an embedding block or your fingertips. Embed any small filler pieces with a pencil eraser tip.

14 ➤ Jiggle the mold. Gently jiggle the mold or tap the sides, leveling and smoothing the surface and pieces as described on page 285. This may take some time on such a large stone. Look closely from several angles to be sure every piece is well-embedded and the surface is smooth, especially if this is to be a tabletop. Wipe the surface with a sponge, concentrating on the areas with tile.

15 ➤ Set the stone aside to harden for 48 hours. Cover the stone loosely with plastic and use the board to transfer it to a safe location. Spray it with water after 24 hours.

16 ➤ Clean up the stone. After 48 hours, gently scrub excess concrete from the tesserae. Remove the stone from the mold and carefully round off the edges. Be very careful scraping the fluted edge — it will chip easily. Rinse the stone well.

17 ➤ Elevate the stone and let it cure. Let the stone cure, elevated on a rack or on pencils, for five more days, spraying it with water every day. Cover it loosely with plastic, making a sturdier stone. After five days the stone will be ready for use, as long as no pressure is applied to it for seven more days.

To enlarge this pattern for a 15½" (40cm) mold, use a copy machine to enlarge it 200% then enlarge the copy 125%.

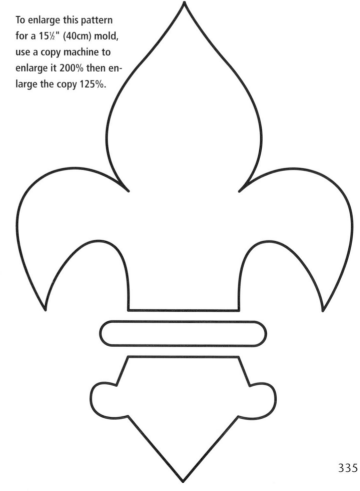

Garden Gloves

This stepping stone was created in the spirit of a **trompe l'oeil,** or "trick the eye" painting in which three-dimensional objects are realistically depicted on a flat surface. I doubt anyone will bend down to try and pick up these gloves, but they would add a lighthearted touch to a garden path, landscaping or porch.

You could make a path of plain gray concrete stepping stones and place this one in the middle. The glove motif would look clever as a small round tabletop for a sunroom that has lots of plants. You could add a border of pebbles or random shapes of mosaic glass. For an easier version of this design, join and round off the fingers to make a pair of colorful mittens.

MATERIALS

square stepping stone mold
12" x 12" x 2" (30cm x 30cm x 5cm)

pencil with eraser

scissors

craft knife

opaque white and translucent
dark blue stained glass

rigid board

dust mask

rubber gloves

7 lbs (3.2kg)
stepping stone concrete mix

mixing bowl

mixing tool

2 cups (472ml) water

3" (75mm) putty knife

optional: tweezers

1 ➤ Enlarge the pattern. Use a copy machine to enlarge the garden gloves pattern on page 339. Make three copies.

2 ➤ Make the templates. Place the mold on one enlarged pattern, centering it over the design. Trace the mold with a pencil. Use scissors to cut out along the traced line to make the Mold Template. Repeat for a second Mold Template. Use a craft knife to cut out just the white gloves from one Mold Template. Then cut out just the blue wristbands from the other Mold Template. The third copy can be your Design Template.

3 ➤ Lay out white tesserae on the template. Arrange the white glass on the Design Template starting with the ten fingers. Look for pieces with rounded edges which will follow the tight curves of the narrow, elongated fingers. Tiny pieces and careful fitting are required. Fairly tight spacing will ensure that the image "reads" easily.

Next, place a white piece in each of the three corners, adjacent to the wristbands. Then outline the rest of the hand, staying within the line, and finish by filling it in.

337

4 ➤ Lay out blue tesserae on the template. Now arrange the dark blue pieces of the wrist-bands. Begin with the four corners of the top glove (the right hand). Next, place the outline pieces. Then fill in the center.

Lay out the other band: place the three corners, outline and fill in. If you follow this order, the illusion of one glove lying on top of the other will be more apparent.

5 ➤ Prepare the mold and the mix. Place the mold on a board. Prepare the mix as described on pages 273–276. Place the white gloves Mold Template on the wet mix surface. Check the time or set a timer for one hour.

6 ➤ Transfer the tesserae. Start transferring the white tesserae for the hands, starting with the key white pieces. Keep the spacing even and fairly tight, about ⅛" (3mm). Let the pieces just rest on the surface for now.

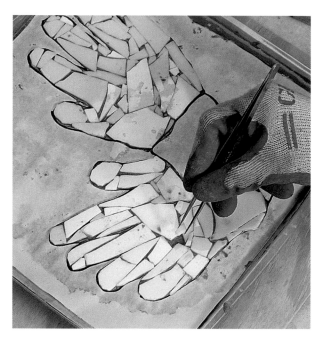

7 ➤ Finish the hands. Outline and fill in the hands. Use tweezers to insert small pieces and adjust others. Be careful to keep the pieces inside the open space in the template.

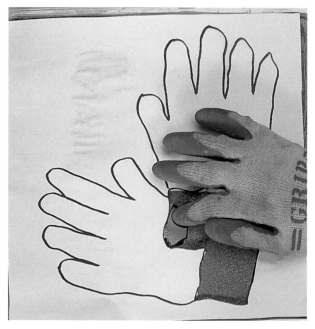

8 ➤ Switch templates and transfer tesserae. Carefully remove the glove template and place the wristband template on the mix. Next, position the blue pieces of the top glove.

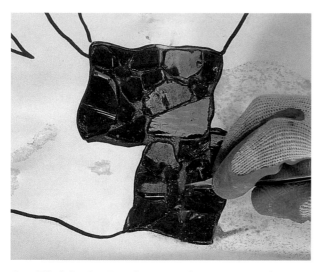

9 ➤ Finish the bands. Transfer the pieces for the bottom glove, placing the corners and outline first. Then fill in and adjust the spacing if necessary.

10 ➤ Embed the tesserae. Carefully peel away the template, then stand back and look at the layout. Does the outline of the entire shape look like a pair of baggy cotton gloves? The pieces should be evenly and tightly spaced, with room for mix to come up between them when you push down. The four fingers of each glove should be close to each other, with a V-shaped space between them. If you see a few gray spaces that still need filling in, add those pieces now.

When you have all the pieces where you want them, begin embedding. Push straight down.

11 ➤ Jiggle the mold. Gently jiggle the mold, leveling and smoothing the surface and pieces as described on page 285.

12 ➤ Set the stone aside to harden for 48 hours. Cover the stone loosely with plastic and use the board to transfer it to a safe location. Spray it with water after 24 hours.

13 ➤ Clean up the stone. After 48 hours, gently scrub the excess concrete from the tesserae as described on page 289. Remove stone from the mold and round off the edges as shown on page 289. Rinse the stone well.

14 ➤ Elevate the stone and let it cure. Let the stone cure elevated on a rack or on pencils for five more days. Cover it loosely with plastic to cure more slowly, which makes a sturdier stone. Spray it with water every 24 hours. After five days the stone will be ready for use, as long as no pressure is applied to it for an additional seven days.

To enlarge this pattern for a 12 " (30cm) mold, use a copy machine to enlarge it 200%, then enlarge the copy 130%.

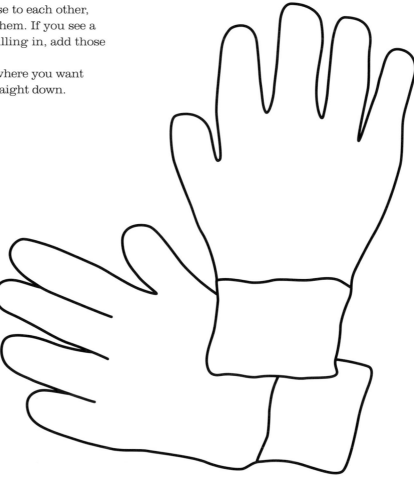

House Number Sign

This house number sign can be made as a wall plaque that hangs on your house or garage, or it can be embedded in a curbside garden. The main consideration here is legibility; in order for the numbers to "read," keep the spacing between the pieces tight, ⅛" (3mm) maximum. This mold will easily fit two to four numerals; if your address is longer, you could build your own mold or buy a longer mold. You could make this project easier by leaving out the background mosaic pieces, but be sure to use a glass color that reads well against the concrete color. Opaque glass is best for legibility because translucent glass tends to fade into the gray concrete background. I chose blue and orange, which are complementary colors and provide a good contrast. You could also choose black and white, a bright color on a white background, yellow on blue or any other contrasty combination. If you can easily distinguish between the two colors when you squint your eyes, you have a good contrast.

Another idea would be to make this a yard sign by inserting two metal stakes, an inch from each end, through the bottom edge of the mold. (See page 371, Garden Stakes and Paperweights.) Use an awl to punch the holes in the plastic mold.

MATERIALS

house sign mold,
12" x 8" x 1" (30cm x 30cm x 25mm)

pencil with eraser

enlarged number patterns

11" x 17" (28cm x 43cm) paper

scissors

craft knife

ruler

clear tape

opaque light blue and orange stained glass

optional: orange glass heart ornament

rigid board

optional mounting device:
2" x 2" (5cm x 5cm) cardboard square 3" x 2" (8cm x 5cm) piece of duct tape

dust mask

rubber gloves

3½ lbs. (1.6kg) stepping stone concrete mix

mixing bowl

mixing tool

1 cup (236ml) water

3" (75mm) putty knife

sponge and small bowl of water

tweezers

optional: embedding block

1 ➤ Enlarge the pattern. Enlarge the numbers you need from page 345. For this mold, the numbers should be about 3 ½" (9cm) tall.

2 ➤ Make the templates. Trace your mold onto a sheet of paper and arrange the numbers so they are spaced about ⅜"(1cm) apart and are no closer than ½" to the edge of the mold. Tape down the numbers. This is your Design Template.

Make a photocopy or tracing of the Design Template. Cut with scissors along the outline of the mold; then use a craft knife to cut out the numbers. Numbers 4, 6, 8, 9, and 0 have holes, and you will need to cut out and save the inside part. This is your Mold Template.

3 ➤ Lay out the numerals on the template. Lay out your glass pieces on the Design Template, starting with the numbers. Carefully follow the tight corners, turns and curves. Look for small pieces with straight edges and curves that match the outlines of the numerals. The numbers will be easier to read if you keep the spacing tight.

4 ➤ Lay out the background on the template.
If you have a heart ornament, position it ⅜" (1cm) from the top edge. Next, find background pieces that fit into the numerals' negative spaces (a triangle for a **4**, two round pieces for an **8**, etc.) and then fill in between each numeral. Place pieces for the four mold corners.

Now outline the numerals. Again, take the time to do a precise layout. Keep spacing fairly tight and consistent.

Finally, outline the entire stone and fill it in. I like to use a variety of sizes and shapes and really mix them up. This makes a more interesting design.

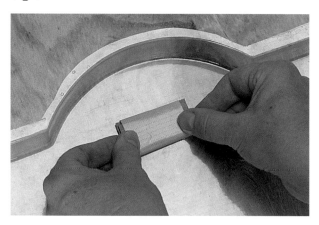

5 ➤ Prepare the mounting device. If you want to hang up your sign, you'll need a recessed area in the back to accommodate a nail or screw. See page 271 for the instructions for making this device.

6 ➤ Prepare the mix. Put on a dust mask and gloves and follow pages 273-276 to prepare the mix. Check the time; this project will take more time than the others since the placement of glass is precise and the entire surface is being covered.

8 ➤ Transfer the numeral pieces. As quickly as possible, transfer the numeral pieces to the mix surface. Keep the pieces inside the paper edge and let them rest on top of the mix for the time being.

Remove the template and make sure the numbers are legible, centered, and level with each other. Make any adjustments and keep an eye on the time.

7 ➤ Place the template on the wet mix surface. Place the Mold Template on the wet mix surface, then carefully place the cut-out paper pieces to create the negative spaces in the numbers that need them. Tweezers are helpful here.

9 ➤ Embed the numerals.
If you embed the numerals now, they will stay in place as you position the background pieces. The pencil eraser head is especially good to push in these small pieces. Work rather quickly, being careful not to shift the pieces as you press them into the mix.

10 ➤ Position the key background pieces. Whether you embedded the numerals or not, now transfer the background pieces in the same order as above: first the heart ornament, numeral negative spaces and the four corners. Then outline the numerals and then the mold border, keeping pieces about ¼" (6mm) from the edge of the mold.

11 ➤ Fill in the background. Fill in the rest of the background. Place the last piece, stand back and take a good look. Move or add any pieces that seem necessary now.

12 ➤ Embed the background. When pieces are spaced this closely together I like to use the embedding block as described on page 281. You could embed the pieces with your finger or a pencil eraser instead.

Push the thickest piece in first, which is the heart. Then embed all the rest. Look for gray spaces that still may need a piece of glass. Add those pieces.

13 ➤ Jiggle the mold and sponge the surface. Gently jiggle the mold, leveling the pieces and smoothing the surface. Sponging the surface will be very helpful after using an embedding block. See page 285.

14 ➤ Set the stone aside to harden for 48 hours. Cover the stone loosely with plastic and use the board to transfer it to a safe location. Spray it with water after 24 hours.

15 ➤ Clean up the stone. After 48 hours, gently scrub the excess concrete from the tesserae as described on page 289. Remove the stone from the mold and round off the edges as shown on page 289. Rinse the stone well.

16 ➤ Elevate the stone and let it cure. Let the stone cure, elevated on a rack or on pencils, for five more days. Cover it loosely with plastic so that it cures slowly, which makes a sturdier stone. Spray it with water every 24 hours. After five days the stone will be ready for use.

tip

The contact-paper technique described on pages 282-284 could also be used for this project. Arrange just the numerals on the Design Template. Adhere the contact paper to the numerals, transfer them to the mix and embed them, then remove the contact paper within about five minutes. Then arrange the background pieces and embed them as explained in the project above.

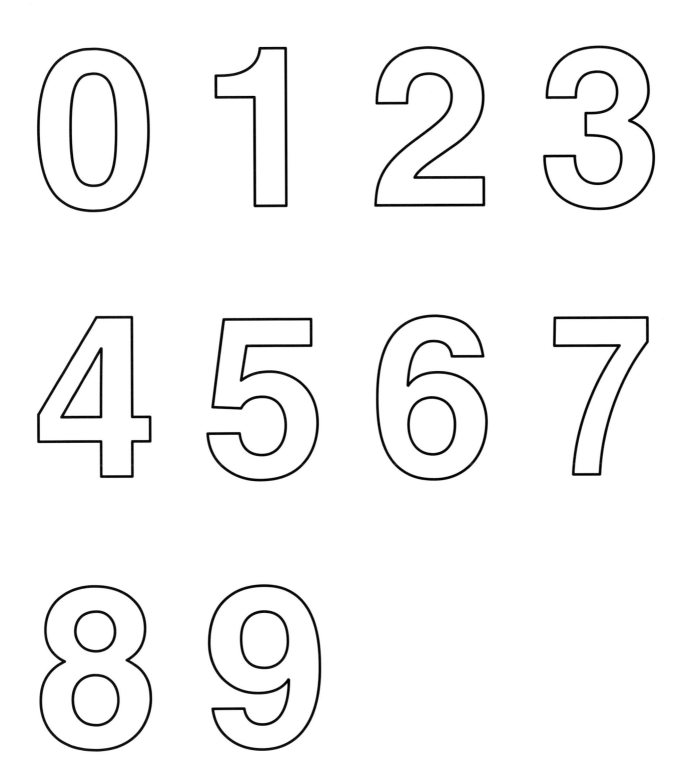

To enlarge these numbers for a 12" x 8"
(30cm x 20cm) mold, use a copy machine to
enlarge them 200%.

345

Lizard

A shiny black reptile and highly polished black rocks are a match made in mosaic heaven! Take your time laying out this project. It's important to find stone shapes that flow into one another, and that smoothly graduate in size from the broad head and shoulders to the pointed tail tip. Laying out a design which includes river rocks, broken plates, marbles, or other irregularly shaped pieces can be frustrating—the pieces tip over, roll off the table and just generally don't stay put. I solve this problem by using a shallow box of sand for laying out the design. The dry sand holds uneven pieces in place no matter which way they are placed.

For variations of this project, think about using different rock colors: dark green, terra-cotta red, even off-white. This design may be made of glass tesserae so you can give your lizard's tail colorful contrasting stripes using the glass on edge. If you plan to use this lizard for a garden path, flip the design over and trace it from the back; then alternate the patterns so your lizards slither one way and then the other as the path unfolds.

MATERIALS

square stepping stone mold
12" x 12" x 1½"
(30cm x 30cm x 38mm)

pencil with eraser

scissors

craft knife

optional: sand in a shallow box or tray

about 50 polished black river rocks, grape-to plum-size

rigid board

dust mask

rubber gloves

7 lbs. (3.2kg)
stepping stone concrete mix

mixing bowl

mixing tool

2 cups (472ml) water

3" (75mm) putty knife

tweezers

embedding block

1 ➤ **Enlarge the pattern.** Use a copy machine to enlarge the lizard pattern on page 351 to fit the size of your mold. Make two copies.

2 ➤ **Make the templates.** Place the mold on one enlarged pattern, centering it over the design. Trace the mold with a pencil and cut on the line with scissors. Use a craft knife to cut out the lizard. This is the Mold Template, and if you're using a tray of sand to lay out your pieces, it is the only template you will need. Otherwise, use another copy of the enlarged pattern or the cut-out lizard as your Design Template.

3 ➤ **Sort the rocks.** First sort the river rocks by size. This will make finding just the right piece much quicker. Try to use flat rocks, not thick, rounded ones that might contact the bottom of the mold when embedded.

4 ➤ Lay out the head, body and tail. If you're using a sand tray, lay the Mold Template on the sand surface. If you prefer, you may instead lay out the rocks on the Design Template; the process is the same.

First make a curving snake figure that is like a backward *S* using twelve to sixteen rocks. Take time to play around with shapes and sizes and to find rocks that fit together well. The first three or four rocks need to touch the design outlines in order to define the smooth upper body curve. When you have an arrangement you like, look at it with squinted eyes to see that you have created a smooth curve. Line up the rocks as closely as possible to the paper template outline without overlapping the edge. If the rocks you have are small, you can make the body two rocks wide, but only between the front and back legs.

For the tail tip, find a flat rock that appears narrow when turned on its side. A good tail tip piece curves and comes to a slight point.

5 ➤ Lay out the legs. The four legs are almost identical: two parts with three or four toes each. Try to find pairs of rocks that match in size and shape. If your bag of rocks did not include rocks small enough for the toes, use the technique on pages 262-263 to smash a few rocks in half.

Remove the template, stand back and squint. Does the shape look like a backward *S* with smooth bends and no kinks? Rearrange the pieces until your lizard looks as if it will slither away.

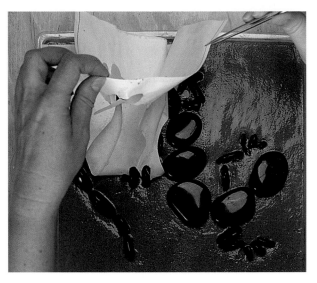

6 ➤ Prepare the mold and the mix. Place the mold on a board. Put on your dust mask and gloves to prepare the mix as described on pages 273-276. Check the time or set a timer for 60 minutes.

7 ➤ Transfer the rocks. Position the Mold Template on the wet mix surface and smooth it down.

Quickly move the rocks to the mix surface, beginning with the head and working down the figure to the tail tip. Then transfer the pieces for the legs and toes. Space the rocks so that they touch. Don't push the rocks in the mix yet; however, you can partially embed broken pieces just enough to keep them in place. Use tweezers to position smaller pieces.

8 ➤ Remove the template. Slowly peel off the paper template. If some rocks overlap the paper, carefully lift the paper around them. Stand back to see if any adjustments are needed. If so, do it now.

9 ➤ Push in the rocks. Rocks are sometimes difficult to push straight down into the mix, even if the concrete hasn't begun to harden. Try to gently seesaw or vibrate the rock while pushing down. Push the rocks in at least three-fourths of the way. Don't push them in too far, or you'll end up with a chain of small "icebergs," the visible portion of the rocks having shrunk while most of the bulk disappears into the mix. Push each piece in, then go back and do it again until all rocks are properly embedded.

If you find that water is pooling around the rocks, soak up the excess with a paper towel.

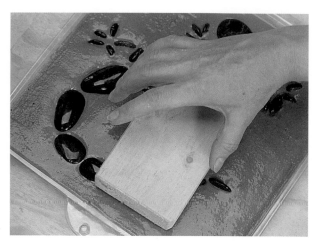

If you want a more level surface, use a weighted block after you have partially embedded the rocks with your fingers, as shown on page 281. This will level the peaks of the rocks. You may choose to embed the rocks completely so that they are flush with the surface of the stone. This surface is better for walking on, but the rocks tend to lose some detail and the space between them grows larger. I prefer to just push in the rocks as in step 9 and just enjoy the bumpy surface of the stepping stone.

10 ➤ **Patch valleys.** When you've finished embedding, you may see a few small valleys or depressions surrounding some of the rocks. You may choose to leave them alone (which would be my choice), or you may fill them in with wet concrete as described on page 293. Keep in mind that if you fill in the valleys or sponge the surface, the rocks will lose some detail and the spacing will not look as tight as before.

11 ➤ **Smooth the mix and jiggle the mold.** If you want a very smooth surface, use the putty knife lightly to even out the surface texture. Gently jiggle the mold.

12 ➤ **Set the stone aside to harden for 48 hours.** Cover the stone loosely with plastic and use the board to transfer it to a safe location. Spray with water after 24 hours.

13 ➤ **Clean up the stone.** After 48 hours, gently scrub excess concrete from the rocks as described on page 288. Remove the stone from the mold and round off the edges as shown on page 289. Rinse the stone.

14 ➤ **Elevate the stone and let it cure.** Let the stone cure, elevated on a rack or on pencils, for five more days. Cover it loosely with plastic so that it cures slowly, which makes a sturdier stone. Spray it with water every 24 hours. When the five days are up, your stone is ready to be used as long as no pressure is applied to it for an additional seven days.

To enlarge these patterns for a
12" (30cm) mold, use a copy
machine to enlarge them 200%.

Pot of Geraniums

The next four projects include some very large "tesserae": a terra-cotta pot, a pair of scrub brushes, a teacup and a plant hook. Even for the experienced mosaic artist, these objects can be tricky to handle and awkward to embed, so take your time planning and laying out these designs. Read through the steps until you have a clear idea of what you'll need to do and in what order.

This wall plaque is a bit whimsical, because the mosaic flowers "grow" out of the three-dimensional pot. The pot has no real function, although you could keep your garden tools or keys in it. If the plaque is hanging on a sunny porch, you could add soil and flower seeds and see what happens, but I prefer just to leave it as it is.

You may come up with other ways to incorporate embedded containers into your mosaic projects. You can cut a small tin pail in half with tin snips and use it in place of the pot. And of course, you can use different colors and substitute daisies or other kinds of flowers for the geraniums.

1 ➤ Saw the pot in half. Use a hacksaw to cut the pot in half vertically. Don't worry about being too precise. The easiest way to do this is to cut halfway down, then turn the pot over and cut down until the second cut joins the first.

2 ➤ Enlarge the pattern. Use a copy machine to enlarge the geranium pattern on page 351 to fit your mold. For a 12" (30cm) square mold, enlarge it 200%. Make two copies of the pattern.

3 ➤ Make the templates. Place the mold on the enlarged pattern, centering it over the design. Trace the mold with a pencil. Use scissors to cut out along the traced line. Use a craft knife to cut out the flowers and leaves, but not the stems or the pot outline. This is the Mold Template; use the other enlarged pattern for the Design Template.

4 ➤ Lay out tesserae on the Design Template. You'll need about 45 orange petal pieces that are similar in size and shape: oval or elongated, about the size of small grapes. Arrange them on the Design Template starting with the flower outlines, then fill in the entire flower area.

Next arrange the green leaf pieces. Start with the key pieces located at the line where the leaves meet the pot rim. Outline

these two corners with green pieces. Place the half-pot on the template to serve as a guide. Next, outline the rest of the leaves, then fill them in. Stay well within the outlines.

Select twelve to fifteen small green stem pieces (glass pieces that will be set on their sides) and set them aside.

5 ➤ Prepare the mounting device. Prepare and position the cardboard and duct tape mounting device as shown on page 271. Since the mold is square, you may want to mark the top of the mold with a piece of tape.

6 ➤ Prepare the mix. Place the mold on a board. Put on your mask and gloves and prepare the mix as described on pages 272-276. Check the time or set a timer for one hour.

7 ➤ Transfer the flower pieces. Position the Mold Template on the wet mix surface. Transfer the flower pieces to the mix starting with the outlines. Fill in each flower with petals, spacing the pieces closely to resemble the flower petals.

8 ➤ Transfer the leaf pieces. Transfer the leaves to the mix surface, starting with the key pieces and the outlines; then fill them in.

9 ➤ Mark the position of the pot. Test the placement of the half-pot now; place it on the template, lining it up with the top dotted line. Check to see if there is ½" to ¾" (12mm to 18mm) between the base of the pot and the edge of the stone. Also make sure that the pot fits between—not on top of—the two leaves. (If it doesn't, you can fix it in a moment.) Then remove the pot.

Use a pencil to make marks through the dotted lines at the four corners of the pot so that there are marks that will remain in the wet mix after the template has been removed.

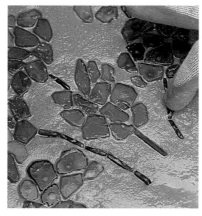

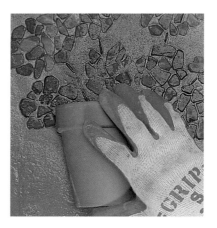

10 ➤ Embed the flower and leaf pieces. If any rearranging is needed to accommodate the pot, do it now. Then embed the flowers and leaves by pushing straight down or use an embedding block.

11 ➤ Remove the template. Before you make the stems, carefully remove the Mold Template.

12 ➤ Create the stems. Mark the position of the stems by drawing light guidelines or dots in the mix with the tip of a pencil. Then begin pushing in green pieces on their edges. Start at the base of a flower and work your way down the stem, going below the pot rim about 1" (25mm). Do this for both of the stems.

13 ➤ Embed the pot. Position the pot no less than ½" (12mm) from the edge. Embed the pot, rocking it gently while pushing down. You want it to go into the mix about 1" (25mm)—most of the way in but not all the way to the bottom. If it does go in too deeply, lift it up a little and jiggle the mold two or three times.

14 ➤ Tamp the mix. Using your gloved fingers, push the mix against the outer pot wall to firm the bond. Do this all around the pot, smoothing as you go.

15 ➤ Jiggle the mold. Gently jiggle and tap the sides of the mold to even out the surface, making sure the pot doesn't shift or sink all the way through the mix. For a more even texture, lightly skim the surface once with the putty knife.

16 ➤ Set the stone aside to harden. Cover the stone loosely with plastic and use the board to set it aside to harden for 48 hours. Spray it with water after 24 hours.

17 ➤ Clean up the stone. After 48 hours, gently scrub excess concrete from the tesserae as described on page 289. Remove the stone from the mold and remove the mounting device as shown on page 288; then round off the edges. Rinse the stone well.

18 ➤ Elevate the stone and let it cure. Let the stone cure, elevated on a rack or on pencils, for five more days. Cover it loosely with plastic so that it cures slowly, which makes a sturdier stone. Spray it with water every 24 hours. After five days the stone will be ready for use.

Pique Assiette Boot Brush

Pique assiette is a French term meaning "plate stealer," or scavenger. It refers to the folk art of using broken china and fragments of pottery to embellish everything from small items to entire houses. Many of these mosaics incorporate uncommon objects. I began with a colorful broken plate, then I selected some other broken tile and glass pieces that coordinated with the plate colors: deep purple, teal green, amber and light blue.

For a variation, you could use the same two brushes in a larger mold and add foot prints of your children and paw prints of your pets. You may want to add fewer mosaic pieces to allow for writing in the wet cement ("Please wipe," "The Smiths," your house number or "Welcome"). This project makes a clever gift for a friend who is tired of muddy shoes! If you use brushes with wooden handles, you should seal the wood first with two coats of acrylic paint.

MATERIALS

square stepping stone mold
12" x 12" x 1½"
(30cm x 30cm x 38mm)

pencil with eraser

paper

two 8"x 2" (20cm x 5cm)
scrub brushes with textured
plastic handles

ceramic plate, tile and glass bits
and pieces

small bowl of water for soaking tile

old towel

rigid board

dust mask

rubber gloves

7 lbs. (3.2kg)
stepping stone concrete mix

mixing bowl

mixing tool

2 cups (472ml) water

3" (75mm) putty knife

ruler

1 ➤ Soak broken ceramic pieces. Read about working with ceramic pieces before starting (see Getting Started page 280). You may soak broken ceramic pieces in water all at once and then do your layout, or soak each piece as you go. Wipe each piece dry before placing it on the template. Pre-soaked tiles are easier to embed than dry ones, and will create a smoother surface.

2 ➤ Make a template. If you want to use a template, trace the mold on a piece of paper; this will be the only template. Place the two brushes in the center of the traced outline, about ⅖" (1cm) apart. Trace a square around the brushes. Then arrange mosaic pieces on the template, starting at the outline of the brushes, staying ¼" (6mm) to ½" (12mm) from the brushes. Next lay the pieces for the outside edges, and finally fill in the middle.

Your other option is to prepare the mix, pour it into the mold and simply start embedding without laying out the pieces on the template first.

3 ➤ Prepare the mix. Place the mold on a board. Put on a dust mask and gloves and prepare the mix as described on pages 273-276. Check the time or set a timer for one hour.

4 ➤ Position the brushes. Position the brushes in the center of the stone ⅖" (1cm) apart.

5 ➤ Embed the brushes. This step will take a bit of muscle to accomplish. Push straight down on a brush and seesaw it from end to end. Try vibrating it. It may be hard to press in, but don't give up. Then embed the other brush. Make sure that the mix comes up between the brushes and that the mix is flush with the submerged handles.

The law of mosaic embedding: "What goes down, must come up." The mix will be significantly displaced by the brushes so you'll notice rising mounds of mix around them.

6 ➤ Smooth the mix. Flatten and smooth the mix with your fingers. Be sure that the brush handles are fully embedded and that the mix comes up and over their edges. Use a finger to smooth the mix between the two brushes. (It will be a little messy.) Then smooth the surface with a putty knife and give the mold a couple of jiggles.

7 ➤ Position the mosaic pieces. Place the pieces beginning with the brush outline, then the mold corners and border, and then fill in the other areas. Be sure to stay ¼" (6mm) to ½" (12mm) from the brushes and the edge of the mold.

8 ➤ Embed the tesserae. If you're feeling confident, try embedding the pieces as you go. Otherwise, finish laying out all the pieces on the mix surface before pushing them all in.

Stand back and look at your design. If you see a few gray spaces or gaps that need to be filled in, add those pieces now. Check the level of the brushes because they tend to rise. Push the brushes in and level them if needed.

9 ➤ Fill in depressions. If you see any exposed irregular ceramic edges, use extra mix to fill these in now, as described on page 293.

10 ➤ Jiggle the mold and sponge the surface. Gently jiggle and turn the mold, leveling and smoothing the surface and pieces. Lightly sponge the surface.

11 ➤ Set the stone aside to harden. Cover the stone loosely with plastic and set it aside for 48 hours. Spray it with water after 24 hours.

12 ➤ Clean up the stone. After 48 hours, gently scrub excess concrete from the tesserae as described on page 289. Remove the stone from the mold and round off the edges. Rinse the stone well.

13 ➤ Elevate the stone and let it cure. Let the stone cure, elevated on a rack or on pencils, for five more days. Cover it loosely with plastic so that it cures slowly, which makes a sturdier stone. Spray it with water every 24 hours. After five days, uncover it and stop spraying it, but wait an additional seven days before using the boot brush.

tip

To hold your boot brush in place or to protect floors: After curing, cut a skid-resistant backing (such as a rubber mesh carpet pad) to match the stone shape. Glue it to the stone bottom with concrete glue or silicone-based glue.

Forget-Me-Not Wall Flower

This project is so much fun! It includes an unexpected feature: a teacup which can hold a tiny potted plant, a bar of soap, or even tea bags. Your creation will be different from mine, but I hope I can inspire you to unpack old jewelry and uncover fun "junk" to include in your plaque. Arrange your design on a paper tracing of your mold, or design it as you go!

Other objects you could embed include: a small terra-cotta saucer as a bird feeder; a large hook to hang your hat; a ceramic soap dish to keep your keys or an antique saucer to hold a votive candle.

MATERIALS

stepping stone mold
(I used a flower-shaped mold)
12" x 12" x 1½"
(30cm x 30cm x 38mm)

pencil with eraser

found objects: old jewelry, glass beads, hardware, mirror and china pieces

smalti, broken tile and stained-glass

rigid board

mounting device:
2"x 2" (5cm x 5cm) cardboard square
3"x 2" (8cm x 5cm) piece of duct tape

dust mask

rubber gloves

7 lbs. (3.2kg)
stepping stone concrete mix

optional: two 2oz. (58g)
packets of charcoal-colored dry pigment

mixing bowl

mixing tool

2 cups (472ml) water

3" (75mm) putty knife

tweezers

1 ➤ **Make a template if desired.** If you want to plan your design, make a template by tracing your mold on a piece of paper. Arrange and rearrange your pieces on this template until you are happy with the design.

If you don't want to use a template, have your bits and pieces ready nearby. You will need to soak any broken ceramic pieces (see page 280).

2 ➤ Prepare the mold for a mounting device.
See page 271 for directions on preparing a mold
with a hanging device.

3 ➤ Prepare the mix. If you want to color your
stone, see page 277 for directions on adding pigment to the mix. Put your mold on a board, put on
your dust mask and gloves and follow the directions on pages 272-276 to prepare the mix. Check
the time or set a timer for one hour.

4 ➤ Position the cup. I started by placing a couple of the larger and more important elements on
the mix: a sprocket from a bicycle and a faucet handle, which I think of as the "flowers" of my design.
Positioning them first helped me choose the placement for the full-size, unbroken teacup.

First, place the cup in the desired position and
gently push it into the mix, just enough to make
an impression.

5 ➤ Start embedding the cup.
Place the lip of the cup on the
mark and start to push it into the
stone at a 45° angle, 1" (25mm)

deep. It's similar to digging in the
dirt with a trowel: push the cup
down and away, then scoop and
push it away and up slightly,
working to gently loosen and lift
the mix—but don't shovel it out.

Keep scooping until a mound
of mix goes about halfway down
into the cup. Stop scooping and
push down on the bottom of the
cup. Vibrate and push the cup
gently to embed the bottom,
then straighten it out into its
final position. You'll probably
have to make several adjustments until it's in the right
place.

6 ➤ Secure the cup. Now the
cup needs to be bonded and secured to the concrete. With a
gloved hand, push the mound of
mix into the cup, leveling it out
as much as possible, pressing it
against the cup and extending it
all the way to the bottom of the
cup. Scoop a bit of mix from else-
where if needed.

t i p

If you are using broken china or broken ceramic tile, briefly soak the pieces in

water and wipe them dry before using them.

7 ➤ Make a shelf. Next, create a concrete shelf beneath the cup to add support. Scrape mix up against the bottom of the cup, forming a ledge underneath. With your fingertips, press around the entire seam where the cup and mix meet.

Optional: Gently, very gently, jiggle the mold to make an even, smooth surface.

8 ➤ Arrange and embed the tesserae. Try to work neatly from now on. You won't want to vibrate the mold after perfectly placing the teacup.

Position the rest of the pieces, keeping them about ¼" (6mm) from the edge. Rearrange them until you are satisfied, keeping an eye on the time. Then start pushing them into the mix, beginning with the thickest pieces and ending with the thinnest. Push straight down; seesaw and vibrate the larger pieces. Very thin, flat pieces, such as bicycle parts or coins, must be pushed in deeply so they will stay in place when the stone has cured.

When you've finished embedding, stand back and look at the stone. Fill in any spaces. Check the thin pieces again to ensure that they are flush with the surface, or even lower.

9 ➤ Smooth the surface. Tap the sides of the mold to even out the surface, but don't vibrate too hard or the heavier pieces may sink out of sight.

10 ➤ Set the stone aside to harden for 48 hours. Use the board to move the stone to a safe location. Cover it loosely with plastic and spray it with water after 24 hours.

11 ➤ Clean up the stone. After 48 hours, gently scrub excess concrete from the tesserae as described on page 289. Remove the stone from the mold, take out the duct tape and cardboard mounting device and round off the edges. Rinse the stone well.

12 ➤ Elevate the stone and let it cure. Let the stone cure, elevated on a rack or on pencils, for five more days. Cover it loosely with plastic so that it cures slowly, which makes a sturdier stone. Spray it with water every 24 hours. After five days the stone will be ready for use.

Sundial

➤ This sundial is designed for decorative purposes, not to tell the time right down to the minute. In order for a sundial to tell accurate time, it must be designed for the latitude and longitude of the place where it will be used. For more detailed information, look up sundials at your local library or on the Internet. The latitude of your city determines the spacing of the numbers and the angle of your pointer, or gnomon. The gnomon I used is actually an iron plant hook. You may use a different object such as a metal plant stake or a bent metal tube.

I kept my design simple by using square tiles. Your sundial may be made using any of the techniques in this book, including adding colorant to the cement. You could also design your sundial with an inscription: "Tempus Fugit" (time flies); "Though silent I speak"; "I tell sunny hours only"; "Every hour has its changes"; or your family name. The plastic stamp I used to make the scrollwork imprint is part of a set of stamps used by cake decorators to make letters in icing. It makes perfect lettering easy because the stamps go right into the wet mix. You can also incise the letters directly into the cement using a craft stick. A chisel-shaped tool such as a screwdriver will make attractive calligraphic letters.

MATERIALS

octagonal stepping stone mold
12" x 12" x 1½"
(30cm x 30cm x 38mm)

pencil with eraser

scissors

craft knife

40 vitreous glass tiles, ¾" x ¾"
(18mm x 18mm)

gnomon: I used a 6" (15cm)
cast-iron outdoor plant hook,
but 8" (20cm) would have been
even better

1" (25mm) diameter flat rock

ruler

rigid board

dust mask

rubber gloves

7 lbs. (3.2kg)
stepping stone concrete mix

mixing bowl

mixing tool

2 cups (472ml) water

3" (75mm) putty knife

craft stick

optional: scrollwork stamp

1 ➤ **Enlarge the pattern.** Enlarge the sundial pattern on page 369. For a 12" (30cm) mold, enlarge it on a copy machine 200%. Make two copies.

2 ➤ **Make three templates.** Place the mold on one enlarged pattern, which will be Template A, centering it over the design. Trace the mold with a pencil. Use scissors to cut out along the traced line. Use a craft knife to cut out and save the geometric cross shape, which you should mark as Template B.

Place the mold on the second copy of the enlarged pattern, centering it over the design. Trace the mold with a pencil and cut along the line. Use a craft knife to cut out the thirteen Roman numerals (just cut a box around each numeral), the large central circle, and a box around the scrollwork at the bottom. This is Template C.

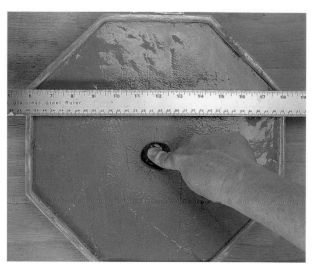

3 ➤ Lay out the tiles on the template. Arrange mosaic tiles on Template B, mixing the colors until you have a pleasing pattern. Leave the middle square blank; this is where the gnomon will be embedded.

4 ➤ Prepare the mix. Place the mold on a board. Put on a dust mask and gloves and prepare the mix as described on pages 273-276. Check the time or set a timer for one hour.

5 ➤ Practice making lines. If this is your first time inscribing lines, see page 286 and make a few lines now. When you're done, smooth and vibrate the mold to erase the practice lines.

6 ➤ Embed a rock prop. The angle of your gnomon should be roughly equal to the latitude of your city. Mine needs to be set at or near 45° because I live in Seattle, which is at 45° latitude. (Bangor, Maine and Toronto, Canada are also at this latitude and would require the same angle.) My plant hook stands at about 60°, and I also want to increase its height, so my solution is to first embed a rock base for my gnomon to lean against. The bottom of the hook will rest on the rock, causing the gnomon to be set at a different angle. Remember, your sundial may not tell the exact time, but setting the gnomon at the correct angle can make it close.

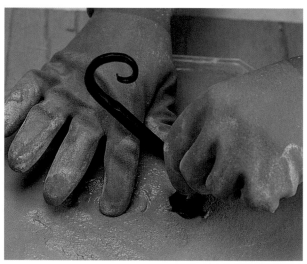

7 ➤ Embed the gnomon. Push the hook into the mix so that it rests on the mold bottom and, if necessary, on the rock. The main arm should extend out of the center of the sundial and reach toward 12 o'clock at a 45° angle.

8 ➤ Fill in the mix. Holding the gnomon with one hand, scrape wet mix to fill in the impression it left. Press down or pat the mix with your gloved hand to even out the surface a little. Hold the hook with one hand and jiggle the mold with the other hand.

9 ➤ Smooth the surface. Try letting go of the hook; it should stand on its own. If not, you need to prop it up so you have both hands free. Use something light that won't sink, such as a tin can. Use your putty knife to smooth the entire surface again.

10 ➤ Use Template A. Position Mold Template A on the wet mix surface, smooth it down and transfer all the mosaic tiles, leaving ⅛" (3mm) between tiles. Work around the hook.

Carefully remove the template. Check to see that the tiles and hook are centered, then embed all the tiles. If the surface needs smoothing or the tiles need leveling, gently tap the sides of the mold. This is your last chance to smooth the surface because you don't want to vibrate the mold after you inscribe the numerals—they will fill in and disappear!

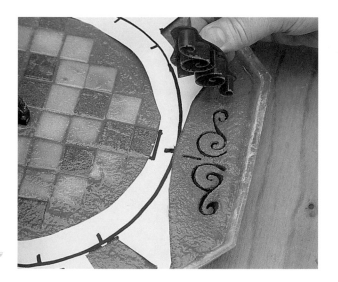

11 ➤ Place Template C. Place Design Template C on the wet mix surface. The numeral boxes should be a minimum of ¼" (6mm) from the edge of the stone and your tiles should be centered in the cut-out circle.

Make the scrollwork impression now, using the scrollwork stamp or drawing the design with a craft stick. If you choose to draw, transfer the design by laying the paper pattern on the mix and making dots with a pointed tool through the design into the mix. Then remove the paper and connect the dots.

12 ➤ Incise the numerals.
Use the craft stick to incise the Roman numerals inside the cut-out boxes. Don't incise the horizontal lines yet. Instead of dragging the stick, use an up-and-down motion, making marks about ¼" (6mm) deep. The lines should look dry and crisp. If they are soggy or filling in with water, wait ten minutes and try again.

13 ➤ Finish the numerals. Remove the template and add the horizontal cross strokes at the top and bottom of each numeral. You may need to go over all the lines two or three times to even them out and clean them up. Don't jiggle the mold or the lines will disappear.

Do not try to make or clean up any incised lines after the concrete starts to harden (after about one hour); it may damage or crumble the stone. If you must, do this after 48 hours, using the tip of a bent paper clip. It is still risky because you may chip or flake the concrete.

14 ➤ Set the stone aside to harden for 48 hours. Use the board to move the stone to a safe location. Cover it loosely with plastic and spray it with water after 24 hours.

15 ➤ Clean up the stone. After 48 hours, gently scrub the excess concrete from the tiles, but don't scrub the numerals. Remove the stone from the mold, being careful of the gnomon. Round off the edges as shown on page 289. Rinse the stone well.

16 ➤ Elevate the stone and let it cure. Let the stone cure, elevated on a rack or on pencils, for five more days. Cover it loosely with plastic so that it cures slowly, which makes a sturdier stone. Spray it with water every 24 hours. After five days, the stone will be ready for use.

To enlarge this pattern for a
12" mold, use a copy machine
to enlarge it 200%.

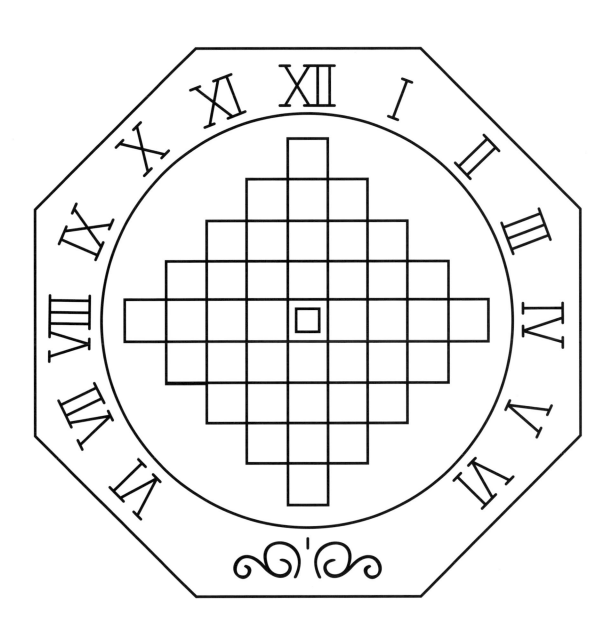

Garden Stakes and Paperweights

Here are some ideas for using up odd tesserae from your other projects. Small mosaics can be paperweights, tiny garden decorations, or with a little ingenuity, fun flower stakes for the garden. "Plant" them in your garden for the summer, then bring them inside for the winter to remind you of warm summer days. I used cookie cutters as molds and found that the lack of a backing was no problem if I set the cookie cutter on a pan covered with sand. If you use a plastic deli container for a mold, just punch a hole in the side for inserting the stake, then plan to cut the mold apart to remove the stone when it has hardened.

All kinds of molds may be used for making paperweights. If you use metal tart pans, aluminum pans or other metal molds, you must paint them with a release agent such as dishwashing liquid. Small plastic deli containers are perfect for making these small mosaics, and you can just throw them away when they become cracked and worn. The instructions show how to make the garden stakes. For paperweights, just follow the same steps except for the ones that show inserting the stake.

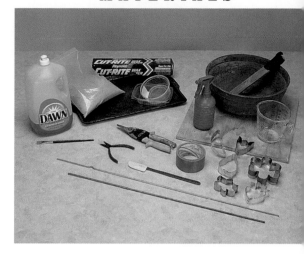

molds:
assorted metal cookie cutters
or deli containers

tin snips

needlenose pliers

duct tape or vinyl tape

metal stakes, 12" to 24"
(30cm to 60cm) long
and ¼" (6mm) diameter

glass nuggets and small pieces
of stained glass

pencil with eraser

scissors

dishwashing liquid, vegetable oil
spray or petroleum jelly

small paintbrush

waxed paper

cookie sheet or rigid board

dust mask

rubber gloves

1½ lbs. (68 kg) (about 2 cups)
stepping stone concrete mix
will make two to three flowers

small mixing bowl

cookie sheet with sand

mixing tool (craft stick)

water

1 cup (288g) fine sand

tablespoon

optional: rubber spatula,
water spray bottle
skid-resistant backing

2 ➤ Cut the cookie cutter.
Prepare the cookie cutter mold by cutting a hole in it for the stake. Use tin snips to cut open the cookie cutter. Cut all the way through.

1 ➤ Lay out tesserae. You can lay out your pieces on a paper tracing of your mold, or you can place the tesserae directly into the wet mix without planning ahead.

3 ➤ Cut small notches. On one end at the halfway point cut a tiny notch about ⅛" (3mm) long. Do the same to the other end.

4 ➤ Bend back the corners. Use needlenose pliers to bend the four notch points out so that when you close the cookie cutter there will be a small opening for the stake to fit through. Pinch the sharp points down for safety.

5 ➤ Tape cookie cutter back together. Pinch the cookie cutter closed and insert the stake through the hole. Use duct tape to tape the cookie cutter closed. Insert the stake.

6 ➤ Apply a release agent. Use a small brush to cover the inside of the metal cookie cutter or tart pan with a thin coat of dishwashing liquid or petroleum jelly.

If the tart pan has an indented design on the bottom, as this one has, fill the indentation with sand to keep the wet mix out.

8 ➤ Fill the molds. Using a rubber spatula or your gloved hand, fill the molds with mix, pushing it down firmly. Push the mix firmly around the stake and smooth the surface. Don't fill it to the top because embedding the pieces will raise the level of mix, possibly overflowing the mold.

9 ➤ Embed the tesserae. Transfer the tesserae and use a pencil eraser to embed. Stay ⅛" (3mm) inside the edges. Tap the sides of the mold a few times and lightly smooth the surface with your fingertips.

10 ➤ Set the stones aside to harden for 48 hours. Cover the molds loosely with plastic. Spray with water after 24 hours.

11 ➤ Clean up the stones. After 48 hours, clean the surface as described on page 289. Untape the cookie cutter and carefully peel it away. (If you used a tart pan, turn it upside down and tap it gently.) Small concrete pieces are very fragile at this stage, so handle them with care. Round off the edges and rinse the stones.

7 ➤ Prepare the baking sheet. Protect the baking sheet with a piece of waxed paper; sprinkle it with a thin layer of sand. Set the cookie cutter on the sand and make sure the stake is level. The edge of my baking sheet did that nicely, but you may need to prop yours up a little more.

Estimate the amount of mix you will need to fill the cookie cutter or mold. If you start with 1 cup (3.4kg) of mix, add 3 tablespoons (45ml) of water and stir well. If needed, add a few drops of water at a time. The thick mix should clump together in your hand and won't seep under the cookie cutter. Check the time or set a timer for one hour.

While you're embedding, if the surface cracks because the mix is hardening or if the stake is bumped, spray the surface once with water, smooth it with your gloved fingers, and continue embedding.

12 ➤ Elevate the stones and let them cure. Let the stones cure, elevated on a rack or on pencils, for five more days. Cover them loosely with plastic to slow the curing process. Spray them with water every 24 hours. After five days the garden stakes will be ready to be "planted." The paperweights need an additional seven days to cure. Cut cork, felt or skid-resistant backing to match the shape of each paperweight and glue it to the bottom.

Gallery

Here are more mosaics that use the same techniques as the projects in this book. Any simple shape can be a source of inspiration for your mosaics. It has been a pleasure sharing my ideas and creations with you. I hope you will spend many fun hours making your own unique mosaics!

Resources

Most mosaic materials can be found at your local craft store. Also look for materials at garden stores, aquarium stores, tile outlets and stained glass stores. Fast-setting concrete is not used in the projects in this book because it sets up too quickly.

CARTER GLASS MOSAIC TILE, DISTRIBUTED BY
HAKATAI ENTERPRISES, INC.
910 Hohokam Dr., Suites 113/114
Tempe, AZ 85281
(888) 667-2429
www.carterglassmosaic.com
➤ Vitreous glass tile in 42 colors

DELPHI STAINED GLASS
3380 East Jolly Road
Lansing, Michigan 48910
(800) 248-2048
www.delphiglass.com
➤ Ceramic tile, smalti, pre-cut stained glass

DIAMONDCRETE
(800) 699-7765
www.diamondcrete.net
➤ Manufacturer of DiamondCRETE fast-setting outdoor cement. Check the web site for stores, plus information about making stepping stones, sealing concrete and Tip of the Month.

DIAMOND TECH INTERNATIONAL
5600 C Airport Blvd.
Tampa, FL 33634
(800) 937-9593
www.dticrafts.com
➤ FlashCrete fast-setting outdoor cement and stained glass pre-cut mosaic pieces

E-Z CRAFT PRODUCTS
2354 Chapman Highway
Sevierville, TN 37876
(800) 311-6529
www.ezcraft.net
➤ Mosaic Mania: packages of color-coordinated stained glass pieces

MILESTONES PRODUCTS COMPANY
15127 NE 24th Street, Suite 332
Redmond, WA 98052
(425) 882-1987
www.milestonecrafts.com
➤ StoneCraft stone mix, color pigment, molds, bags of mosaic glass, ceramic tiles, pebbles, stone lettering stamps and tools, and stepping stone kits

MOSAIC MERCANTILE
P.O. Box 78206
San Francisco, CA 94107
(877) 9-MOSAIC (toll-free)
www.mosaicmercantile.com
➤ Mosaic tile, kits and accessories

MOSAIC TILE SUPPLY
10427 1/2 Unit A Rush Street
South El Monte, CA 91733
http://mosaicsupply.com/
➤ Manufacturer of vintage Italian mosaic tile, tools, stained glass, smalti, and polished abalone for mosaics

MOUNTAINTOP MOSAICS
Elm Street PO Box 653
Castleton, VT 05735
(800) 564-4980
mountaintopmosaics.com/
➤ Vitreous glass mosaic tile, smalti, friendly advice

QUIKRETE COMPANIES
(800) 282-5828
www.quikrete.com
➤ Manufacturer of Concrete Patcher

SEA GLASS, INC.
7000 Boulevard East
Guttenberg, NJ 07093
(973) 344-2222
www.seaglassinc.com
➤ Chunky glass in various colors

SPECTRUM GLASS COMPANY, INC.
P.O. Box 646
Woodinville, WA 98072-0646
(425) 483-6699
www.spectrumglass.com
➤ Manufacturers of art glass

STAINED GLASS WAREHOUSE
97 Underwood Road
Fltecher, NC
(888) 616-7792 (toll-free)
www.stainedglasswarehouse.com
➤ Molds, concrete, stained glass

SUNSHINE GLASSWORKS
111 Industrial Pkwy.
Buffalo, NY 14227
(800) 828-7159
www.sunshineglass.com
➤ Molds, mosaic glass tile, stained glass

TABULARASA
Order smalti diectly from Italy from the Web site: www.tabularasa.com/

WITS END MOSAICS
5224 West State Road 46, Box 134
Sanford, FL 32771
(407) 323-9122
www.mosaic-witsend.com
➤ Smalti, glass and ceramic tiles, glass nuggets, books and tips

Mosaic Organizations and Web Sites

Mosaic Matters, an online magazine
http://www.asm.dircon.co.uk

British Association for Modern Mosaics
www.bamm.org.uk/index.htm

The Society of American Mosaic Artists
www.scsu.edu/sama

Cole Sonafrank's links to Mosaic Forums, Resources & Studios
http://kokomo.gi.alaska.edu/MosaicLinks.html

Author's Web Site

www.sdonnellydesign.com

WREATHS

for Every Season

by June Apel with Chalice Bruce

Table of Contents

page 380 Introduction   **page 382** Wreathmaker's Toolkit   **page 384** Choosing Your Base

page 386 Selecting Flowers   **page 387** Basic Techniques   **page 388** Bowmaking 101   **page 391** Wreath Makeovers

392
‹ The Spirit of Spring

424
Summer Glory ›

Spring Medley **394**

Picture of Spring **400**

Easter Basket Wreath **406**

Sherbet Pinwheel Wreath **412**

Keepsake Wreath **418**

426 Lilac Picnic Chandelier

432 Seaside Wreath

438 Americana Wreath

442 Garden View Wreath

448 Terra Cotta Pot-Topper

454
‹ Fall Homecoming

Fall Bounty Wreath **456**

Pumpkin Garland **462**

Country Roads Wreath **466**

Cornhusk & Curls Wreath **470**

Cornucopia Dessert Wreath **478**

484
Merry Winter ›

486 Winter Berry Wreath

492 Glitter 'n' Glow Candle Ring

498 Sugarplums Wreath

504 Sweetheart Wreath

page 510 Resources

Wreaths Make the Seasons Go 'Round!

Living in the hills of Western Pennsylvania, surrounded by woods and cornfields, I am blessed with a perfect view of nature's annual journey from spring to winter and back again. It's a wondrous show to behold, and glorious inspiration for creating wreaths for every season.

In this book, step by step and season by season, I'll show you how easy it is to make wreaths to brighten every room of your home, handmade gifts from your heart (the best kind!), and even your own original versions of wreaths you've admired in stores or catalogs, only for a lot less money. Along the way, I'll share favorite tricks I've learned in 30 years of wreathmaking—little ways to make your crafting more enjoyable and rewarding.

While materials lists and instructions detail precisely what you need to recreate each wreath as shown, use them as guidelines rather than rules. Take creative detours according to your own whims and fancies. I've included variations on every project to illustrate some of the endless possibilities. If, in the end, your wreath doesn't look exactly like mine, good for you! That means it's uniquely yours!

Making a wreath is a great way to pause and celebrate life's simple pleasures—nature's bounty, old-fashioned decorating romance, the satisfaction of creating something with your own hands. I hope the simple steps in this book will lead you far beyond the 20 projects featured here, into a joyful lifetime of wreathmaking.

Best wishes for season after season of celebration!

—June Apel

To help you choose the best wreath project based on the amount of time you want to devote and your skill level, use these helpful ratings at the beginning of each project. And don't be afraid to tackle the more challenging wreaths—the step-by-step photos and instructions will guide you through every project. Have fun!

TIME

⏱ Can be completed in an afternoon

⏱ ⏱ Can be completed in a day

⏱ ⏱ ⏱ Can be completed in a weekend

DIFFICULTY

❀ **EASY** (You couldn't mess up if you tried!)

❀ ❀ **INTERMEDIATE** (A bit more involved, but you can do it!)

❀ ❀ ❀ **ADVANCED** (Requires a little extra patience and finesse.)

Wreathmaker's Toolkit

Three Rules for Making Great Wreaths

Okay, so they're more like suggestions than rules. Just keep them in mind and you can't go wrong.

1. DON'T SKIMP ◆ When I make a wreath, I like it to be substantial. Be generous with your flowers and other decorations. It's probably the easiest secret to good-looking wreaths.

2. BUILD TO LAST ◆ If you're going to make a wreath—especially if you're making it as a gift—take the time to do it right. Sometimes the smallest details like securing materials with glue *and* wire can make the difference between a wreath that lasts a few months and one that lasts a few years.

3. DON'T MIX MEDIA ◆ Mixing dried flowers and silk leaves on the same wreath creates an odd effect. Keep natural with natural and artificial with artificial.

Wherever you find your inspiration—a stroll through the craft store, your own backyard or the pages of this book—this chapter will help you make the most of it. Here you'll find information on basic tools, techniques and supplies...everything you need to create your own one-of-a-kind wreaths!

Basic Supplies and Tools ›

Most craft stores carry the basic supplies and tools you need to create beautiful wreaths. You can also buy any hard-to-find materials from your local florist.

◆ **florist greening pins** Sometimes referred to as S-pins, greening pins are used for securing large flower heads, bows and other materials to your base. I always buy mine in bulk because I go through them so quickly.

◆ **florist wire (paddle wire)** Sold in a variety of gauges (the lower the gauge, the heavier the wire), florist wire comes in handy for a multitude of uses. A 28-gauge works well for most tasks, from making bundles to attaching materials to your base. The thread-like 30-gauge is nice for lightweight tasks where you want the wire to be inconspicuous, such as securing moss to a base or tying a bow. Use a heavier gauge wire for heavy-duty tasks, like attaching the branch in the Garden View Wreath (page 442) or making hanging loops. Keep a variety of colors (green, silver, black, gold) on hand and use whichever blends in best.

◆ **stem wire** This wire is used to add length to a flower stem and to make "picks." Use heavier gauges for making hanging loops for your wreaths. The light, fabric-wrapped stem wire makes wonderful grapevine-like tendrils (see the Pumpkin Garland, page 462).

◆ **coiled florist wire** Because it doesn't kink like the paddle wire, I prefer using heavier-gauge coiled wire to make my hanging loops.

◆ **straight pins** Among other miscellaneous uses, pins are handy to use as an alternative to hot glue when working on foam forms. The shorter ones are most convenient.

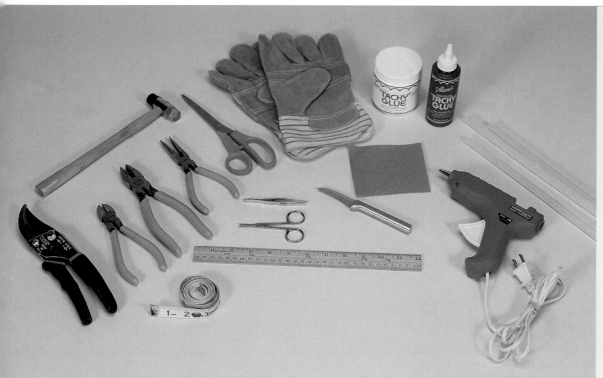

Tools (CLOCKWISE): Gloves, craft glue, very fine sandpaper, small knife, glue gun and glue sticks, ruler, tweezers, cuticle scissors, tape measure, pruners, assorted pliers, tack hammer, scissors.

♦ **needle and thread** Always good to have on hand when you're working with fabrics and bows. You never know when you might need a stitch.

♦ **floral tape** This self-sealing tape is used for hiding wire stems and hanging loops.

♦ **twine, narrow ribbons and embroidery threads** Keep a variety of colors around for tying and attaching bows.

♦ **floral and acrylic spray paint** I occasionally use paint to perk up colors, to add bright silver and gold accents (buy the 14K kind for maximum sheen), and to salvage dried flowers or leaves that have lost their color but are in good condition otherwise. For best results, apply multiple light coats, allowing to dry after each coat.

<TIP>
Spraying your materials in a cardboard box will help confine the overspray.

♦ **aroma oils** There are a multitude of scents from which to choose—floral, fruity, spicy, you name it. I prefer oils to aroma sprays because they're more economical. Aroma oils will stain flowers and ribbons, so be sure to apply carefully with an eyedropper. Use sparingly—a drop or two is all you need.

♦ **acrylic paint and paintbrush** Basic colors (white, green, brown) are handy for disguising wires and raw edges. You'll need a variety of colors for the eggs in the Easter Basket Wreath, the birdhouse in the Garden View Wreath, and other accents.

♦ **clear acrylic spray** Use sparingly. A couple of thin coats will help protect and preserve your dried flowers. It's an especially good idea for candle rings and other wreaths that will be handled and moved a lot. Expect a slight darkening of colors; test on individual flowers before spraying the whole wreath. You can use any finish, from matte to gloss, depending on the effect you're after.

♦ **glue gun and glue sticks** The glue gun is the MVP of wreathmaking tools! Don't bother buying the top-of-the-line—it will soon be covered with bits of dried flowers and moss. Do buy the longer glue sticks—they're a bit more economical, plus you don't have to stop as often to reload.

♦ **craft glue** Keep two types on hand: thicker glue in a jar for applying small, individual flowers; and all-purpose glue in a bottle for other applications where fast drying is not a concern.

♦ **tweezers** Just the thing for working with delicate little flowers and for picking glue strings off your finished wreath.

♦ **scissors** At the very least, get a good pair of standard scissors for cutting ribbon. Small, cuticle-type scissors come in handy for detail work, like snipping small flowers, reshaping a leaf and trimming fine ribbons. I also keep utility shears for cutting fine wires.

♦ **assorted pliers** Needlenose pliers are especially useful for bending heavy wires and making hanging loops. You will also need a pair of wire-cutters for working with heavy wire and silk flower stems.

♦ **pruners** Handy for trimming thick dried flower stems and grapevines.

♦ **ruler or tape measure**

♦ **small knife** Handy for shaping florist foam.

♦ **gloves** A little extra protection for working with grapevines or thistles.

♦ **small tack hammer** For anchoring florist pins into fabric- or ribbon-covered foam bases.

♦ **very fine sandpaper** Among other random uses, I use sandpaper to touch up miniature birdhouses and other wooden accessories.

Choosing Your Base

♦♦♦ Choosing the right base for your wreath will not only make your wreath look its best, it will also make your crafting easier and more enjoyable. Here are some tips on working with the most common bases.

Straw >

This is my personal favorite. Not only are straw bases your cheapest option and easy to find in a wide range of sizes and shapes, they're also extremely versatile, easy to work with (they take gluing well and are easy to pin into), and appropriate for covering with anything from leaves to fabric. Straw bases are never perfectly round which, I think, only adds to the handcrafted charm of your finished wreath. Before you add a hanger or begin decorating, take a moment to decide on the most pleasing orientation of your wreath. Once you decide on the top, mark it with a piece of narrow ribbon that can be removed later.

Grapevine >

Grapevines are another inexpensive and fun base to work with. They offer a nice, wide surface area, plenty of places to wire your bundles, and lots of little nooks and crannies to tuck in decorations and stems. A grapevine wreath is a great choice if you're after a rustic or country look, or if you want to leave some of the base exposed, either left natural or spray painted for added color.

Grapevines come in many sizes and charming, irregular shapes. So, again, take a moment before you start decorating to decide which side you want to be the top. If you have access to grapevines, you can even make your base from scratch! (See page 408 for easy instructions.)

Foam >

If a nice, smooth finish and uniform shape is what you're after, a foam base is an excellent choice. This base works very well with lace and fabrics, lending itself to polished, Victorian looks. It also works well with silk flowers to make a lightweight wreath—especially nice for people with plastered walls who prefer using adhesive hooks to nails.

Because the foam is so dense, you may need to use your trusty tack hammer to insert florist pins, especially when your wreath is covered with fabric or ribbon. Hot glue will melt the foam, so opt for a low-temperature glue gun.

Metal Ring >

Sold at most craft stores, these welded rings are perfect when you need a strong, thin, perfectly round base—especially for horizontal formats like the Lilac Picnic Chandelier (page 426) and the Pumpkin Garland (page 462). They're also fun to use in combination with another wreath base. (See Sugarplums Wreath, page 498.)

Bay Leaf and Other Ready-to-Decorate Bases >

If a quick and easy wreath is what you want, consider starting with a plain base of bay leaves, lemon leaves, pine, cedar, pussy willow, grasses, baby's breath… the list goes on and on. It's the most expensive of the base options discussed here. To make sure you're getting the most for your money, give the wreath a gentle shake to check for excessive shedding and to make sure leaves are attached securely.

Etc. >

Keep your eyes open for unusual and unconventional wreath opportunities, like the Terra Cotta Pot Topper (page 448) or ways to make your own base, like the Americana Wreath (page 438). Wooden curtain hoops make great little bases for miniature wreaths; use them to cheer up cabinets, table settings and gift wraps.

Hanging Tips

♦ ♦ ♦ ♦ ♦ ♦ ♦ ♦ ♦ ♦ ♦ ♦ ♦ ♦ ♦ ♦ ♦

• Be sure to position your hanging wires far down enough so they won't be visible from the front of your finished wreath.

• One hanger or two? Use two if your wreath is especially heavy, or if it's a heart or some other odd shape that's hard to balance with one hanging wire.

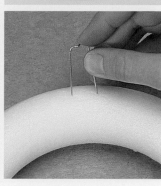

Straw: Adding a Hanger

Store-bought wreath hangers work well with straw bases. Put a dab of hot glue on the points of the hanger, insert, and glue again to secure. Alternately, it's also easy to make your own hanger. Simply slide your wire through the straw several times, forming a loop, then secure with glue.

Grapevine: Adding a hanger

Cut a generous length of wire, around 10" (25cm), and secure one end by twisting it around a few vines. Bend your wire to create the hanging hoop, and secure the other end in the same manner. Trim off excess wire. Use floral tape to cover any sharp points and camouflage the hanger.

Foam: Adding a hanger

Dip a floral pin in thick craft glue and insert into your wreath at a 45° angle, using a tack hammer as necessary. Squeeze on a dab of hot glue to secure. This type of hanger is only appropriate for a relatively lightweight wreath.

Adding hanging tabs.

Use this type of hanger for any ribbon- or fabric-covered base. Make a ring out of florist wire. (Wrap the wire around two fingers three times; on the fourth pass, twist the wire around the ring to secure.) Cut a short length* of ribbon. Fold in the raw ends to meet in the center and glue them down. Slip the ring onto your ribbon, and glue the ribbon in half. Glue the tab to the back of your wreath.

* The size of your finished tab should be proportionate to the size of your wreath—big enough to secure to and support your wreath, yet small enough so that the hoop doesn't show from the front of your wreath.

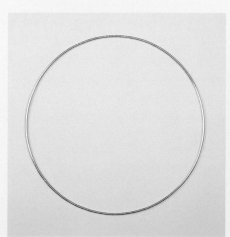

Metal Ring

Bay Leaf Wreath

Pine Wreath

Selecting Flowers

The Dried Wreath >

Dried plants—flowers, grasses, pods, foliage, etc.—are my favorite wreathmaking materials. I love the natural look and smell of them. I love gathering and drying my own. And I love the variety of colors and textures—from the earthy tones of goldenrod, ferns and mosses to the cheerful shades of larkspur and peonies, from delicate delphiniums to sassy sunflowers. I even enjoy the way the colors of a dried flower wreath fade and mellow over time, creating a cozy "antique" patina. It's like having a whole new wreath!

You can reasonably expect a dried flower wreath to hold its color and shape for up to a year. To avoid premature fading, display your wreath away from direct sunlight. Flip to page 391 for simple ways to revive your wreath when it does start showing its age.

The Silk Wreath >

Today's craft stores offer a staggering variety of silk flowers, foliage and artifical berries—a virtual garden of wreathmaking materials from which to pick! Silk wreaths outlive dried wreaths, holding their colors and shapes for several years—although they, too, will fade if displayed in direct sunlight. Silk wreaths are an appropriate choice for bathrooms, front doors and other sheltered outdoor displays.

Quality silk flowers don't come cheap, however, you can save money just by thinking ahead. Craft stores typically operate a season ahead of the rest of the world, so picks and flowers commonly go on sale early in the season. And you'll find even better deals at the end of the season and after holidays. With a quick spray of silver, those clearance-priced spring berries would be dandy.

Caring for Your Wreath >

An occasional dusting will help keep your wreath looking its best. A small paintbrush is the safest option for dried flower wreaths. For silk wreaths you could try using a hair-dryer (on the lowest setting), short bursts of pressurized air (the kind you use to clean computer keyboards) or a silk flower cleaner. If your bow looks flat, plump it up with a warm curling iron.

Dried, Preserved or Freeze-Dried?

SILICA GEL PRESERVED
Silica gel preserves the natural colors and shapes of flowers for a close-to-fresh look.

AIR-DRIED
Air-drying plants darkens the colors, changes the shapes, and results in a beautiful look very distinct from the fresh version. This is the most durable and longest lasting of these three options, and easy to do yourself.

FREEZE-DRIED
The most expensive of these three procedures, freeze-drying comes closest to maintaining that "fresh flower" color and shape.

Favorite Flowers for Air-Drying

amaranth ◆ artemesia ◆ baby's breath ◆ caspia ◆ celosia ◆ coneflower (I dry primarily for the centers—the petals will not keep their shape) ◆ dill ◆ dusty miller ◆ everlastings ◆ feverfew ◆ fountain grasses ◆ goldenrod ◆ holly ◆ hydrangea ◆ ivy ◆ larkspur ◆ lavender ◆ nigella ◆ peonies (even though it breaks my heart to cut them off the bush!) ◆ pussy willow ◆ Queen Anne's lace ◆ roses ◆ common sage ◆ statice ◆ strawflower (it's especially important to pick and hang these just as they're beginning to open) ◆ sweet Annie ◆ tansy ◆ wheat ◆ yarrow

Basic Techniques

Bundling >

Bundling will give your wreath a full, well-balanced look. It's also a far more efficient alternative to attaching flowers one by one. Sometimes you'll make bundles of the same type flower, as in the Sherbet Pinwheel Wreath (page 412). More often, you'll make mixed bundles. Note: Some flowers, such as sanfordii, are too fragile to bundle; it's best to add these flowers individually at the end.

Continuous Wiring >

This is a quick and handy technique for covering your base with flower bundles, as well as artificial picks, moss and other materials. Start by securing the end of your paddle wire around your base. Glue a row of flower bundles to your wreath, and wrap the wire taut across the stems and around the back of your wreath. Place the next row of bundles so that their heads hide the stems of the previous bundles. Wrap with wire. Continue until your wreath is completely covered. Cut and fasten the wire, and secure with a dab of hot glue.

Working With Hydrangea >

I use a lot of hydrangea in my wreaths, both as a filler and as a feature flower. It's nice and full, comes in a variety of colors, and is relatively inexpensive. It's also very fragile, so here are a few tips to make working with hydrangea a little easier.

Bundling and wiring
When making bundles using an assortment of flowers or grasses, keep the longer, spikier ones in back; the rounder, fuller ones in middle; and the smallest ones in front. The size of your bundles should be in proportion to the size of your wreath. Secure the stems with a few twists of 28-gauge florist wire.

Attaching hydrangea to your wreath
Break large hydrangea heads into smaller pieces—they're easier to work with this way, plus you can cover more area. Apply hot glue to your wreath, set the hydrangea in place, and secure it at the stem with a florist pin. Hold in place and apply light pressure for thirty seconds or so, just until the glue sets.

Touching up bare spots
Hydrangea will shed as you work with it. Don't just throw away these individual florets, use them to fill in bare spots. Apply using tacky glue and tweezers.

Bowmaking 101

Too many people are intimidated by the prospect of making a bow. Fact is, if you can make a loop and tie a knot, you've got what it takes to make a fabulous bow! If there is a "secret" to bowmaking, it's this: Use wired ribbon. Really. You simply can't make a bad bow with wired ribbon. You'll probably pay more than you would for non-wired ribbon, but it's so easy to shape and such a joy to work with that the extra investment is well worth it.

The Stacked Bow >

Nine times out of ten, I use some variation of this basic "stacked" bow. All you do is make two easy-as-pie bows and tie them together to form one nice, full bow.

But wait—it gets even better! Once you get the hang of it, you can make little adjustments and variations to create all kinds of bows! Create a layered look by using a satin bow on the bottom and a sheer ribbon on top. Work with four or five narrow ribbons at once to create a confetti-type bow like the one I use on the Sherbet Pinwheel Wreath (page 412). To create a bigger, fuller bow, simply make more loops per layer. Bigger yet? Just add more layers. The bow possibilities are endless…and, in these five simple steps, yours for the making!

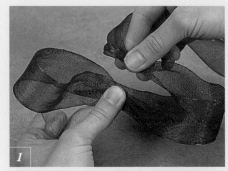

step 1
Begin by making two loops to establish the width of your bow.

step 2
Make two more loops of roughly the same size.

step 3
With a generous length of narrow ribbon, tie off the center of your bow tightly. (Don't trim off this ribbon yet, you'll be using it in step 5.) Cut the tail of your bow to the desired length. You now have the bottom layer of your bow.

step 4
Repeat steps 1 and 2, making a second four-looped bow slightly smaller than the first one. This will form the top layer of your bow.

step 5
Tie the two layers together using the tails of the narrow ribbon from step 3, keeping the knot on the back of your bow. Trim off the narrow ribbon or use it to attach your bow to your wreath. Arrange and fluff the loops, and there you have it…a beautiful, professional-looking bow! I knew you could do it!

The Flat Bow ›

Here's another easy bow to make when you want a simple, understated effect.

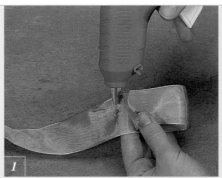

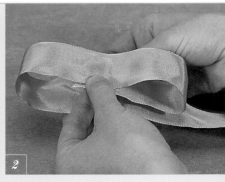

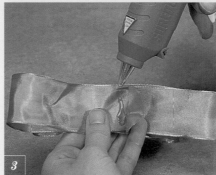

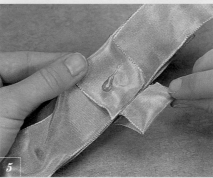

step 1
Bring in one end of your ribbon to make a loop. Secure the end with a dab of glue.

step 2
Make a second, equal loop and secure in the center with glue. If you like, you can use a pin to mark the center of your bow.

step 3
Make a second set of loops slightly larger than the first. Again, secure in the middle with glue.

step 4
Cut a length of ribbon approximately three times the ribbon's width. Glue one end to the back of your bow.

step 5
Bring the ribbon around the front of your bow, fold under the raw edge and glue down on the back of your bow.

step 6
Cut another length of ribbon twice as long as you want the tails. Fold this ribbon in half at a slight angle and glue to the back of your bow.

step 7
Finish off tails by folding the ribbon in half and cutting at an angle.

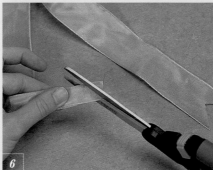

The Overlay Bow >

Say you find the perfect sheer ribbon for your wreath, only its pattern gets lost in a regular stacked bow. I have just the trick for you! You'll need equal lengths of a sheer ribbon and a base ribbon which should be in a coordinating color that accentuates the sheer ribbon's pattern.

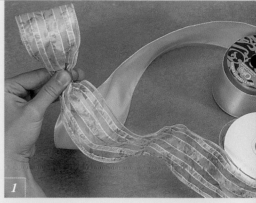

step 1

Layer your sheer ribbon on top of your base ribbon. Follow the directions on page 14 for making a stacked bow.

step 2

Finish your bow by squeezing a few drops of glue along the edges of the tails to secure the two
ribbons together.

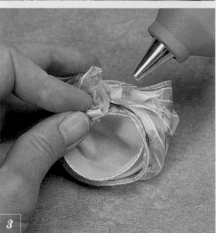

step 3

Make a loop of ribbon and secure the ends with glue.

step 4

Tie the glued seam of your loop with a length of narrow ribbon and attach to the center of your bow.

Wreath Makeovers

No matter how carefully you construct your wreath and how diligent you are to keep it out of direct sunlight, the day will come when your wreath starts showing its age. Just a few minutes of attention might make a world of difference. Here are a few tricks to revive a tired wreath:

♦ Replace the bow. Sometimes a fresh ribbon is all that's needed.

♦ Give it a little "trim." Simply snip off any stems that are broken or flowers that are faded. (Great additions to potpourri!)

♦ Replace key flowers that are faded or discolored, or simply add new flowers.

♦ A can of spray paint can go a long way, as the following makeovers illustrate.

♦ If your wreath is just too far gone, be sure to salvage any pods, berries, picks, etc. you might use in a future wreath.

Summer-to-Winter Makeover >

Before
This lemon-leaf base was a fine little decoration for my kitchen—until, that is, the leaves turned a drab brown and the roses faded.

After
First, I sprayed the entire wreath gold, roses and all. I added some silver accents (baker's fern and pinecones), a few pink pepperberries and finished with glitter and a bow.

Winter-to-Spring Makeover >

Before
This spruce wreath was my best buy of the season! It held all its needles through winter and beyond. Come spring, it was still in perfect condition, but almost completely drained of color. Besides, who ever heard of a spring evergreen wreath?

After
I sprayed the wreath a pretty yellow…added a ring of spring blooms—roses, veronica, rice flower, larkspur and hops—and voila! I'm the only house in the neighborhood with a spring spruce wreath!

The Spirit of Spring

♦♦♦ Winter softens into spring. I love the simple things about this time of the year—wild violets freckling woodland floors, the return of familiar birdsongs, the smell of green in the air. Time to open the windows wide and let the fresh air in!

Nothing airs out and perks up a room like your very own handmade wreath. Go with soft pastels and cheery colors for springtime. Incorporate the season's most jubilant blooms—tulips, daffodils, peonies, hydrangea, cherry blossoms and pansies. Add spring floral scents of violet, lilac, hyacinth and lily of the valley (Just a hint, like it's drifting in on a breeze).

The wreaths in this chapter are guaranteed to breathe the spirit of spring into your home. I recommend the Sherbet Pinwheel for playful souls, the Picture of Spring for artistic types, and the Spring Medley for those whose thoughts turn to romance this time of year. You'll also find a sweet-as-sugar Easter wreath, and the pretty and practical Keepsake Wreath—just the project for a rainy April day.

1

(above) EASTER BASKET WREATH; (opposite page starting from upper left, clockwise) SPRING MEDLEY, KEEPSAKE WREATH, SHERBERT PINWHEEL WREATH, PICTURE OF SPRING

Spring Medley

♦♦♦ ANY ROOM WILL FEEL A LITTLE SUNNIER WITH THIS SUMPTUOUS MEDLEY OF BLOOMS—THE FANCY, CASCADING BOW IS SIMPLY ICING ON THE CAKE! THIS STYLE OF LEMON LEAF WREATH IS VERY POPULAR THESE DAYS; YOU'LL SEE THEM IN VIRTUALLY EVERY HOME DECORATING CATALOG FOR ANYWHERE FROM $50 TO $120, DEPENDING ON THE SIZE AND COMPLEXITY (THIS SPRING MEDLEY WOULD PROBABLY RUN AROUND $90). BETWEEN YOU AND ME, IT'S RELATIVELY EASY TO MAKE (YES, EVEN THE BOW!)—AND FOR A LOT LESS MONEY. JUST THINK: YOU DON'T HAVE TO PAY FOR SHIPPING, PLUS YOU GET THE PLEASURE OF MAKING IT YOURSELF!

TIME

DIFFICULTY

2 straw wreaths: one 14" (36cm) and one 18" (46cm)—try to find wreaths that fit together snugly (see step 1)

9-12 dried peonies (pink)

3 heads dried hydrangea (light green)

6-9 dried rose heads (yellow)

nigella orientalis

starflowers (natural)

larkspur (white)

rice flower (white)

sanfordii

silver queen sage

ti tree (pink)

lemon leaves (salal)

feather fern

pepperberries (pink)

5 yards (4.5m) of 1½" (4cm) wired taffeta ribbon (pink) for bow

florist wire

florist pins

hot glue gun

Substitute Your Favorites

♦ **FEATURE FLOWERS**: freeze-dried roses, magnolias, crabapples

♦ **"RADIATING" FLOWERS**: amaranthus, baby eucalyptus, fescue grass, flax, heather, lavender, lepto, pennyroyal, bracken fern, flowering oregano

♦ **FILLER FLOWERS**: Australian daisies, feverfew, lemon mint, rodanthe, coxcomb, yarrow, hops, globe amaranth, strawberry flowers

step 1

Make the double base. Press the smaller wreath flush inside the larger wreath. Glue along the seam, and wire to secure. Attach a wire for hanging (see page 385).

Secret to Success

◆ ◆ ◆ ◆ ◆ ◆ ◆ ◆ ◆ ◆ ◆ ◆ ◆ ◆

As you add each type of flower, arrange them first and glue in place only when you're happy with the placement and spacing. Use florist pins as needed.

Puff Up Your Peonies

◆ ◆ ◆ ◆ ◆ ◆ ◆ ◆ ◆ ◆ ◆ ◆ ◆ ◆

If your dried peonies are a little too "mushed," steam them just until the petals start to soften, then blow into the center to puff open. Stand upright and allow to dry.

step 2

Build a base of lemon leaves. Using a dab of hot glue (and florist pins as needed), secure the base of each leaf to the straw base. Fill in the outer and inner edges first, then fill in between, placing leaves in random directions. Completely cover the straw base.

step 3

Add peonies and hydrangea. Cut the peony stems to about 3" (8cm). Evenly space three clusters of peonies around your wreath. Glue and insert stems into the straw. (If you're having trouble, use a screwdriver to poke the holes.) For added dimension, let your peonies sit above the lemon leaves rather than nestling them. Center a head of hydrangea between each cluster of peonies; break one of the heads in half, leaving room in between to add your bow later. (See page 387 for special tips on working with hydrangea.)

step 4

Add roses. Evenly place roses in clusters of three or four. (Don't forget to save that space for your bow!) Glue into place.

step 5

Add nigella and starflowers. Break off sprigs of nigella and cluster in a few spots around the inner perimeter of your wreath. Make bundles of starflowers and insert them randomly around the center and inside edge

step 6

Add larkspur. Cut the larkspur into 3" to 4" (8cm to 10cm) sprigs and cluster around the outside of your wreath, establishing a radiating effect that will be accentuated with the flowers to follow.

step 7

Add rice flowers and sanfordii. Make small bundles of rice flowers. Use these bundles and sprigs of sanfordii to fill in around the peonies, roses and hydrangea. (You're still saving room for your bow, right?)

step 8
Add silver queen sage and ti tree. Make 3" to 5" (8cm to 13cm) bundles of silver queen sage and ti tree, and arrange in a radiating pattern around the outside of your wreath.

step 9
Add feather fern. Break off 3" to 5" (8cm to 13cm) pieces of feather fern and work them in along the outer perimeter of your wreath. (It's always best to add your most delicate drieds toward the end.)

step 10
Add pepperberries. Almost done! For the final dried element, add small clusters of pepperberries randomly around your wreath, filling in any holes.

step 11
Now for the bow. There's a simple secret to this lush, sprawling bow: Make two stacked bows with 15" to 20" (38cm to 51cm) tails and "stagger" them in the space you've been saving. Use glue and a florist pin per bow to secure.

step 12
Arrange the tails. Finesse the tails to cascade down and around your wreath, tucking under flowers here and there. Use florist pins in strategic places to secure—just be sure they are hidden by your flowers.

♦♦♦ The Spring Medley... instant sunshine!

Lemon leaves quickly lose their color in direct sunlight, so choose a nice, sheltered spot to display your beautiful Spring Medley. If you really enjoy this style of wreath, don't stop at spring. You can follow the same basic steps to create a medley for any season! The only rule is to have one featured element—in this case, the peonies. Try sunflowers for summer, yarrow for fall, and pomegranates for winter! For the other flowers, just aim for a variety of textures and sizes.

variation

Go monotone!

This is a wonderful wreath to do in a monotone scheme. For my "shades of white" variation, I featured freeze-dried gardenias, artemesia, eucalyptus leaves and starched antique lace.

Picture of Spring

♦♦♦ SPRING IS FOREVER BLOOMING IN THIS GLEEFUL LITTLE TRIO! IT'S THREE TIMES THE FUN—
A WONDERFUL WAY TO START YOUR WREATHMAKING YEAR, A GREAT DECORATIVE SOLUTION
FOR ANY NARROW, HARD-TO-DECORATE WALL AND A SUPER SPRINGTIME GIFT. DESPITE THE
INTRICATE APPEARANCE, IT IS RELATIVELY EASY AND INEXPENSIVE TO MAKE, ES-
PECIALLY IF YOU USE LEFTOVER ROSES FROM YOUR CHRISTMAS CRAFTING.
THE HARDEST PART IS DECIDING HOW TO DISPLAY YOUR TRIO. WILL IT BE
THE RIBBON? THE FRAME? BOTH? I COULDN'T MAKE UP MY MIND, SO I'LL LET
YOU DECIDE FOR YOURSELF!

TIME
⏱ ⏱ ⏱

DIFFICULTY
☘

three 6" (15cm) foam
wreaths

assorted dried flowers
in various stages of
bloom: spray roses
(pinks and white),
larkspur or delphinium
(white, blue, pink),
Australian daisies,
ammobium (yellow),
plus a few miniature rosebuds

1 large bunch of preserved
evergreen ming fern

10 yards of inexpensive, 1"
(2.5cm) ribbon (green)

3 yards of 1½" (4cm) wired
ribbon for bow (optional)

3 small buttons (optional)

picture frame, opening should
measure no less than 8" x 24"
(20cm x 61cm)

6 brads

fishing line

sharp knife

florist wire

tweezers

craft glue

acrylic spray

hot glue gun

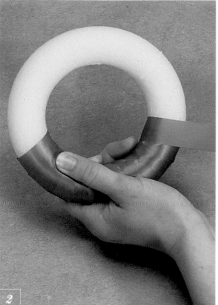

step 1

Flatten the backs. Use a knife to carefully slice about one-third off the back of each wreath. This will make them sit nicely against the wall.

‹NOTE›
Some craft stores sell foam wreaths that come with one flat side. This will save you a step.

step 2

Wrap in ribbon. Wrap each wreath with green ribbon, securing the beginnings and ends of your ribbon with a dab of hot glue. Add a tab at the top of each wreath for hanging (see page 385).

step 3

Make ming bundles. Cut your ming into short sprigs. Use florist wire to tie small bundles about the size of large grapes.

step 4

Cover wreaths with ming. Work your way around the front of each wreath, hiding the stem of each ming bundle behind the head of the next. Cover wreaths #1 and #2 solidly, creating a lush, grassy-looking surface. For wreath #3, just be sure to cover the inner and outer perimeters well; you can be sparing in between. Use scissors to neaten your ming as necessary.

step 5

Separate flowers by bloom-stage. Separate each type of flower into three groupings: buds (for wreath #1), partially opened flowers (for wreath #2) and full blooms (for wreath #3). Take care not to mix up your flowers; decorate each wreath only with its designated bloom-stage.

Timesaver

◆ ◆ ◆ ◆ ◆ ◆ ◆ ◆ ◆ ◆ ◆ ◆ ◆ ◆ ◆ ◆ ◆ ◆ ◆ ◆

For a different look that's quicker to achieve, cover with soft sheet moss or reindeer moss instead of ming.

step 7
First, wreath #1. Using tweezers and craft glue, add sprigs of larkspur around the rose clusters.

step 8
Add ammobium buds, mini rosebuds and some Australian daisy buds, and wreath #1 is done! Apply a light coat of acrylic spray.

tip

If your larkspur is too delicate to dip in glue, carefully squeeze a drop of glue directly on the wreath and use tweezers to set the flowers in place.

step 6
Start with the roses. Arrange and glue your roses in six groupings around your first two wreaths. Be extra generous with the roses on wreath #3. Next, take each individual wreath to completion.

♦WREATH #2

step 9
Now onto wreath #2. Fill in around the roses with larkspur.

step 10
In go the ammobium.

step 11
And finally the Australian daisies. Finish with a light coat of acrylic spray. Two wreaths down, one to go!

step 12
Now for wreath #3. This time, cover virtually the entire wreath with larkspur, allowing the ming to peek out around the inner and outer edges.

step 13
Add ammobium, fill in any holes with Australian daisies, and wreath #3 should be drenched in blooms! Don't forget the acrylic spray.

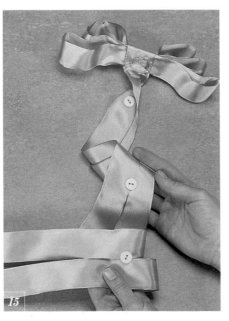

step 14
Frame the wreaths. Arrange the trio within your inverted frame. When you're happy with the spacing, use a ruler to mark off the top of each wreath on both sides of the frame. These marks indicate where to nail brads; be sure to leave enough sticking out so you can string fishing line horizontally from brad to brad, making it as taut as possible. Suspend the wreaths by bending the hanging loops downward to hook over the fishing line.

step 15
Add ribbon hanger. Instead of (or in addition to) framing your trio, you could display them on a pretty ribbon. Make a flat bow (see page 389) with long, 30" (76cm) tails. Arrange your trio vertically along the tails and mark off the top of each wreath. Stitch a button at each point, being certain to catch the inner edge of each tail in your stitches. Hang the wreaths on the buttons.

♦♦♦ Three cheers for your Picture of Spring!

Aren't your little wreaths beautiful? This simple format—themed groupings of small wreaths—offers endless variations, both in the materials you use and how you choose to display your finished wreaths. You could make a multi-colored trio of rosebud hearts and display them horizontally on a small branch. Create a variety of kitchen-herb samplers to adorn your cabinet doors. Or make a four-seasons quartet using artificial floral mini-picks—daffodils for spring, sunflowers for summer, leaves for fall, and poinsettias for winter.

variation

A merry little foursome!

Cover each small foam heart with a different type of preserved greenery, such as cedar, baker's fern, juniper and boxwood. Create the snow-dusted look by lightly drybrushing with white acrylic paint or liquid snow. I decorated my foursome with mini pinecones, jingle bells, brunia and coordinating bows.

Easter Basket Wreath

♦♦♦ HERE'S A NEAT TWIST ON WREATHMAKING. FIRST, I'LL SHOW YOU HOW TO MAKE YOUR OWN GRAPEVINE WREATH FROM SCRATCH. THEN YOU'LL SEE HOW TO TURN YOUR ORDINARY WREATH INTO A FUN-FILLED EASTER BASKET—A CHARMING DECORATION FOR FRONT DOOR, CHILD'S ROOM OR BUNNY TRAIL! FOR ADDED FUN, GET YOUR FAVORITE KIDS TO PITCH IN AND PAINT THE EGGS. SAVE A FEW FROM EACH YEAR (BE SURE TO MARK NAMES AND YEARS DISCRETELY ON THE BOTTOMS) AND BESTOW THEM ON THE KIDS WHEN THEY'RE OLDER AS THE START OF THEIR OWN FAMILY EASTER TRADITION.

TIME

DIFFICULTY

what you'll need

17" (43cm) metal ring

ten to fifteen 5' (1.5m) grapevines

8 stems silk tulips
(assorted spring colors)

artificial grass

stuffed Easter bunny and baby peep

miniature basket

12 decorated eggs (wood, ceramic or papier maché, the lighter the better)

3 yards (2.7m) of 2½" (6.3cm) ribbon for bow

24" (61cm) of 2½" (6cm) lace with one decorative edge

7 yards (6.3m) of 1½" (3.8cm) plisse ribbon (yellow); you can substitute grosgrain or any ribbon with body

20" x 20" (51cm x 51cm) piece of chicken wire; your hardware store will cut it for you by the yard, or buy it pre-packaged at a craft store

2 pieces of cardboard, about 20" x 12" (51cm x 30cm) each

2 blocks of florist foam

white masking tape

brown florist tape

florist wire

duct tape

hot glue gun

Save a Step

I'll show you how to create your own base out of grapevines, but you can get the same general effect by purchasing an oval grapevine wreath, about 20" x 15" (51cm x 38cm). Get the narrowest diameter you can find so your basket "handle" doesn't look out of proportion.

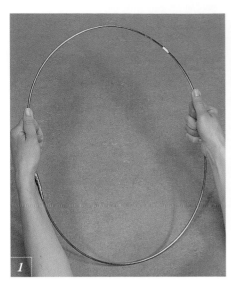

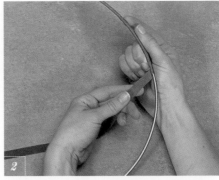

step 1
Shape hoop. Wrap duct tape around the weld of your metal ring to keep it from splitting. With the taped joint on the side, squeeze the ring into an oval shape.

step 2
Wrap hoop with tape. Wrap the entire hoop in brown florist tape so you won't notice it through the grapevines.

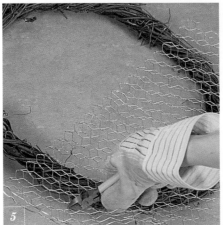

step 3
Entwine hoop with grapevine. Start by wiring on the end of a grapevine and wrapping it firmly around your hoop. (Use heavier vines first, saving the finer vines for the top layers of your wreath.) Take your time, pruning off any wild, unwieldy offshoots as you go. But try to save as many curlicues as possible—they'll add a nice sense of whimsy to your basket.

Before You Start

◆ ◆ ◆ ◆ ◆ ◆ ◆ ◆ ◆ ◆ ◆ ◆ ◆ ◆ ◆

Soak grapevines in water for one hour or, better yet, overnight. This makes them much more flexible and easier to work with.

step 4
Wrap, wrap, wrap. To start a new grapevine, tuck the end under previous vines and continue wrapping, always in the same direction. Continue until your grapevine wreath is about 1½" to 2" (3.8cm to 5cm) in diameter. Select the best-looking side to be the "handle" (or top) of your basket. Turn over and attach wire for hanging (see page 385).

step 5
Cut your basket. Wearing heavy gloves for protection, fold your chicken wire in half; you should now have a 10" x 20" (25cm x 50cm) piece. Carefully cut out the shape of your basket, using the bottom half of your wreath as a guide and adding about an inch (2.5cm) all around.

step 6
"Sew" chicken wire in place. Shape your chicken wire basket, bending it around to "hug" the grapevine. Flip your wreath over and use florist wire to tack the chicken wire to the grapevine every 3" to 4" (8cm to 10cm), starting at the top corner and working all the way around.

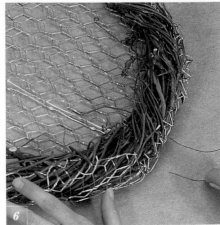

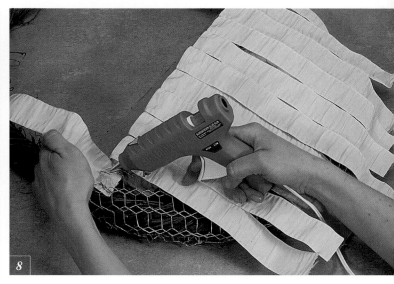

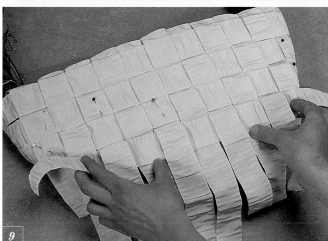

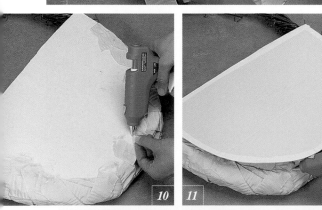

step 7

Finish basket base. Again using the bottom half of your wreath as a guide, cut both pieces of cardboard to size, this time adding about an inch (2.5cm) above the top of the chicken wire. Cut blocks of florist foam to fill the inside of your basket. Glue one of your cardboard pieces to the back of your wreath. Allow to dry, using weight or clamps to ensure a good, tight bond.

step 8

Attach vertical ribbons. For the vertical weaves of your basket, cut eight lengths of plisse ribbon at 14" (36cm) and four lengths at 10" (25cm). With the longer pieces in the center, arrange your ribbons across your chicken wire frame; the ribbons should butt against each other, and there should be at least ½" (1.3cm) overhang at the top and bottom of your basket. Secure only the top of each ribbon with a fine line of glue right where the ribbon folds behind the chicken wire. If you glue too far down there won't be room for your first horizontal weave.

step 9

Weave your basket. For the horizontal weaves, cut three lengths of plisse ribbon at 23" (58cm) and three lengths at 18" (46cm). Using the longer pieces at the top of your basket, weave into your vertical ribbons; there should be at least a ½" (1.3cm) overhang on either side. Cut additional lengths of ribbon as needed to completely cover the height of your basket.

step 10

Secure loose ends. Make sure all your ribbons form a nice, tight weave. Then turn your wreath over and glue down the loose ends to the cardboard. (If you want to be very diligent and ensure an extra-long life for your basket, use a needle and thread to tack each corner of your weave.)

step 11

Finish the back. Use masking tape to finish off the edge of your second piece of cardboard and glue in place on the back of your wreath. Again, clamp or weigh down and allow to dry.

step 12

"Plant" tulips. Now the real fun begins! Arrange tulips on one side of your wreath, inserting the stems into the florist foam.

step 13

Position and secure bunny. Snuggle your bunny into your tulips and carefully glue him into place.

step 14

Add mini-basket and build egg base. Glue your bunny's basket into place. Cut a few small pieces of florist foam and glue into the right side of your basket to serve as a base for your eggs.

step 15

Trim with lace. Carefully glue the lace along the top edge of your basket, securing both ends around the back of the wreath.

step 16

Pile in your eggs. Position your eggs and hot glue them into place. It's easiest to arrange half of them as the base layer, then stack your favorites on top.

step 17

Fill in with grass. Fill in around your bunny and eggs with little tufts of artificial grass. (The handle of a paintbrush comes in handy for tucking grass into tight spots!) Trim any unruly excess.

step 18

Add the bow. Make a bow. (I used an overlay bow—see page 390 for instructions.) Use a stem of wire, slipped through the back of your bow and bent in half, to secure your bow in the florist foam at the base of your tulips. Place your little peep into bunny's basket and you're done!

♦♦♦ Have a happy holiday with your Easter Basket!
If the bunny is a little too cute for your taste, leave him out and add more flowers. If you're making this as a gift, just pin Mr. Bunny in place so he can be removed later, and tuck some real candies into the mini-basket!

variation

Harvest Basket
For a rustic fall variation of the basket wreath, replace the ribbon with woven cornhusk—either natural or fabric-dyed, as I've used here. Fill with crabapples, gourds, artichokes, etc., either freeze-dried or artificial. Other adornments include assorted grasses, wheat, salal leaves and bittersweet.

411

Sherbet Pinwheel Wreath

what you'll need

TIME

DIFFICULTY

◆◆◆ AS PLAYFUL AS THE FIRST BREEZE OF SPRING, THE SHERBET PINWHEEL MAKES A LIGHT-HEARTED DECORATION FOR A CHILD'S BEDROOM, HALLWAY, POWDER ROOM OR ANYWHERE YOU WANT TO ADD A WHIRL OF COLOR. IT'S SWEET AND SIMPLE TO CREATE; ONCE YOU TRANSFER THE PATTERN TO YOUR WREATH, IT'S AN EASY MATTER TO FILL IN WITH DRIFTS OF CANDY TUFT. IT'S LIKE COLORING IN A COLORING BOOK!

2 foam wreaths, 12" (30cm) and 8" (20cm)

candy tuft (one bunch each of five spring colors)

Australian daisies

assortment of very narrow (⅛" [3mm] to ¼" [6mm]) satin and sheer ribbons for bow; select colors that coordinate with your candy tuft

raffia

6 yards (5.4m) of inexpensive 1" (2.5cm) ribbon (white)

florist wire

straight pins

florist pins

craft glue

hot glue gun

tweezers

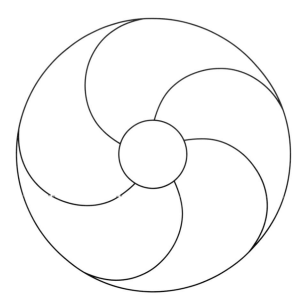

Sherbet Pinwheel Template

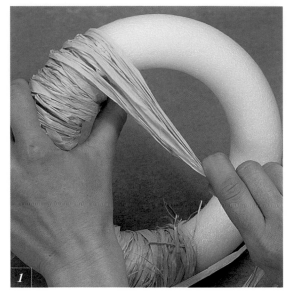

step 1

Raffia-wrap small wreath. Wrap the smaller wreath with raffia as necessary to achieve a good, tight fit inside the larger wreath.

step 2

Double your base. Insert the small wreath flush inside the larger wreath. Glue the seam and wrap with florist wire. Wrap the entire double-form in raffia to achieve a full, even surface to work on.

step 3

Wrap with ribbon. Wrapping your base with one continuous ribbon can be cumbersome, so try cutting your 1" (2.5cm) ribbon into 3-yard (2.7m) lengths. When you come to the end of a ribbon, glue it down, glue the next piece on top and secure both with a straight pin. Keep all your pins on one side of your wreath so you can hide them with the candy tuft.

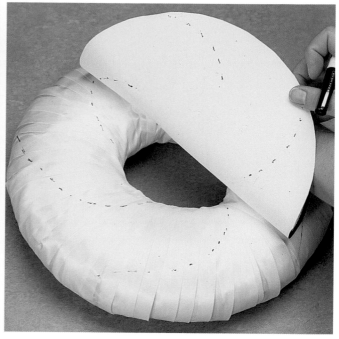

step 4

Transfer the pattern. Enlarge the pattern from page 40 to approximately 12" (30cm) wide or the diameter of your prepared base. Transfer the pattern to the front of your wreath (the side with the pins), using a sharp-point marker to poke through the pattern every inch or so. Turn over and attach a wire for hanging. (see page 385).

step 5

Make bundles of candy tuft. Cut your candy tuft into small sprigs. Use fine-gauge florist wire to tie small, single-color bundles about the size of large grapes.

step 6

Color your pinwheel. Now you're ready to fill in each section of your pinwheel pattern with a different color candy tuft! Take a minute to plan the most pleasing sequence of colors, then grab your glue gun and fill in one section at a time. Start from the inside and work your way out, hiding the stems of one bundle behind the head of the next for a solid, mossy effect. When you're done, check for any small holes or gaps; fill in with bits of candy tuft.

step 7

Outline with daisies. Working a couple inches (5cm) at a time, squeeze a thin line of glue between color sections and use tweezers to place Australian daisy heads. Arrange your daisies with a bit of zigzag to give your wreath a little extra personality.

step 8

Add a "confetti" bow. Make a stacked bow with your narrow ribbons (see page 388) and attach with a florist pin.

♦♦♦ The Sherbet Pinwheel Wreath—a real whirl of fun!

As long as you keep your wreath out of direct sunlight, the glorious colors should last a good, long time. If they do fade, try masking each section and perking up with florist spray. Or, better yet, make another Pinwheel Wreath! You can create the same pattern with different effects using caspia, hydrangea, rice flowers, mini roses, Australian daisies and other flowers that are available in an assortment of colors. The method of application will vary depending on the flower.

variation

Design your own
If you're a doodler, have fun creating an original pattern of your very own. I've colored in this swirly design with three shades of globe amaranth.

Keepsake Wreath

what you'll need

◆◆◆ IF (LIKE ME) YOU HAVE DRAWERS AND SHOEBOXES STUFFED WITH SNAPSHOTS, TICKET STUBS, GREETING CARDS AND OTHER RANDOM "TREASURES," THIS WREATH IS FOR YOU! THE KEEPSAKE WREATH OFFERS A PRETTY AND PRACTICAL ALTERNATIVE FOR KEEPING ALL THOSE SPECIAL MEMENTOS TOGETHER IN ONE PLACE. I CREATED THIS ONE FOR MY DAUGHTER'S WEDDING DAY, BUT YOU MIGHT CREATE ONE IN HONOR OF A MILESTONE ANNIVERSARY, A FAMILY REUNION OR A FAVORITE PET. THIS WREATH FEATURES AN INVITATION, A POEM (FRAMED), A ROSETTE FROM THE BRIDE'S SHOE, JEWELRY, GARTER, THE CORK FROM THE COUPLE'S FIRST CHAMPAGNE TOAST, FAVORS, AND EVEN A COUPLE OF COOKIES FROM THE DESSERT TABLE! A TRUE HEIRLOOM TO PASS ON FROM GENERATION TO GENERATION, THE KEEPSAKE WREATH IS A GREAT "SPRING CLEANING" PROJECT TO WORK ON WHILE YOU'RE WAITING FOR YOUR SEEDS TO SPROUT!

TIME
⏱

DIFFICULTY
☘

14" (36cm) foam base

polyester batting

preserved flowers: 2 small heads of dried hydrangea, 2 stems of spray roses, 3 to 5 rose heads and a few ivy leaves (or substitute your own significant flowers, silk or dried)

10 yards (9m) of 2½" (6.4cm) lace with at least one finished side

8 yards (7m) of narrow (¼" to ¾" [6mm to 19mm]) burgundy ribbon; I used two coordinating ribbons for interest, but you can use the same ribbon if you prefer

3 yards of 1½" (1.3cm) wired ivory satin ribbon for the bow

small framed snapshots and assorted mementos

corsage pins (optional)

florist pins

straight pins

hot glue gun

Preserve Special Occasion Cookies

◆ ◆ ◆ ◆ ◆ ◆ ◆ ◆ ◆ ◆ ◆ ◆

Melt paraffin wax. Quickly dip cookie, completely covering in a thin layer of wax. Allow to cool. Repeat.

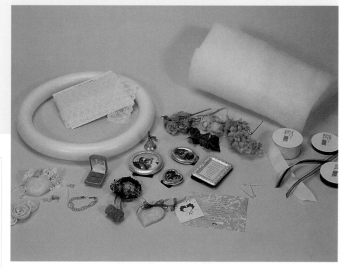

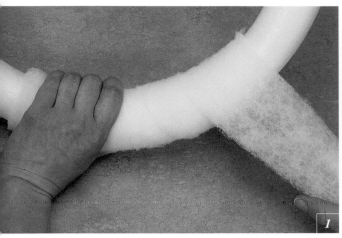

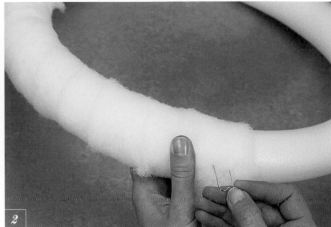

step 1

Wrap base with batting. Cut polyester batting into 3" (8cm) wide strips. Use a dab of glue and a florist pin to secure the beginning of the first strip to your foam base. Wrap the strip around your base so it's taught but not tight, keeping a consistent overlap to achieve a nice, even layer of padding.

step 2

Add more strips. When you come to the end of a strip, secure it along with the beginning of the next strip using a dab of hot glue and a florist pin. Continue until your wreath is completely covered with a generous, even layer of padding. Go around a second or even a third time, depending on the look you want to achieve.

step 3

Top with lace. Now cover your padded wreath with one continuous piece of lace. Begin by securing one end with a dab of glue and a florist pin.

step 4

Keep an even overlap. Wrap your wreath with the lace, keeping it taught but not tight and maintaining an even overlap all the way around. When your wreath is completely covered, secure the end of your lace with a florist pin and attach a wire for hanging (see page 385).

step 5

Spiral with narrow ribbon. Cut a 4-yard (3.6m) length of narrow ribbon. Pin it to the front of your wreath, near the point where your lace ends. (Later, you will place your bouquet in this area to hide the rough edges and pinheads.) Spiral the ribbon evenly around your wreath, and pin the end near the same point you started.

step 6

Crisscross. Repeat with the remaining 4-yard length of narrow ribbon, this time going in the opposite direction to form a crisscross pattern around the front of your wreath.

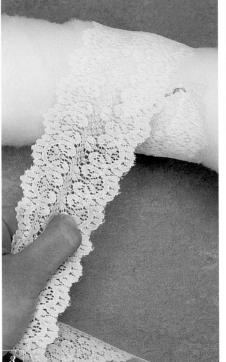

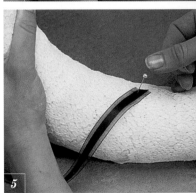

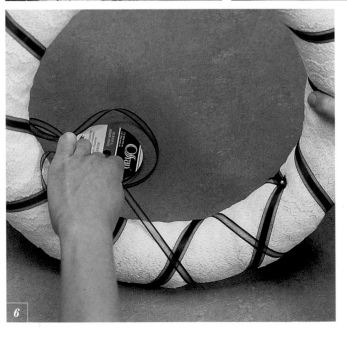

step 7

Place one head of hydrangea on top of a stem of spray roses. Secure the stems with a dab of glue.

step 8

Add a rose or two at the base of your hydrangea. Fill in with additional rose heads and ivy leaves as desired. You've just completed half of your bouquet. Repeat the same basic layering—spray rose, hydrangea, rose—to create the second half.

step 9

Place one half of your flower "bouquet" to hide the ends of your lace and narrow ribbons. Secure with hot glue and a straight pin.

step 10

Secure the second half of your bouquet in the same way, leaving 3" to 4" (8cm to 10cm) of space between to attach your bow.

step 11

Make a stacked bow (I made a layered variation—see instructions on page 388) and attach in the center of your bouquet using a piece of fine ribbon.

step 12

Arrange your picture frames. Start by placing your picture frames and other larger mementos in a balanced arrangement around your wreath. Secure them in place using the crisscross ribbons.

step 13

Add mementos. Arrange your mementos around your wreath until you're happy with the spacing and placement. Use either the crisscross ribbons or corsage pins to secure.

♦♦♦ Love and cherish your Keepsake Wreath!

The Keepsake Wreath is intended to be more of a "scrapbook" than a year-round wall decoration. Take it out on anniversaries or whenever you feel like a stroll down memory lane. For the rest of the time, package your wreath with the same love and attention you used to assemble it. Choose a sturdy, generously sized box that opens and closes easily. (Some packaging stores sell boxes specially made for wreaths.) Use acid-free tissue to cushion and protect your wreath, and store it in a low-humidity area. You might even want to cover your box with a pretty wrapping paper!

variation

Oh baby!

For a baby theme, replace the lace with gingham ribbon and fashion the "bow" out of a piece of baby's blanket and a favorite stuffed toy. Attach booties, birth announcement, silver cup and other sweet little mementos of babyhood.

423

Summer Glory >

◆◆◆ Summer erupts. Greens so green they almost hurt the eyes…glorious riots of butterflies and blooms…childhood memories floating on the breeze. A person could just sit all summer long and take it in. But of course there are flowers to water, weeds to pull and wreaths to make!

This is the time to gather and dry peonies, roses, hydrangea, daisies and other favorite flowers. (Be sure to dry enough to see you through the winter!) Keep your eyes open for little pinwheels, pretty seed packets, interesting twigs, mosses and other unique additions for your wreaths. Add sweet hints of summer with aromas of rose, heather, peach, apple and vanilla.

On the following pages, you'll find wreaths to dress up picnics and terra cotta pots, wreaths inspired by garden views and strolls along the seashore, plus a quick and easy star-shaped wreath that will brighten your summers for years to come.

(above) TERRA COTTA POT-TOPPER; (opposite page starting from upper left, clockwise) LILAC PICNIC CHANDELIER, GARDEN VIEW WREATH, AMERICANA WREATH, SEASIDE WREATH

2

Lilac Picnic Chandelier

♦♦♦ THERE IS NOTHING MORE ROMANTIC THAN A SUMMER PICNIC—ESPECIALLY WHEN SERVED BENEATH THIS CHANDELIER WREATH AT DUSK. ASIDE FROM BEING AN ENCHANTING GARDEN DECORATION, THE LILAC PICNIC CHANDELIER OFFERS A WONDERFUL USE FOR A GLASS CLOCHE AFTER IT HAS SERVED ITS PURPOSE OF NURTURING SPRING SEEDLINGS. IN KEEPING WITH THE EASY-GOING SPIRIT OF PICNIC ENTERTAINING, THIS WREATH IS FUN AND SIMPLE TO CREATE. IT'S BEST WHEN SERVED WITH ONE LOADED PICNIC BASKET, A NICE, SOFT BLANKET (PREFERABLY RED GINGHAM) AND A PERFECT SUMMER DAY.

TIME

DIFFICULTY

TIME

DIFFICULTY

metal ring ; I used a 10" (25cm) ring, but you should choose the size that supports your cloche

natural raffia

4 slip rings and 1 S-hook

60" (152cm) of fine chain, cut into 3 equal pieces

6 silk lilacs

silk hydrangeas with leaves (4 white, 2 green)

stem of green berries

6 yards (5.4m) of ½" to 1" (1.3cm to 2.5cm) sheer ribbon for bows

glass cloche or garden bell

florist wire

hot glue gun

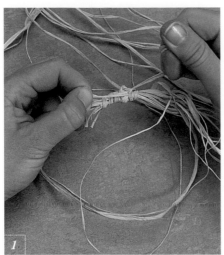

step 1

Attach raffia to ring. Take a few strands of raffia and knot an end onto your metal ring. Secure with a dab of hot glue and allow to dry.

step 2

Wrap. Wrap the raffia tightly around the ring, making sure no metal shows through. Add new strands of raffia as needed; overlap the end of a strand with the beginning of a new strand, secure with a dab of glue, and bind tightly with a single piece of raffia.

step 3

Attach slip rings. Attach three of the slip rings, evenly spacing them around the metal ring.

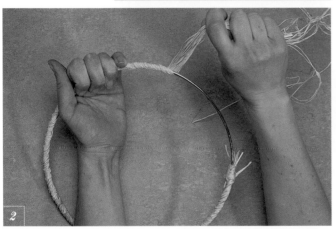

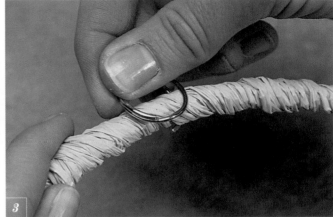

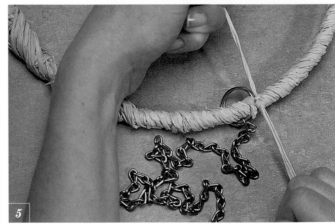

step 4

Add chain. Attach a length of 20" (51cm) chain to each slip ring.

step 5

Secure hoops. Use a piece of raffia to tie each slip ring in place, being sure to keep all three knots on the same side of the ring. This will be the bottom of your chandelier. Trim excess raffia.

step 6

Glue in place. Add a dab of hot glue to ensure the hoops won't budge.

step 7

Complete the hanging chain. Slip the top of all three chains onto the fourth slip ring. (Be sure to slip them on in order to ensure your chandelier hangs level.) Through the completion of your wreath, let the chain hang down through the center of your wreath to keep it out of the way.

step 8

Start with your lilacs. Wire on your lilacs to hang down evenly around the hoop. (Remember, the hanging chain indicates the top of your chandelier, so make sure you're hanging your lilacs in the right direction. And be careful not to wire up your chain as you go!)

step 9

Top with white hydrangea. Cut the leaves off your hydrangeas and set aside; you'll be using some of them in step 11. Cut your white hydrangea into florets. Use florist wire to fill in the top of your hoop with the hydrangea.

step 10

Fill in with green hydrangea. Now cut the green hydrangea into florets. Use florist wire to intersperse them among the white hydrangea, filling in any thin spots.

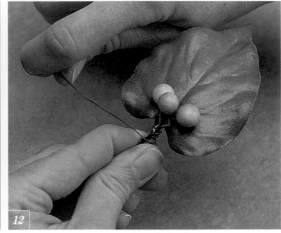

step 11
Make berry clusters. "Harvest" your berry stem by pulling or cutting off each berry, being sure to leave a stem of wire. Twist together into groups of three.

step 12
Make berry picks. Wire each berry cluster to the base of a hydrangea leaf.

step 13
Camouflage stems. Wrap berry wires and leaf stem with green florist tape.

step 14
Attach berry picks. Use your glue gun to intersperse the berry picks randomly among the hydrangea.

step 15
Finish with bows. Make three stacked bows (see page 14) and attach to the base of each hanging chain.

430

♦♦♦ **Feast your eyes on your finished Lilac Picnic Chandelier!**
Use the S-hook to suspend your Lilac Picnic Chandelier from a favorite tree. Then simply anchor a candle in your cloche using white sand or salt, and carefully slip it into the wreath. All that's left to do now is pack up the picnic basket! If you'd like to use a chandelier wreath as an indoor accent—suspended in a bay window, perhaps—consider creating a dried version using globe amaranth, rose buds, yarrow and other durable flowers.

variation

Tabletop wreath
Start by cutting a circle of 2" (5cm) thick foam large enough to anchor your cloche and serve as the base of your wreath. Remove a small circle of foam from the center to fit snuggly around the knob of your cloche, then press the cloche firmly down into the base to embed. Build your wreath directly on the foam. (I used peonies, love-lies-bleeding and other dried flowers.)

Seaside Wreath

what you'll need

◆◆◆ TWO OF MY FRIENDS RETURNED FROM A FUN-FILLED TRIP TO ARUBA WITH THE LOVELY SEASHELLS THAT INSPIRED THIS WREATH. IT'S SWIMMING WITH WHIMSICAL STARFISH AND AN ASSORTMENT OF OCEAN-HUED DRIED MATERIALS—GLOBE THISTLE "URCHINS," TING TING "SEAWEED," WAVES OF CASPIA AND GYPSY GRASS. ALL THAT'S MISSING IS THE SAND BETWEEN YOUR TOES! I MADE A SEASIDE WREATH FOR EACH OF MY FRIENDS—ONE WITH DRIED FLOWERS AND ONE WITH SILK (SEE PAGE 63). IT'S NO TICKET TO ARUBA, BUT I HOPE IT SERVES AS A LASTING, YEAR-ROUND REMINDER OF THE WONDERFUL TIME THEY HAD THERE.

TIME
🕐 🕐

DIFFICULTY
🌸 🌸

14" (36cm) grapevine wreath

caspia in two shades of blue

gyspy grass, whitewashed blue

hydrangea, 3 heads green and 2 heads blue

assortment of blue dried flowers— everlastings, globe thistle, baby everlastings, sea holly, eucalyptus

ting ting, green

maidenhair fern

small piece of driftwood, about 10" (25cm) long

starfish—1 large, 3 medium and various small ones

assorted seashells

10 yards (9m) of ⅛" (3mm) blue satin ribbon

florist wire

hot glue gun

Substitute Your Favorites

◆ ◆ ◆ ◆ ◆ ◆ ◆ ◆ ◆ ◆ ◆ ◆ ◆ ◆

You can make this wreath as simple or elaborate as you like. Take a stroll down the dried-flower aisle of your neighborhood craft store and pick out any sea-worthy elements you find, such as German statice, frosted mint, diamond eucalyptus, lepto, nigella, poppy pods, scabiosa, springerii fern, curly willow and veronica.

step 1

Secure the driftwood. Position the driftwood along the bottom of your wreath. Use a piece of florist wire to secure each end. Turn your wreath over and attach wire for hanging (see page 385).

step 2

Begin building your background. Make small, mixed bundles of the lighter caspia and gypsy grass. Use these bundles to cover the inside and outside edges of the top half of your wreath.

step 3

Fill in with hydrangea. Use pieces of green hydrangea to fill in between caspia/gypsy grass bundles on the top half of your wreath. (See page 387 for special tips on working with hydrangea.)

step 4

Get darker and keep going. Repeat steps 2 and 3 to cover the bottom half of your wreath, this time using darker caspia in the gypsy grass bundles and blue hydrangea to fill in between. Use these flowers to help camouflage the wire securing your driftwood. Now you have a rich, variegated background on which to "paint" your ocean scene!

step 5

Start with your "star" fish. Place your largest starfish on one side of your wreath, establishing your focal point. Work in your larger shells and starfish, concentrating them on the
bottom, or the "ocean floor" of your wreath. Once you're happy with the arrangement, glue into place.

step 6

Add everlastings and globe thistle. Glue these randomly around your wreath.

step 7

And now for the little touches. Intersperse sprigs of sea holly and small bundles of baby everlastings around the top half of your wreath. Add some small shells and starfish around the entire wreath. (For an extra touch of fun, use two small shells and a small faux pearl to create a treasure-filled oyster!)

435

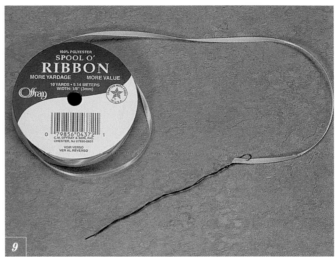

step 8

Create starfish burst. Bring more focus to your large starfish with a burst of eucalyptus, ting ting and maidenhair fern. Place a few stems of each radiating out from the top of your starfish, angled out slightly from your wreath for added dimension. Use a dab of glue at the base of each stem to secure.

step 9

Thread your "needle". Cut a small slit at the end of your narrow ribbon. Thread a 6" (15cm) length of florist wire through the slit, bend the wire in half and twist. This is your ribbon-weaving needle.

step 10

Make "ripples" of ribbon. Pass your ribbon under and around flowers, in essence weaving your ribbon into your wreath. Aim for random but even coverage all around your wreath.

♦♦♦ Splash into summer with your completed Seaside Wreath!

The Seaside Wreath is at home in the bedroom, family room, home office (for quality daydreaming!) and even the bathroom, as long as it's not exposed to a lot of steam. (Otherwise, consider making a silk version.) If the ocean isn't your idea of a dream vacation, how about making a Mountain Wreath with an earthy assortment of dried mosses, pinecones and leaves?

variation

Swimming in silks

You can create a stunning seaside wreath using silk materials—a much more durable option if you intend to display your wreath in a bathroom. Add a few fish, seashells and some coral pieces to complete your silk seascape.

Americana Wreath

what you'll need

♦♦♦ DON'T YOU LOVE THE SIMPLE THINGS IN LIFE? TAKE THIS WREATH, FOR EXAMPLE. BIND SOME BRANCHES TOGETHER, TOSS IN A ROSE, TIE ON A BOW AND THERE YOU HAVE IT—THE PERFECT PATRIOTIC TOUCH FOR THE FOURTH OF JULY! FOLLOW A FEW SIMPLE STEPS TO PREPARE YOUR BIRCH (OR TO MAKE ANY TYPE OF WOOD LOOK LIKE BIRCH!), AND THE NATURAL BEAUTY OF THIS STAR WILL SHINE ON LONG AFTER THE FRESH ROSE FADES. FUN AND FOLKSY, THE AMERICANA WREATH IS AT HOME INSIDE OR OUT, ON SCREEN DOOR OR GARDEN GATE. I LIKE MINE ON THE GARDEN SHED!

TIME

DIFFICULTY

5 relatively straight branches of roughly the same length (20" [51cm]) and diameter (1" [2.5cm]); I prefer white birch, but any wood will do

1 fresh red rose

3 yards of 1" (2.5cm) blue wired ribbon for bow

coping saw

sanding block or sandpaper

white gesso

acrylic spray

twine

strip of plastic (I cut mine from a milk jug)

2 slip rings

florist water tube

florist wire

hot glue gun

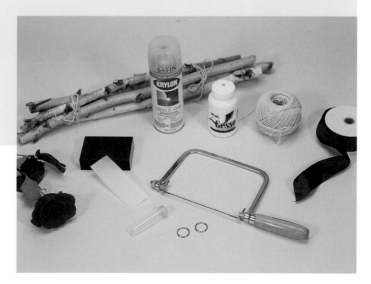

Template for flower tube holder

We think of birch as being pretty white, but chances are the branches you find will look a little dingy. So here's an easy way to brighten and protect them:

1. SAND ♦ Start by using a sanding block or sandpaper to remove any dirt and loose bark from your branches.

2. PAINT ♦ Brush each branch with gesso, avoiding the ends to allow the natural wood to show.

3. WIPE ♦ Use a paper towel or rag to wipe off enough gesso to achieve a white-washed effect. Allow to dry.

4. DE-NUB ♦ Cut off any "nubs" to expose spots of natural wood. If you painted over any of the ends of your branches, cut off a thin slice to expose the natural wood.

5. SEAL ♦ Spray branches with acrylic spray and allow to dry. This will protect the finish and give it a pretty, transparent shine. Now your branches look like the bright, white birch we all know and love! And they'll stay that way.

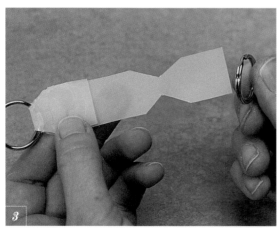

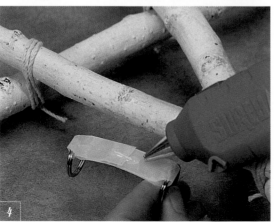

step 1

Arrange your star. Arrange your branches into a star shape. Every branch is shaped a little differently, so take a few minutes to experiment and find the best fit.

step 2

Tie the joints. Tie the branches together at each intersection with a piece of twine. Secure with a simple square knot and trim ends. Attach a wire hoop at the top point for hanging (See page 385).

step 3

Make a flower tube holder. Cut a strip of plastic using the template on page 65. Slip on the slip rings to rest in the notches. Fold over the plastic and secure with dab of hot glue.

step 4

Attach the tube holder to the wreath. Squeeze a strip of glue on the back of your tube holder and glue in place.

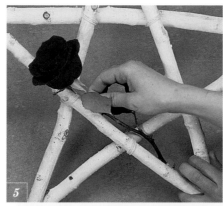

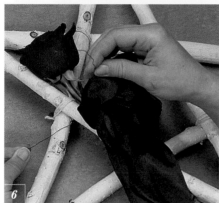

step 5

Add one red rose. Trim the stem as necessary and insert it into the tube, allowing the birch to support the rose.

step 6

Add bow. Make a stacked bow (see page 388) and attach with florist wire.

♦♦♦ A Star is Born!

For a less patriotic theme, choose a different color for your bow, replace the red rose with a sunflower or zinnia, or skip the flower altogether. The simple beauty of this birch star is bright enough to stand on its own. And best of all, you made it with plenty of time left over to relax and enjoy a nice, icy glass of tea. Mmm, gotta love those simple things!

variation

Window to winter

Birch is such a great material to work with—especially if you can get it free from your backyard. Using three pieces per side, I made this dimensional rectangle and decorated it with twisted wisteria vines, juniper, pepperberries and frosted canella berries.

Garden View Wreath

what you'll need

◆◆◆ THIS IS MY FAVORITE WREATH TO GIVE AS A GIFT BECAUSE IT IS SO OPEN TO PERSONAL-IZATION. CHOOSE COLORS, FLOWERS AND ACCESSORIES WITH THE RECIPIENT IN MIND. YOU COULD EVEN INCLUDE THEIR NAME ON A RUSTIC LITTLE SIGN: "LAURIE'S GARDEN" OR "WELCOME TO KIRK'S WOODS" OR "JAMIE WEEDS HERE!" CRAFT STORES OFFER ALL KINDS OF FUN MINIATURE ACCESSORIES TO BRING YOUR SCENE TO LIFE—GARDEN BENCHES, BUNNIES, WIND CHIMES, BICYCLES, CROQUET SETS, TIRE SWINGS, YOU NAME IT! LITTLE DETAILS LIKE THESE INVITE PEOPLE TO LEAN IN AND LOOK CLOSER. SO—ARE YOU READY TO GET "PLANTING"?

TIME

DIFFICULTY

18" (46cm) straw wreath; I like straw wreaths because they offer a nice, wide surface to work on, but if weight is an issue, you can substitute a foam base

2-3 heads assorted hydrangea

assorted dried flowers—I used German statice, caspia, sweet Annie, candy tuft, Australian daisies, rice flowers and sanfordii

sheet moss

reindeer moss

preserved boxwood

2-3 small sponge mushrooms

3-4 small, thin river rocks

15" (38cm) tree branch (look for one that's forked at one end)

two 4½" (12cm) lengths of ½" (1.3cm) dowel rod

twig fence

a variety of miniature accessories—I used a watering can, terra cotta pots, wheelbarrow, old-fashioned reel mower, straw hat, welcome sign, vegetables, beehive and bees, birds, bird's nest and eggs, unpainted birdhouse, garden tools, and, for my gazing ball, a tiny glass bauble and an unfinished pedestal

acrylic paints

florist pins

florist wire

fishing line or twine

hot glue gun

Other Ideas for Mini Flower Gardens

◆ ◆ ◆ ◆ ◆ ◆ ◆ ◆ ◆ ◆ ◆

silver sage ◆ red cedar ◆ veronica ◆ larkspur ◆ gypsophilia ◆ flowering oregano ◆ pepperberries ◆ lepto ◆ dudinea ◆ baby's breath ◆ beech

step 1

Start with a moss background. Dampen moss and cover the entire wreath, securing well using glue, florist pins and wire. Attach a wire for hanging on the back (see page 385). Make sure your hanging wire is a secure one—this wreath has some weight to it.

step 2

Place mushroom ledges and stepping stones. Glue in your sponge mushrooms, clustered to one side of your wreath. Starting on the opposite side, stagger your river rock stepping stones to lead toward the center of the wreath where you'll place your gate. Use florist pins underneath as needed for added support. (You'll camouflage the pins later.) Now you have little "ledges" for displaying your miniature decorations!

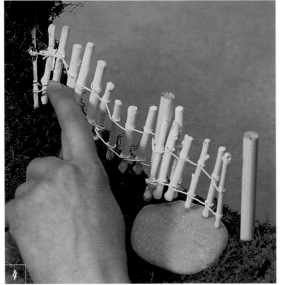

step 3

Plant the tree and fence posts. Place your "tree trunk," trimming it as necessary to fit. Glue into place and hold firmly against your wreath for a few minutes while the glue dries to ensure a tight bond. Sharpen one end of each piece of dowel (a pencil sharpener works great for this!), squeeze a dab of glue onto each point, and insert into straw to mark the placement of your gate.

step 4

Place the fence. Use florist pins and glue to secure the outer ends onto the wreath. Glue the inner ends to the dowel posts, leaving a couple of inches (5cm) of overlap on one side to form your gate.

step 5

Add foliage. Glue boxwood "branches" onto your tree.

step 6

Plant hydrangea shrubs. Break hydrangea heads into smaller pieces, and glue down the opposite side of your wreath. (See page 387 for special tips on working with hydrangea.)

step 7

Add tree blossoms. Now that you have your foundation built, it's time for the details! First, glue small sprigs of German statice into your boxwood branches.

step 8

Plant your flower garden. Snuggle the beehive into place among the hydrangea. Next, make small bundles of each of your assorted flowers. Start gluing these in under your hydrangea and work your way down.

step 9

Add some shrubbery. Glue a little shrubbery alongside your tree trunk. Here, I've used a few sprigs of yellow caspia and sanfordii.

step 10

Fill your flower pots. Glue a tiny bit of moss into the bottom of each mini terra cotta pot. Fill with tiny bundles of assorted flowers.

445

step 11

Make your gazing ball. Paint your pedestal base gray to look like stone. When it's dry, glue your bauble on top. Voila! A gazing ball! (I bet, with a little thought, you can come up with your own clever tricks for creating original garden accessories!)

step 12

Load your wheelbarrow. Glue larger veggies on bottom and smaller on top.

step 13

Accessorize. Now for the really fun part! Fill your bird's nest with eggs and nestle among the tree branches. Perch a birdie on the fence post. Glue your welcome sign to the tree. Park your wheelbarrow on the ledge and lean your garden tools against the tree. Arrange your flower pots and other accessories on your stepping stones. Buzz a few bees around the hive.

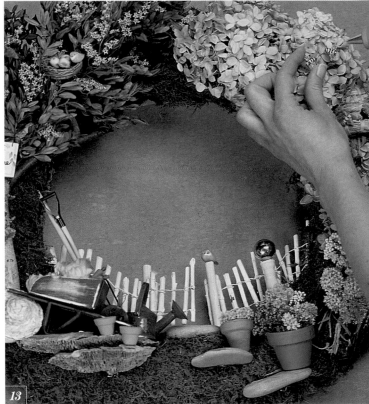

step 14

Hang birdhouse. Use acrylic paints to decorate your birdhouse and allow to dry. Suspend from a tree branch using fishing line or twine.

step 15

Touch up with moss. Glue small tufts of reindeer moss under stones and ledges, at base of flower garden, or wherever you need to soften rough edges and hide florist pins.

Wasn't that fun? Now any room in your home can have a picturesque view! (Just be extra careful to use a secure hook or nail to hang this one, as it has some weight to it.) Don't forget to keep your eyes open for fun little additions to use in your next Garden View. Let your imagination loose, and every scene you create will be a true original!

variation

Get even more detailed

I made this wreath in memory of our dear neighbor Bob, an avid gardener. The arbor is a piece of wire covered with dried morning glory vines and mini rosebuds. I made the fence from balsa wood. The apples are unfinished mini apples I purchased from a craft store and dyed red. The wall is fashioned from real stone glued onto a piece of foam.

447

Terra Cotta Pot Topper

♦♦♦ THERE'S SOMETHING SWEET AND OLD-FASHIONED ABOUT GIVING GIFTS FROM THE GARDEN. AND I NEVER MET AN HERB GARDENER WHO WASN'T HAPPY TO DISCOVER A NEW USE FOR HIS EVER-ABUNDANT HARVEST! THE TERRA COTTA POT TOPPER IS QUICK AND EASY TO PUT TOGETHER—ESPECIALLY IF YOU MAKE THE CHICKEN-WIRE BASE AHEAD OF TIME. (YOU MAY EVEN WANT TO MAKE A FEW, JUST TO HAVE ON HAND!) ADORN WITH HANDFULS OF FRESH-CUT HERBS (SMELLS WONDERFUL!), ADD SOME BERRIES (I USE FREEZE-DRIED, BUT FRESH WILL WORK JUST AS WELL) AND FINISH WITH FRESH SUNFLOWERS, DAISIES, ZINNIAS OR WHATEVER'S BLOOMING IN YOUR BACKYARD. BY ITSELF OR FILLED WITH GOODIES, THE TERRA COTTA POT TOPPER MAKES A UNIQUE AND NEIGHBORLY GIFT.

TIME

⏱

DIFFICULTY

☘

piece of chicken wire at least 36" x 6" (91cm x 15cm)

floral moss

8" (20cm) terra cotta pot

fresh herbs (I used marjoram, oregano, sage, dill, thyme and chives)

freeze-dried berries (18 strawberries and 9 blackberries)

3 fresh mini sunflower heads

2 yards (1.8m) of ½" (12mm) gingham ribbon

natural raffia

copper plant tag

florist wire

green florist tape

hot glue gun

Wreathmaker's Garden

In addition to beautifying your landscape, these plants yield foliage, berries, vines and other materials you can use in your wreaths all year round.

arborvitae ♦ birches ♦ bittersweet ♦ boxwood ♦ crabapple ♦ English ivy ♦ fountain grasses ♦ grapes ♦ hydrangea ♦ junipers ♦ lilacs ♦ maple ♦ morning glory ♦ mosses ♦ oaks ♦ pines ♦ pussy willow ♦ pyracantha ♦ roses ♦ spruces ♦ wisteria ♦ yews ♦ and don't forget assorted herbs and flowers!

449

Work Ahead Tip

◆ ◆

If you're making this as a gift, you can work up to step 3 ahead of time. When you're ready to add your herbs and flowers, simply mist your moss with water.

step 1

Make a moss-filled tube. Cut a piece of chicken wire about 36" x 6" (91cm x 15cm). Place a strip of damp moss along the center and form the wire into a tube. (Soaking your moss in water beforehand will help keep the herbs and flowers fresh a little longer. Squeeze out excess water before using.)

step 2

Sew it up. Use florist wire to sew together the seam of your tube. (Careful of sharp edges!)

step 3

Top your pot. Wrap the tube around your pot, molding the chicken wire to hug the top edge. Use florist wire to connect the ends of the tube.

step 4

Add chives. Gather three bunches of chives. Arrange evenly around the top of your wreath, leaving a few inches of overhang on the ends. Use florist wire to tack each chive bunch to the chicken wire in two or three places.

step 5

Add herb bundles. Make two bundles of assorted herbs. Using a long piece of raffia, join them—stem to stem—to form one double-ended bundle. Use the raffia to tie the bundle to the chicken wire, centered above a bunch of chives. Top the other two chive bunches the same way.

step 6

Add raffia bows. Now for a little touch of raffia. Attach a small, simple bow to the center of each herb bundle.

step 7

Wire strawberries. Cut 8" (20cm) wires, bend in half, and insert into your strawberries. Use a dab of hot glue to secure. Allow to dry.

step 8

Bundle strawberries. Make six bundles, each with three strawberries and a small bunch of herbs. Twist together the strawberry wires to secure. If necessary, wrap each stem with green florist tape to camouflage.

step 9

Add strawberries. Space the strawberry bundles evenly around your wreath, bending each wire stem to "hook" into the chicken wire.

step 10

Add blackberries. Wire the blackberries the same as you did the strawberries. Twist together three clusters of three berries each, and wrap each stem with green florist tape to camouflage. Use the stems to hook the berry trios under each raffia bow.

step 11

Add sunflowers. Cut the stem of each sunflower about 3" (8cm) long. Using needlenose pliers or some other handy hole-poking tool, make three holes evenly spaced around the top of your wreath. Insert flowers, securing with florist wire if necessary.

step 12

Final touches. Make three simple gingham bows and attach under each sunflower. Tie the plant tag on with one of these bows to use as a gift tag.

◆◆◆**Add a dash of kindness to someone's day with your completed Terra Cotta Pot Topper!** Fill your pot with goodies (seeds, gloves, tools, lotion, etc.) and present to your favorite gardening friend. She's sure to appreciate the thought as well as the herbs, which will dry naturally and can be pinched off and used for cooking. No need to limit your "toppers" to terra cotta pots. For a get-well gift, present a jar of homemade chicken soup with a mini topper of lavender. For a cat lover, top a ceramic water bowl with fresh catnip and little kitty toys. Top a pail, a basket, a watering can with dried flowers, silk flowers, "found" art…oh, the top-abilities!

variation

Baker's gift wreath
Here's a sweet-smelling wreath you can make for a friend who likes to bake. Form a chicken-wire base on the rim of a pretty mixing bowl and wrap with cheesecloth to soften. Create a pattern using star anise, whole nutmeg, allspice and bay leaves. Tie on gingham bows, cinnamon sticks and cookie cutters, then fill with baking goodies.

Fall Homecoming

♦♦♦ My idea of perfection is a fall day. I never feel more at home on this earth than I do on a crisp autumn afternoon, surrounded by the crescendo of colorful leaves, kaleidoscope skies, fields of gold and the familiar smell of wood burning in the air. Inside, the house is filled with the comforting smells of cinnamon and apple pie, of cloves, mulberry and spices. It all makes you want to slow down, sit back and breathe deeply.

The wreaths in this chapter celebrate the season with colorful leaves, acorns, goldenrod, berries, cornhusk, grapevines, gourds, citrus peels and other autumn treasures. The palette ranges from the earthy tones of the Country Roads Wreath to the vibrant golds and reds of Fall Bounty. Whether you prefer the rustic style of Cornhusk & Curls, the casual elegance of the Pumpkin Garland, or the fresh and edible Cornucopia Dessert Wreath, these projects will welcome the warm pleasures of fall into your home.

(above) PUMPKIN GARLAND; (opposite page starting from upper left, clockwise) FALL BOUNTY, CORNUCOPIA DESSERT WREATH, CORNHUSK & CURLS, COUNTRY ROADS WREATH

3

Fall Bounty Wreath

◆◆◆ THIS WREATH CELEBRATES THE FULL GLORY OF FALL IN A RAGE OF SILK FLOWERS, VELVET

LEAVES, BEADED BERRIES AND RIBBONS. YOU WOULDN'T GUESS TO LOOK AT IT,

BUT THIS WREATH IS ACTUALLY INEXPENSIVE AND FAIRLY SIMPLE TO AS-

SEMBLE. YOU COULD EASILY MAKE A SMALLER VERSION FOR HALF THE

PRICE—EVEN LESS IF YOU KEEP YOUR EYES OPEN FOR SILK FLOWER SALES

AND BARGAINS. IF YOU'RE GOING TO SPLURGE, SAVE IT FOR THE FOCAL FLOWERS.

TIME

⏱ ⏱ ⏱

DIFFICULTY

♣ ♣

2 straw wreaths, 18" (46cm)
and 24" (61cm)

4-6 inexpensive bunches of
assorted silk mums with leaves
(about 60 medium and large
heads in coordinating fall colors)

grapevine, about 35" (89cm) long,
ideally with a split

4-5 stems of assorted small silk
filler flowers (such as stock or
straw flowers)

1-2 stems of "focal" silk flowers
(I used ranunculus)

1-2 stems of silk Japanese lanterns

2 bunches of velvet leaves
(about 30 leaves)

two 5-yard (4.5m) lengths of
1½" (3.8cm) wired ribbon
in coordinating fall colors

2-3 stems of artificial berries

10 beaded berry picks

florist wire

florist pins

hot glue gun

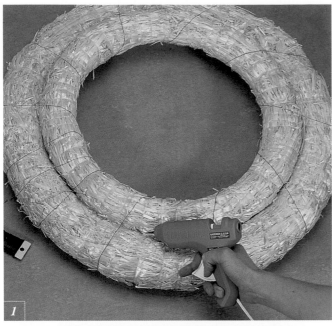

step 1

Build the double-decker base. Center the smaller wreath on top of the larger one. (No need to press flush—tiering will give the wreath added dimension.) Glue along the seam and wrap with wire to secure. This nice wide base is the hidden secret behind this wreath's full, lush look. Attach wire for hanging (see page 385).

step 2

Clip your flowers. "Harvest" your mum bunches, clipping off individual flowers, leaving 2" to 3" (5cm to 8cm) stems.

step 3

Camouflage your straw base. Using the leaves you just clipped off, cover the inner and outer edges of your wreath. Overlap the leaves slightly as needed for a solid, uniform coverage. This will hide any straw that may show around the flowers, giving your wreath a nice, finished look.

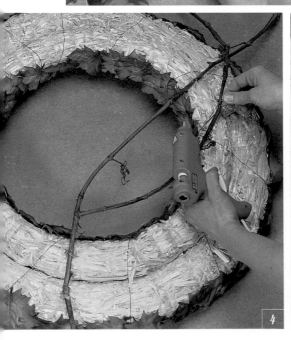

step 4

Secure the grapevine. Place your grapevine across the bottom half of your wreath. Pin and glue on each side to secure.

step 5

Biggest flowers first. Use your largest mums to form your base layer. It's a good idea to first place the flowers (poke the stems right into the straw) and then—once you're sure they are distributed evenly around your wreath—go back and glue into place. (This way you won't run out of flowers when you're 90 percent done!) This first layer of flowers should sit flush against your wreath.

step 6

Next layer: smaller mums. Again, it's a good idea to place all your smaller mums first, then go back and glue in place. Vary the height of this layer of flowers to add depth, nestling some among the larger mums and allowing others to sit slightly higher.

step 7

Work in your filler flowers. Cut your filler flowers into small sprigs and arrange around your wreath as desired. I like to concentrate mine around the grapevine.

step 8

Add the Japanese lanterns. Cut your Japanese lanterns into small pieces—clusters of three or five pods—and arrange as desired around your wreath.

step 9

Add velvet leaves. Cut your velvet bunches into individual leaves and glue around your wreath as desired. For fun, glue one or two "tumbling" across your grapevine.

step 10
Weave in ribbon. Work one of your ribbons through the wreath, weaving under and around the flowers, tacking down with florist pins as needed. Repeat with second ribbon. Aim for a relatively even coverage over the entire wreath.

step 11
Add berries. Cut your berry sprays into small sprigs. Distribute these sprigs along with your berry picks around your wreath as desired and glue into place.

step 12
Finish with your "focal" flowers. For the final touch, cut your focal flowers down to stems of 2" to 3" (5cm to 8cm), concentrate them within one quadrant of your wreath and glue into place.

♦♦♦ A brilliant burst of fall!
This wreath is worthy of a featured spot over a fireplace or on a sheltered front door. You'll be sorry when it's time to pack it away for the winter. The good news is that you can use the same techniques to create a "bountiful" silk wreath for any season!

variation

Spring fling!
Add a blast of spring to any room with assorted silk flowers. Have fun incorporating butterflies, ladybugs or other little camouflaged surprises.

Pumpkin Garland

what you'll need

TIME

DIFFICULTY

♦♦♦ HALLOWEEN JUST WOULDN'T BE HALLOWEEN WITHOUT PUMPKINS! IF YOU'RE IN THE MOOD FOR A MORE ELEGANT ALTERNATIVE TO THE TRADITIONAL JACK-O-LANTERN, I HAVE JUST THE THING. THE PUMPKIN GARLAND IS A GREAT WAY TO USE THOSE PRETTY, BEADED GRAPES THAT ARE SO POPULAR THESE DAYS. IT'S WHAT ALL THE BEST-DRESSED PUMPKINS WILL BE WEARING THIS FALL! AND BEST OF ALL, IT'S SUPER SIMPLE TO MAKE—THE HARDEST PART WILL BE CHOOSING YOUR FAVORITE PUMPKIN.

a few wisteria vines; instead of wisteria, you can use a metal hoop wrapped in raffia (see page 54)

3 bunches of beaded grapes, velvet grapes or beaded berries

1 large head of dried green hydrangea

3 yards (2.7m) of 1½" (3.8cm) wide wired green silk ribbon for bows

12 velvet ivy leaves

light-gauge, green cloth-covered stem wire for tendrils

pumpkin

florist wire

hot glue gun

Before You Start

♦ ♦ ♦ ♦ ♦ ♦ ♦ ♦ ♦ ♦ ♦

Soak wisteria in water for one hour or, better yet, overnight. This makes it much more flexible and easier to work with.

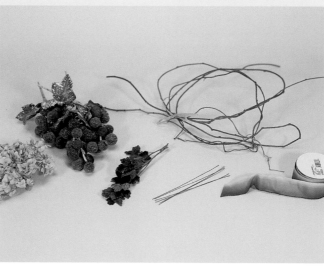

step 1
Make a custom-fit wreath. Start by forming a wreath of wisteria about halfway down your pumpkin. Twist the wisteria around itself, adding vines until you achieve the width desired and the wreath sits about an inch lower than where you'd ultimately like it. (This will allow for the shrinkage that occurs as the wreath dries.) Allow the wreath to dry overnight.

step 2
Add grapes. Wire on the grape bunches, evenly spaced around your wreath.

step 3
Add hydrangea. Break the hydrangea into pieces and use it to fill in around grape clusters, leaving space between to add bows.

step 4
Add bows. Make three small stacked bows (see page 388) and wire on between the grape clusters.

step 5
Add velvet leaves. Squeeze a dab of glue onto each stem, and slip in velvet leaves here and there around your wreath.

step 6
Add "tendrils". Using the end of a paintbrush or similar form, curl wires around and around to make curlicues. Glue the tendrils here and there around your wreath as desired.

◆◆◆ What a treat!

It's that easy to turn an ordinary pumpkin into a festive centerpiece, and the average jack-o-lantern into a Greek gourdish god! Make several garland-topped pumpkins to create a dramatic grouping for your table, kitchen counter or stairway. When your pumpkin is past its peak, you can still use your garland around the base of a hurricane.

variation

A basket case

Give a favorite basket the same special treatment. I used a metal hoop wrapped in raffia for the base of this wreath. If needed, use S-hooks to suspend your finished wreath from the rim of your basket.

465

Country Roads Wreath

what you'll need

♦♦♦ THE MAKINGS FOR THIS ALL-NATURAL WREATH CAME FROM THE BACKROADS OF INDIANA COUNTY, PENNSYLVANIA—MY VERY OWN "WEED GARDEN!" GRAB YOUR PRUNERS AND HEAD OUT TO A QUIET COUNTRY LANE OR MEADOW WHEN THE WEEDS AND WILDFLOWERS START COMING INTO BLOOM (IN MY NECK OF THE WOODS IT'S AROUND JUNE). EARLY FALL IS THE BEST TIME FOR HARVESTING GOLDENROD—TRY TO GET IT JUST BEFORE ITS PRIME, WHEN IT'S NICE AND GOLDEN. FALL IS ALSO THE TIME TO GATHER THISTLES, MILKWEED PODS, ROSE HIPS AND, OF COURSE, ALL THOSE GORGEOUS LEAVES. DON'T WORRY ABOUT FINDING THE EXACT MATERIALS SHOWN HERE. USE THE PLANTS NATIVE TO YOUR AREA AND YOUR WREATH IS GUARANTEED TO BE A TRUE ORIGINAL.

TIME

DIFFICULTY

oval grapevine base—mine is about 15" x 30" (38cm x 76cm)

dried goldenrod

assortment of air-dried flowers, wild grasses and berries (I used black-eyed Susans, crown of corn, millet, milkweed pods, wild roses, elderberries, bittersweet, sunflowers and thistles sprayed burgundy for extra contrast)

Queen Anne's lace (preserved in silica gel)

assortment of preserved fall leaves (purchase in craft store or make your own by following the simple instructions on this page)

curly gold raffia

acrylic spray

florist wire

hot glue gun

Preserving Autumn Leaves

♦ ♦ ♦ ♦ ♦ ♦ ♦ ♦ ♦ ♦ ♦ ♦ ♦ ♦ ♦ ♦ ♦ ♦

1. **START WITH LEAVES** that are unblemished, intact and colorful. The colors will darken slightly, so be sure to start with the brightest leaves you can find.
2. **WORKING ON AN IRONING BOARD** or a cotton towel topped with newspaper, sandwich your leaf between two sheets of wax paper. Make sure the leaf is nice and flat. Slip the wax paper between two paper towels.
3. **WITH A DRY IRON** on low to medium setting, press your leaf "sandwich." The heat will soften the wax paper, lightly coating and preserving the leaf in wax. (Use fresh wax paper for each leaf. The paper towels, which absorb wax from the outside of the paper, will have to be replaced every few leaves or so.)

step 1

Create a base of goldenrod. Attach wire for hanging to the grapevine base (see page 385). Make bundles of goldenrod. Use glue and wire (see "Continuous Wiring" on page 387) to secure downward-hanging bundles to your wreath, hiding the stem of each bundle with the head of the next. Start at the bottom of your wreath and work your way up first one side and then the other, until you have a solid base of goldenrod.

step 2

Insert bundles and add thistles and milk pods. Make small bundles of various grasses and flowers. Arrange the bundles evenly around your wreath, gluing the stems and tucking them in between goldenrod bundles. Cut short stems of thistles and milk pods and glue them randomly around your wreath as desired.

step 3

Add wild roses, berries and bittersweet. Cut into short stems and sprigs. Insert randomly around your wreath as desired and glue into place.

step 4

Add your most delicate drieds last. Glue Queen Anne's lace, sunflowers and preserved leaves around your wreath as desired. At this point, take your wreath outside and apply a generous coat of acrylic spray to minimize shedding and help preserve the colors.

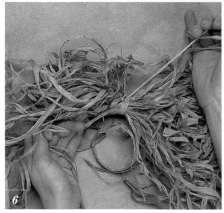

step 5

Make the bow. This bow couldn't be easier to make. Start by separating your raffia into two equal bunches. Take one length of raffia and make a loop on one end, leaving the other end hanging down as a tail. Do the same with your second length of raffia. With loops opposite each other, bring the two bunches together to form one complete bow.

step 6

And tie! Now take an extra piece of raffia and tie the two together in the center. Attach the raffia bow to the top center of your wreath using florist wire.

♦♦♦ The Country Roads Wreath—proof that one person's weed is the wreath-maker's treasure!
This wreath may shed quite a bit because of all the natural ingredients, so it's best displayed on a screened-in porch or other sheltered spot. The colors will fade and mellow with age. Personally, I like the resulting look, but if you prefer, you could always add some fresh assorted bundles and newly preserved leaves to perk it up. Or better yet, take a stroll through the country to gather the makings for your next wreath!

variation

Mountain memories
There is something about making an original piece of art out of natural "found" materials. It's like bringing a little piece of the outdoors into your home! In this case, I covered a straw base with overlapping layers of paper beech bark that had been soaked in water until pliable. Once that dried, I added fungi, moss, twigs, feathers and a neat little stone "vase" filled with a few simple dried flowers.

469

Cornhusk & Curls Wreath

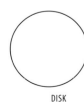

what you'll need

◆◆◆ LOOK OUT ANY WINDOW OF OUR HOME AND YOU'LL SEE CORNFIELDS. I'M NEVER MORE APPRECIATIVE OF THE VIEW THAN I AM IN THE FALL WHEN THE STALKS DRY AND MELLOW, FORMING THE PERFECT BACKDROP FOR THE SEASON'S VIBRANT PALETTE OF OR-ANGES AND GOLDS. THESE FIELDS ALSO PROVIDE ME WITH A VERY CONVEN-IENT SUPPLY OF CORNHUSK—A FAVORITE CRAFTING MATERIAL OF MINE FOR TWENTY-FIVE YEARS. I HOPE YOU'LL TRY THIS WREATH AND DISCOVER FOR YOURSELF THE EARTHY PLEASURE OF WORKING WITH CORNHUSK.

TIME

DIFFICULTY

twig swirl wreath, about 32" (81cm)

8-10 oranges

5 acorns and 10 acorn caps

ten 10" (25cm) cinnamon sticks

one bag of dried cornhusk, dyed with fabric dye (see sidebar); for a more natural wreath, leave the cornhusk un-dyed (Most craft stores sell inexpensive bags of cornhusk, but if you have permis-sion to harvest husk from a field, remember that the fine, inner husk closest to the cob is easiest to work with.)

brown lemon (salal) leaves

tallow berries

dried oak leaves

2 yards (1.8m) of 3" (8cm) wide burlap ribbon

5 small buttons

aroma oil, clove or other autumnal scent (optional)

⅜" (10mm) dowel rod

knife or peeler

twine

craft glue

brown florist tape

semi-gloss acrylic spray

spray bottle of water

very narrow curling iron

florist wire

hot glue gun

Dyeing Cornhusk

◆ ◆ ◆ ◆ ◆ ◆ ◆ ◆ ◆ ◆ ◆ ◆ ◆ ◆ ◆

Follow the directions on the box of fabric dye, mixing colors and muting with tea bags to achieve the desired color. (Color will lighten as the husk dries.) To avoid mold, spread husks out on newspaper to dry.

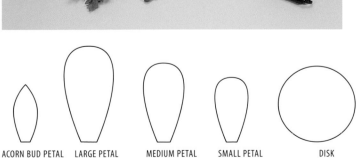

ACORN BUD PETAL   LARGE PETAL   MEDIUM PETAL   SMALL PETAL   DISK

Template for Cornhusk Flowers
Enlarge 200% to bring up to actual size.

You will need to make five flowers for this wreath. Using the templates on page 471, cut twelve large petals, ten medium petals, ten small petals and two circles per flower. Cut along the grain of the cornhusk and don't worry about cutting perfect petals—variations add to the charm of your flowers. Start by gluing together the two disks with the grains running in opposite directions for strength. (Keep the glue along the edges of the circles, because you'll be running a wire through the center later.)

tip
♦

To make your cornhusk easier to work with, place it between paper towels and flatten with a dry, warm iron.

♦ MAKING CORNHUSK FLOWERS

step 1
Place the base petals in two layers: glue six evenly spaced along the edge of the disk, then six more on top and between these.

step 2
Now do the same with your medium petals—two layers of five petals each.

step 3
Finally, your small petals—again, two layers of five.

step 4
Cut an 18" (46cm) length of wire. Twist the center of the wire around the "nub" of an acorn cap. Use glue to secure and allow to dry.

472

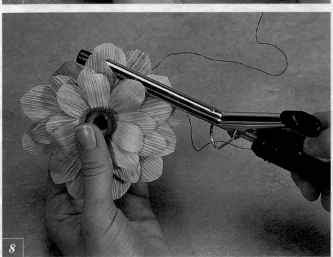

step 5

Poke both ends of the wire down through the center of your cornhusk flower.

step 6

Use a button on the back of your flower to secure the wire. Just run through the holes and twist, twist, twist.

step 7

If you'd like to add a little curl to your flower, spritz it lightly with water and allow to dry naturally.

step 8

You can also use a warm curling iron to shape dry petals, curling the edges under slightly.

◆MAKING ACORN BUDS

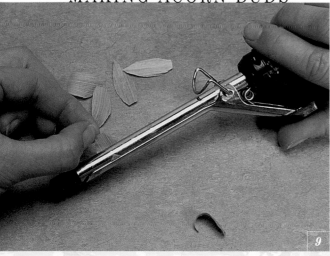

step 9
Spray five acorns with acrylic spray and allow to dry. Using the bud template on page 471, cut five to seven petals per bud. Use a warm curling iron to "flip" each petal. (Tip: If you don't have a curling iron, use twine to curl your petals around a dowel rod, spritz with water and allow to dry.)

step 10
Glue petals onto the base of your acorn.

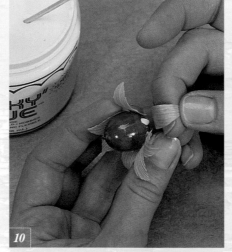

step 11
Choose caps slightly larger than your acorn buds and wire as described in step 4. Glue acorn buds into the caps.

step 12
Finish your buds by wrapping stems in brown florist tape.

◆MAKING ORANGE CURLS

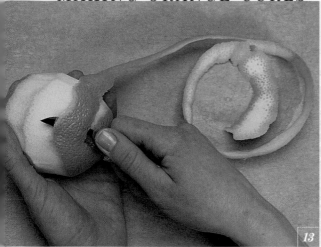

step 13
With a knife or peeler, slice long, narrow strips of peel from your orange. You can experiment with different widths to achieve different looks. You'll want about fifteen to twenty-five curls in all.

step 14
Twist the peels around the dowel, secure with a piece of twine, and allow to dry. I find that I get the best results with air-drying—especially when I set the dowels on a warm radiator. It usually takes a few days, but time will vary depending on temperature and humidity. Alternatively, you can dry the curls overnight in a very low (130°F or 55°C) oven.

step 15
Gently slip the dried curls off the dowel and apply a light coat of acrylic spray.

tip
◆

Wiping your dowel rods with just the tiniest dab of vegetable oil will make your dried curls much easier to remove.

step 16
Make cinnamon cross. Use a dab of glue to make an "X" out of two cinnamon sticks.

step 17
Make burlap bow. Make a basic bow out of a 15" (38cm) length of burlap ribbon by bringing both ends in to overlap in the middle.

step 18
Make cornhusk flower "bouquets". Layer the cornhusk flower, cinnamon stick cross and burlap bow, then use the wire from the cornhusk flower to secure. Add a dab of glue for good measure. Make five bouquets in all.

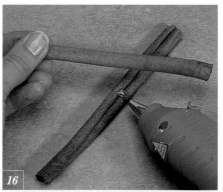

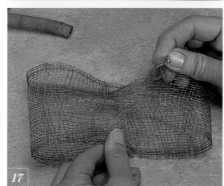

step 19

Swirl in salal. Add a dab of glue to each leaf and slip them between the twigs. Overlap leaves in a radiating pattern around the inside of your wreath. Create a second circle of salal leaves around the first one. (I used the more golden leaves from my bunch on the inner circle and the browner ones on the outside.)

step 20

Attach bouquets to wreath. Space the bouquets evenly around the inside of your wreath, using the wire stems on each bouquet to secure them in place. Attach wire for hanging (see page 385).

step 21

Add tallow berries. Glue a line of berry clusters between each cornhusk bouquet.

step 22

Add orange curls. Glue the curls radiating out from behind each bouquet.

step 23

Add acorn buds. Squeeze a dab of glue on the end of your acorn bud wires and insert them around the wreath as desired.

step 24

Finish with oak leaves and aroma. Slip the orange oak leaves between the twigs to "frame" your cornhusk flower arrangements. Use a little dab of glue to secure each one in place. If you like, apply a drop or two of aroma oil to your leaves.

♦♦♦ **Enjoy your finished Cornhusk Wreath!**

If you enjoyed making these simple flowers, try coming up with your own flower variations. Cornhusk is so inexpensive that you can afford to experiment. If cornhusk is not for you but you like the design of this wreath, try using dried sunflowers instead.

variation

Cornhusk & curls heart

Lemon curls and cornhusk daisies (with dried black-eyed Susan centers) add the finishing touch to this layered heart wreath. Start by placing a row of salal leaves around the inside, baby's breath on the outside, then fill in between with rows of sweet Annie, lavender and larkspur. Fill in as needed with hydrangea.

Cornucopia Dessert Wreath

♦♦♦ THIS WREATH DOES DOUBLE DUTY! USE IT AS A COLORFUL CENTERPIECE FOR THANKSGIVING DINNER, PERHAPS SURROUNDING AN ARRANGEMENT OF FRESH FLOWERS. AFTERWARD, THE WREATH BECOMES A GRAND AND EDIBLE CENTERPIECE FOR YOUR DESSERT SPREAD. IF YOU WANT TO GO ALL-OUT, CLEAN OUT A PUMPKIN TO PLACE IN THE CENTER OF YOUR WREATH AND FILL IT WITH PUNCH OR FRUIT DIP. YOU CAN ASSEMBLE THE MAJORITY OF THIS WREATH THE DAY BEFORE, PLACING THE PERISHABLE FRUITS AND FRESH FLOWERS AT THE LAST MINUTE.

TIME

DIFFICULTY

18" (46cm) florist wreath form with wet foam

fresh flowers and ivy leaves (I used roses and chrysanthemums)

assorted nuts (walnuts, Brazil nuts, pecans, almonds, filberts)

assortment of dessert fruits (aim for a variety of sizes and colors—I used assorted pears and apples, tangerines, grapes, plums, kumquats, strawberries and blueberries)

fresh cranberries

round toothpicks (the longer the better)

sugar glue (see recipe below)

plastic wrap

florist pins

needle and thread

Recipe for Sugar Glue

Beat one egg white until frothy. (If you prefer, use a powered egg substitute.) Add 1 cup (127g) powdered sugar, about a third at a time, beating after each addition. Beat five minutes longer until stiff.

tips
♦

♦ To give your fruit a bit of sheen, polish with a paper towel and just a dab of vegetable oil.
♦ To protect your table from any moisture, place a pad or folded towel under the tablecloth.

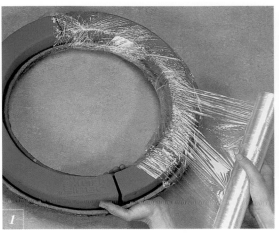

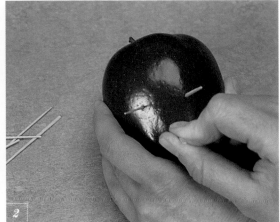

step 1
Prepare oasis. Immerse florist foam in water until saturated and wrap with plastic wrap.

step 2
"Pick" your largest fruit first. A good, general rule for assembling this wreath is to work from your largest ingredient to your smallest. So starting with your biggest fruit—in my case the red apples—insert two or three toothpicks, which you'll use to anchor your fruit in the foam.

step 3
Nestle in apples. Place four apples evenly spaced around the top of your wreath. Don't be afraid to push—the idea is to "nestle" your fruit into the foam, using the toothpicks to hold the fruit in place. Think of your wreath in fourths, adding about the same amount of each fruit to each quadrant to achieve a full, balanced look.

step 4
"Pick" and place apples and pears. Fill in the top of your wreath with larger fruit, leaving space to add flowers later.

tip

Don't place your fruits to sit perfectly straight; you'll get a more pleasing effect by angling them this way and that.

step 5

Add a ring of ivy leaves. Using florist pins, cover the
lower edge with a skirt of slightly overlapping ivy leaves.
This will camouflage the wreath form and create a nice, finished look.

step 6

"Pick" and place fruit. Using picks, place the brown
pears, green apples, tangerines and plums randomly
around your wreath. Fill in the side of your wreath, leaving
space to add flowers.

step 7

Add flowers. Now it's time to fill in those spaces you've
been saving. Holding the stems under water, cut them
down to about 4" (10cm). Use needlenose pliers to poke
holes in your foam and insert flowers.

step 8

Go nuts! Arrange the nuts around your wreath. Some will nestle between fruits. Otherwise, use a dab of sugar glue to hold in place.

step 9

Weave in cranberry garland. Using a needle and thread, string four 2' (1.2m) lengths of cranberries. Weave the cranberry garland between and around your fruits, securing the ends with florist pins.

step 10

Accent with smallest fruits. Pick and place kumquats. Break grapes into small clusters and arrange around the top of the wreath. Skewer two or three blueberries per toothpick and insert around wreath as desired.

step 11

Finish with ivy leaves. Just slip a few ivy leaves around your flowers, and you're set!

◆◆◆ A grand finale!

Now if only everyone can save room for dessert! Not just for Thanksgiving, this wreath will make any occasion—from casual summer barbecue to formal affair—feel special. Fora variation, you can apply the same idea on a smaller scale using vegetables to dress up individual place settings. Form a circle out of a piece of heavy wire, sized to fit around a small bowl or custard cup. Using fine green wire, cover the circle with fresh parsley, then decorate with mini carrots, radish "roses", olives, cherry tomatoes, etc. Add dip and serve!

Merry Winter

♦♦♦ The smell of fresh pine, snow falling soft as a lullaby, baking cookies into the wee hours of the morning…Factor in winter's sleigh-full of wreath-makings—from ivy and poinsettia to jingle bells and gingerbread men—and it truly is the most wonderful time of the year!

In this season of decorating merriment, anything goes for wreaths. Deck them out in traditional greens and reds, magical silvers and golds, Victorian mauves and pinks, or a sweet, candy-colored palette.

If you're short on time (and who isn't this time of year?) you'll appreciate the Winter Berry and Sugarplums wreaths. Short on gifts for the names on your list? You can make a Glitter 'n' Glow Candle Ring in the time it takes you to find a parking spot at the mall! For full-fledged winter romance, there's the Sweetheart Wreath, which is the very top of the mood-setting scale.

(opposite page starting from upper left, clockwise) GLITTER 'N GLOW CANDLE RING, SUGARPLUMS WREATH, SWEETHEART WREATH, WINTER BERRY WREATH

4

Winter Berry Wreath

what you'll need

◆◆◆ HERE'S A CHRISTMAS QUICKIE! DECORATE A PLAIN BAY LEAF BASE WITH GARLANDS OF IVORY LACE AND PEPPERBERRIES...SUSPEND IT FROM A DECKED-OUT BOW...AND BEFORE YOU KNOW IT, YOU'LL BE LOOKING AT A WREATH-FULL OF CHRISTMAS CHEER. JUST ADD MULLED APPLE CIDER, A CRACKLING FIRE AND HOLIDAY SINGING IN THE BACKGROUND, AND YOU'VE GOT ALL THE MAKINGS OF AN EVENING OF OLD-FASHIONED HOLIDAY ROMANCE.

TIME

DIFFICULTY

16" (41cm) bay leaf wreath

dried cedar

ivory lace (you can substitute baby's breath or candy tuft)

pepperberries (red)

mini pinecones

burgundy brunia flowers (you can substitute canella berries or mini rosebuds)

5 freeze-dried rose heads (ivory)

4 yards (3.6m) of 1½" (3.8cm) wired ivory satin ribbon

2 yards (1.8m) of narrow ribbon

florist wire

hot glue gun

step 1

Work in cedar. Start by adding a little extra texture to your bay leaf wreath by gluing sprigs of cedar throughout.

step 2

Plan your pattern. Swirl a narrow piece of ribbon around your wreath to indicate where you will place your flowers. Leave space at the top to add your roses later.

step 3

Start with the ivory lace. Using the ribbon as a guide, glue in your ivory lace sprig by sprig. (Do not bundle—you're aiming for a more elongated effect.) Remove the ribbon as you go.

step 4

Glue in clusters of pepperberries. Aim to create the impression of a pepperberry garland twisting around the ivory lace.

step 5

Add pinecones. Glue the mini pinecones in clusters of two or three, concentrating them along the edges of your "garlands."

step 6

Make "holly berry" clusters. Wire a cluster of three brunia flowers together by the stems, then add a dab of glue to secure. (Okay, they're not really holly berries. But who's to know?)

step 7

Glue on berry clusters. Concentrate the clusters around the pinecones.

step 8

Add roses. Arrange the roses at the top of your wreath and glue into place.

step 9
Accent with pinecones and berry clusters. Really make your roses "pop" by filling in around them with pinecones and berry clusters.

step 10
Make hanging ribbon. Make a stacked bow (see page 388) leaving 15" (38cm) long tails. Make a 1½" (4cm) hanging hoop out of heavy wire. (Wrap the wire around two fingers three times, then twist with an additional wire to secure.) Attach the hoop to the back of your bow with a piece of narrow ribbon.

step 11
Attach ribbon. Carefully flip your wreath over. With the bow centered directly above your roses and a few inches above the top edge of your wreath, glue the tails trailing down each side. Reinforce in two or three spots per side with wire—double the wire, thread under the wreath frame and twist securely.

step 12
Fancify bow. Add a little arrangement of pinecones, brunia clusters and bay leaves to the center of your bow.

◆◆◆ A whirl of Christmas cheer!
There you have it—and with
plenty of time left to finish wrapping your gifts! Now that you
know how easy it is to dress up a
plain wreath, you can add a swirl
of color to any season! Come spring,
I think I'll try pink baby's breath
and globe amaranth in assorted
pastels. Yellow caspia, bittersweet
and tallow berries would make a
pretty variation for fall.

variation

Same swirl, different stuff
You really need to start with a nice base to
pull off this type of wreath, since sections are
left exposed. An airy fern wreath was the
inspiration for this whirl of pink, featuring
pink rodanthe, burgundy sweet Annie, pink
rice flowers and yellow strawflowers.

Glitter 'n' Glow Candle Ring

◆◆◆ THIS FESTIVE LITTLE WREATH TURNS AN ORDINARY GLASS HURRICANE INTO A SPARKLING CENTERPIECE—THE PERFECT TOUCH OF CHRISTMAS CHEER FOR YOUR COFFEE TABLE. DURING THE DAY, THE RICH PINKS AND GOLDS BRIGHTEN ANY ROOM. AT NIGHT, WHEN THE CANDLELIGHT STRIKES, YOU'LL LOVE THE DAZZLE OF THE GLITTER AND THE GLOW OF THE GLASS BULBS. AND COME GIFT-GIVING TIME, THIS GEM OF A WREATH IS PERFECT FOR THE FRIENDS ON YOUR LIST—IT'S SO QUICK TO MAKE AND A CINCH TO CUSTOMIZE USING THEIR FAVORITE COLORS!

TIME
⏱
DIFFICULTY
❀ ❀

- grapevine wreath—I used a 9" (23cm) wreath, but choose the size that best accommodates your hurricane
- dried sweet Annie (burgundy)
- dried hydrangea (light green/pink)
- six 1" (2.5cm) glass ball ornaments
- 12 small pinecones
- 12 acorns
- coxcomb
- pepperberries (pink)
- preserved cedar (gold)
- grapevine tendrils
- gold spray paint (I prefer the 14K gold kind for more sheen)
- pink spray paint
- very fine glitter
- hurricane
- florist wire
- acrylic spray
- hot glue gun

tip
◆

Dried materials are highly flammable. Always use a hurricane with this wreath—never use it directly surrounding a lit candle.

493

step 1

Spray wreath. Spray your wreath with gold paint. While you're at it, spray your cedar, pinecones, acorns and grapevine tendrils. Allow to dry.

step 2

Start with cedar and sweet Annie. Fill in the bottom of your wreath in a radiating pattern, alternating sprigs of cedar and sweet Annie.

step 3

Add hydrangea. Tint hydrangea with a light dusting of pink spray paint. Break the hydrangea into small pieces and use it to fill in the top of your wreath. (See page 387 for special tips on working with hydrangea.) Remember—your hurricane will be in the center, so there's no need to cover the inner perimeter.

step 4

Add glass balls. Arrange glass balls around your wreath as desired. Once you're happy with the spacing, glue into place.

step 5

Wiring pinecones. Use a wire that is strong enough to hold the pinecone, but fine enough to slip between the petals. Simply work the wire in between petals at the base of the pinecone and twist to secure. Trim wire, leaving enough to attach the pinecone to your wreath.

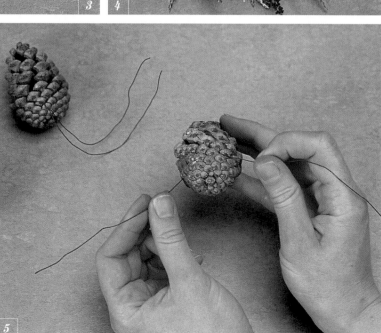

step 6

Add pinecones. Use wire stems to secure the pinecones here and there around the wreath.

step 7

Add acorns. Cluster acorns, cap down, around your wreath.

step 8

Add coxcomb. Break into small pieces and glue around wreath as desired.

step 9

Add pepperberries. Break pepperberries into small clusters and glue around the wreath as desired. Be sure to fill in any sparse spots.

step 10

Glitter up! Spray your wreath with a light coat of acrylic spray and immediately sprinkle with glitter.

step 11

Top with tendrils. Glue gold tendrils randomly around the wreath. Don't nestle them too far down—let them stick out to add texture and dimension to your wreath. The only thing missing now is a candle in your favorite Christmas aroma!

♦♦♦ Glimmer, shimmer and glow!

I love the pink and gold tones of this candle ring—but when you make yours, use whatever colors tickle your fancy, from silver monotones to a mix of glorious jewel tones. You can follow the same directions to create a full-sized wall wreath—just be sure to fill in the inner perimeter with hydrangea.

variation

Glittery wall wreath

I love this festive combination of dried red roses, rice flowers, pepperberries, pinecones (painted with artificial snow) and seashells. Pearly balls and snowflakes (they're actually buttons!) are icing on the cake. Start by covering a little straw base with preserved cedar, and finish with a generous sprinkling of glitter.

497

Sugarplums Wreath

what you'll need

♦♦♦ IF YOU'RE SHORT ON TIME BUT BIG ON CHRISTMAS, HERE'S A SPECIAL GIFT FROM ME TO YOU: A QUICK AND WHIMSICAL WAY TO DRESS UP A PLAIN EVERGREEN WREATH! PART OF THE BEAUTY OF THIS DESIGN IS THAT, AFTER CHRISTMAS, YOU CAN SIMPLY RE-PLACE THE CENTER HOOP WITH A MORE GENERIC WINTER-THEMED ONE. THAT WAY, YOU GET MORE USE OUT OF YOUR PRETTY EVERGREEN WREATH, AND YOUR FAMILY DOESN'T MOCK YOU FOR LEAVING CHRISTMAS DECORATIONS UP THROUGH FEBRUARY!

TIME
⏱

DIFFICULTY
✤

24" (61cm) fresh or artificial evergreen wreath (use a wreath pre-strung with lights for additional twinkle)

metal hoop—I used a 12" (31cm) hoop, but you should choose a ring slightly larger than the center of your wreath

3 yards (2.7m) of inexpensive, 1" (2.5cm) green ribbon

7 yards (6.3m) wired 1½" (3.8cm) red satin ribbon

3½ yards (3.2m) wired 1½" (4cm) sheer red ribbon

artificial candy picks—I used 25, but how many you need will vary depending on the size of your picks and hoop

8 beaded berry picks

16 candy canes

8 rubber bands

8 peppermint sticks

1 stem of white glitter stars

florist wire

hot glue gun

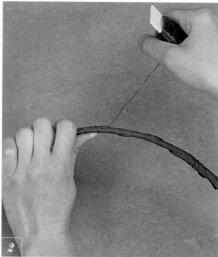

step 1

Wrap hoop in ribbon. Instead of trying to wrap the entire hoop with one continuous piece of ribbon, cut your ribbon into 2' to 3' (61cm to 91cm) lengths, securing the ends with glue. Don't worry about being perfect here. You're just trying to camouflage the hoop. As long as no gold shows, you're set.

step 2

Use wire to secure ribbon. Wrap, wrap, wrap, spiraling the wire around your hoop every inch (2.5cm) or two to hold the ribbon in place.

step 3

Tie on ribbons. Cut 15" (38cm) pieces of ribbon—sixteen satin and eight sheer. Sandwich one sheer piece between two satin pieces and tie onto your hoop, leaving about twice as much on the outside as on the inside. (No need to measure—just eye it.) Tie on the remaining ribbons the same way, evenly spacing them around the hoop.

step 4

Now for the candy! If necessary, trim the stems of your picks down to 2" or 3" (5cm or 8cm) to make them easier to work with. Using continuous wiring (see page 387), attach your candy picks to the front of your hoop. (Careful not to catch your ribbons in the wire!)

step 5

Add mounting wires. Cut four 3' (91cm) pieces of heavy wire and attach them evenly around the back of your hoop. Thread each wire under the hoop and twist so that you're left with two equal tails.

step 6

Mount hoop on wreath. Center the hoop on the front of your evergreen and attach with the wires. (Don't cut the excess wire, just tuck it in so you can remove the hoop and re-use it next year.)

step 7

Add berries. Slip in berry picks, centered at each ribbon. Use the stem of the pick or a piece of wire to secure.

step 8

Make candy cane hearts. Use a rubber band to connect two candy canes at the base. Angle the tops of the candy canes to form a heart shape and add a dab of glue to secure. Hold for a minute or two until the glue sets. Repeat with the rest of your candy canes to make eight hearts in all.

step 9

Attach hearts. Twist a piece of wire around the rubber bands at the base of your hearts. Position hearts between ribbons and secure with wire.

step 10

Now the peppermint sticks. Work in the peppermint sticks evenly around your wreath, slipping between candies to hold in place.

step 11

Finish with glittery stars. Clip off individual stars, leaving a wire stem on each. Glue the stars randomly around your wreath. Let them extend above the candy picks rather than nestling them in the wreath.

◆◆◆ **Sweet!**

Shape the ribbons into nice, neat waves and hang the wreath. If only gift-shopping were this quick and easy! After the holidays, all it takes is a few minutes to remove the sugarplum hoop, pack it away for next year, and replace it with a hoop of your choice—say a simple hoop of pinecones or a romantic ring of poinsettias.

variation

Even simpler!

A hoop, some glittery silk rose picks and an evergreen base. Put them all together, and you've got a simply elegant display for Thanksgiving through Valentine's Day!

503

Sweetheart Wreath

what you'll need

♦♦♦ THIS WREATH IS ONLY FOR THE UTTERLY ROMANTIC AT HEART. SUGARY PINK FREEZE-DRIED ROSES AND A SWEET LITTLE BOX OF CANDIES ARE DELIVERED WITH LOVE ON A SATIN-WRAPPED HEART. WITH THE ROSES SIMPLY PINNED IN PLACE, THIS WREATH MAKES AN EXTRA-SPECIAL GIFT—ESPECIALLY FOR FELLOW CRAFTERS WHO CAN REMOVE THE ROSES AFTER VALENTINE'S DAY FOR USE IN THEIR NEXT PROJECT... PERHAPS A GIFT FOR YOU! EVEN THE LEAST CRAFTY RECIPIENT CAN USE THE ROSES IN POTPOURRI OR SIMPLY ARRANGE THEM IN A PRETTY BOWL.

TIME
⏱ ⏱

DIFFICULTY
❀ ❀ ❀

18" (46cm) foam heart

6" x 1" (15cm x 2.5cm) round florist foam

12 freeze-dried roses—pink, 1½" to 2" heads (3.8cm to 5cm), or use silk or velvet rose heads

assorted dried fillers (baker's fern, baby's breath, caspia)

12 rose stems

9 yards (8.1m) of 1½" (3.8cm) satin ribbon (wine) for wrapping base

3½ yards (3.2m) of ⅞" (2.2cm) organza ribbon (wine) for bow

aroma oil—rose or other "romantic" fragrance (optional)

2 sheets of patterned tissue paper

small heart-shaped paper doilies

shallow, heart-shaped box with lid, about 5" (13cm) wide (papier maché or any lightweight material)

artificial candies—I made truffles out of polymer clay, topped with candy sprinkles—or wrap small foam balls in candy foils (If you're making this as a gift wreath, you may want to attach a real box of chocolates!)

polyester fill

pink spray paint

white acrylic paint

decorative-edge scissors

embossing foil and stylus

florist pins

hot glue gun

rubber bands

small sponge

Template for embossed gift tag

step 1

Begin wrapping points in ribbon. Cut two pieces of satin ribbon, about 6" (15cm) each. Arrange ribbons along either side of the top point as shown, gluing ends on the opposite side of the wreath. Do the same for the bottom point, then flip the wreath over (this will be the front of your finished wreath) and repeat, being sure to glue ribbon on the opposite side. It may look messy now, but trust me—it will pay off.

step 2

Finish points. Now cover each point with three short, slightly overlapped horizontal ribbons as shown. Again, secure all ends on the opposite side of the wreath, and finish both points on the back of your wreath before doing the front points.

step 3

Wrap it up. Wrap each side of your heart with a continuous length of satin ribbon, keeping a taut and even overlap. Secure each end on the back of the wreath with a dab of glue. Add two wires at the top of your heart for hanging. (See page 385 for instructions.)

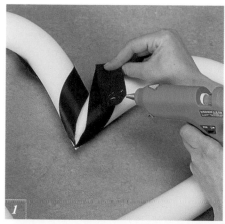

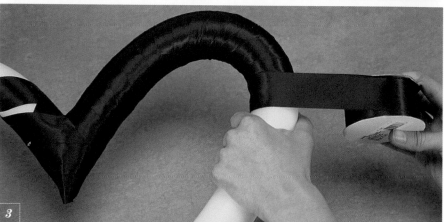

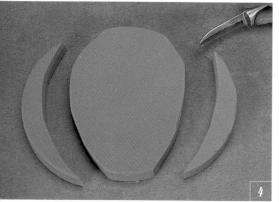

tip

If your ribbon attracts lint try spraying it with a static removal spray.

step 4

Shape base for bouquet. Cut your florist foam into an oval shape.

step 5

Attach roses. Arrange your roses on the oval base, using florist pins to secure. (Roses can be removed and reused.)

step 6

Add caspia and baby's breath. Fill in around the roses with sprigs of caspia and baby's breath. To maintain the "removability" of the roses, take care to glue these fillers to the foam and not to the roses.

step 7

Attach stems. Use a rubber band to bundle together the rose stems. Insert into the bottom edge of the florist foam.

step 8

Arrange tissue. Place both pieces of tissue paper (wrong sides together) under your arrangement. Lie your bouquet diagonally on your tissue. Add a strip of polyester fill along the stems to give them more bulk.

step 9

Fold over tissue. Fold up the bottom point of the tissue to form a triangle behind your bouquet, leaving 1"–2" (3cm–5cm) of stems exposed at bottom. Trim off excess tissue. Wrap your bouquet in the tissue like you'd wrap a baby in a blanket—fold in one side, and then the other. Roll down the top of the tissue to frame your bouquet. Glue tissue to the back of florist foam and secure with a few florist pins.

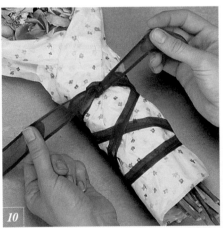

step 10

Wrap stems with ribbon. Cut a piece of organza ribbon about 24" (61cm) long. Starting with the center of the ribbon at the bottom of your stems, criss-cross up and around as shown. When you reach the top of your stems, tie the ribbon off in a square knot.

step 11

Add a bow. Make a stacked bow of organza ribbon (see page 14) and tie on using tails from the square knot. Position the bouquet diagonally across the heart and secure in place with florist pins and hot glue. (If you like, you can skip the glue so the entire bouquet can be removed and used as a pretty tabletop display.)

step 12

Add sprigs of baker's fern. Arrange around the outside of the bouquet, taking care to glue them to the tissue or the florist foam and not the roses.

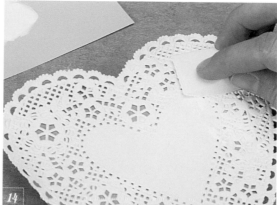

step 13

Paint heart box. Apply a light coat of spray paint to the box and lid. Repeat as necessary, allowing to dry between coats.

step 14

Stencil box design. Center your doily on your box lid. Use white acrylic paint to sponge over the doily and transfer the pattern to your box lid. (Before stenciling your lid, it's a good idea to practice on a piece of scrap cardboard first.)

step 15

Line box with doilies. Unless your doily fits your box perfectly, you'll have to do some cutting and piecing here. Just remember that the left side will show and the right side will be hidden under the lid.

step 16

Truffle time! Now arrange and glue your candies in the left side of your box. You can cheat and fill the right side with tissue—nobody will ever know.

step 17

Emboss gift tag. Cut a 2½" (6cm) square of embossing foil using your decorative-edge scissors. Use your stylus and the pattern on page 505 (or your own original design) to emboss your gift tag. It's a good idea to do this on top of a thick piece of cardboard, a section of newspaper or some other surface that has some give.

step 18

Attach box of candies. Experiment with your candy box until you find the placement and angle you like best. Glue onto wreath and hold in place for a few minutes while it dries.

step 19

Add lid, gift tag and aroma. Now glue the lid atop your box and tie on the gift tag. If you like, add a drop of two of aroma oil behind the roses.

♦♦♦ **Valentine romance, straight from the heart!**
Pinning in the roses is not only a great perk for gift-giving, as I've already mentioned. It's also a clever way to "renew" this wreath every year. Simply pin in a fresh dozen roses every Valentine's Day—the rest of the wreath should hold up just fine.

variation

Spread a little love!
You can make sweet little hearts like these in no time! Gather small foam hearts, pretty ribbons and assorted dried flowers and spend a fun afternoon making mini Valentine wreaths for all your friends. They make great decorations for gift-wrapping, too!

Resources

Flyboy Naturals

15550 Old Highway 99 South
Myrtle Creek, OR 97457
(800) 465-5125
Fax: (541) 863-7757
E-mail: flyboy@wizzards.net
www.flyboynaturals.com
♦ specializes in freeze-dried flowers, fruits and vegetables

D&P Flowers

3657 G 7/10 Rd.
Palisade, CO 81526
(970) 464-0558
Fax: (970) 464-5332
E-mail: dpflo1000@aol.com
www.dpflowers.com
♦ specializes in naturally dried and freeze-dried flowers

Flying B Bar Ranch

1100 McMullen Creek Rd.
Selma, OR 97538
(541) 597-2418
Fax: (541) 597-2050
E-mail: roses@webtrail.com
www.webtrail.com/roses
♦ specializes in freeze-dried garden roses; carries over 60 different varieties

The Flower Mart.com

P.O. Box 1809
Hillsboro, OR 97123
(800) 733-0506
Fax: (503) 628-0647
E-mail: sales@theflowermart.com
www.theflowermart.com
♦ specialists in fine dried and preserved florals

Dried Flowers Direct

3597 Skyline Dr.
Penn Yann, NY 14527
(315) 536-2736
E-mail: drieds@linkny.com
www.driedflowersdirect.com
♦ growers of wholesale and retail dried flowers from Keuka Flower Farm

Donna's Weed Barn

Route 985
Boswell, PA 15531
(814) 629-6708
♦ dried flowers and floral supplies

The material in this compilation appeared in the following previously published North Light Books and appears here by permission of the authors. (The initial page numbers given refer to pages in the original work; page numbers in parentheses refer to pages in this book.)

McGraw, MaryJo.   Greeting Card Magic with Rubber Stamps © 2000.   Pages 1, 5-127 (6-129)
Jessee, Peggy.   Quick & Easy Decorative Painting © 2000.   Pages 3, 6-125, 127 (130-252)
Donnelly, Sarah.   Easy Mosaics for Your Home and Garden © 2001.   Pages 1, 4-126 (253-376)
Apel, June and Bruce, Chalice. Wreaths for Every Season © 2002.   Pages 1, 4-142 (377-510)

Other fine North Light Books are available from your local bookstore, art supply store or direct from the publisher.

07   06   05   04   5   4   3   2

Library of Congress Cataloging in Publication Data

Big Book of Crafts / edited by editors of North Light Books—1st ed.
         p. cm.
     ISBN 1-58180-550-0 (hc. : alk. paper)

COVER DESIGNER: MARISSA BOWERS
PRODUCTION COORDINATOR: SARA DUMFORD

Metric Conversion Chart

TO CONVERT	TO	MULTIPLY BY
Inches	Centimeters	2.54
Centimeters	Inches	0.4
Feet	Centimeters	30.5
Centimeters	Feet	0.03
Yards	Meters	0.9
Meters	Yards	1.1
Sq. Inches	Sq. Centimeters	6.45
Sq. Centimeters	Sq. Inches	0.16
Sq. Feet	Sq. Meters	0.09
Sq. Meters	Sq. Feet	10.8
Sq. Yards	Sq. Meters	0.8
Sq. Meters	Sq. Yards	1.2
Pounds	Kilograms	0.45
Kilograms	Pounds	2.2
Ounces	Grams	28.3
Grams	Ounces	0.035

Try your hand at these other fun crafts -
NORTH LIGHT BOOKS MAKES IT EASY!

You can create your own tabletop fountains and add beautiful accents to your living room, bedroom, kitchen and garden. These 15 gorgeous step-by-step projects make it easy, using everything from lava rock and bamboo to shells and clay pots. You'll learn to incorporate flowers, driftwood, fire, figurines, crystals, plants and more to create works of art that will have friends buzzing for years to come.

ISBN 1-58180-103-3, paperback, 128 pages, #31791-K

Create unique, colorful crafts, including greeting cards, journal covers, picture frames, wall hangings and more with a world of exciting fabrics. All you need to get started are some old clothes, buttons, coins, cording, faux jewelry and other embellishments. Simple decorative techniques, such as fabric stamping, collage and basic stitching, are clearly explained inside, requiring no prior knowledge of sewing or quilting.

ISBN 1-58180-153-X, paperback, 128 pages, #31902-K

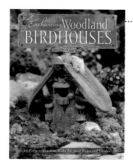

Create rustic, whimsical houses perfect for use indoors and out. Lucinda Macy provides step-by-step instructions and full-color photos that make every project easy. There are 13 designs in all, including birdhouses, decorative fairy and gnome homes, and garden homes for toads. Each one can be embellished with acorns, moss, seedpods, twigs and other natural materials.

ISBN 1-58180-071-1, paperback, 128 pages, #31793-K

Perfect for kids, crafters and animal lovers, this fun guide will teach you how to paint irresistible likenesses of your favorite family pets on rocks. Whether furry, feathered or finned, you'll learn to capture the charm of your pets with step-by-step instructions and easy-to-use acrylic paints that guarantee immediate, good-looking results! Projects include a range of cats and dogs, as well as fish, rabbits and other beloved critters.

ISBN 1-58180-032-0, paperback, 128 pages, #31552-K

Use rubber stamps to decorate candles, jewelry, purses, book covers, wall hangings and more. 16 step-by-step projects show you how by using creative techniques, surfaces and embellishments, including metal, beads, embossing powder and clay - even shrink plastic!

ISBN 1-58180-128-9, paperback, 128 pages, #31829-K

These books and other fine North Light titles are available from your local art & craft retailer, bookstore, online supplier or by calling 1-800-448-0915.